Nietzsche's *The Case of Wagner* and *Nietzsche Contra Wagner*

Edinburgh Critical Guides to Nietzsche
Series editors: Keith Ansell-Pearson and Daniel Conway

Guides you through the writings of Friedrich Nietzsche (1844–1900), one of modernity's most independent, original and seminal minds

The Edinburgh Critical Guides to Nietzsche series brings Nietzsche's writings to life for students, teachers and scholars alike, with each text benefitting from its own dedicated book. Every guide features new research and reflects the most recent developments in Nietzsche scholarship. The authors unlock each work's intricate structure, explore its specific mode of presentation and explain its seminal importance. Whether you are working in contemporary philosophy, political theory, religious studies, psychology, psychoanalysis or literary theory, these guides will help you to fully appreciate Nietzsche's enduring significance for contemporary thought.

Books in the series

Nietzsche's *The Birth of Tragedy from the Spirit of Music*, Tracy B. Strong and Babette Babich
Nietzsche's *Philosophy in the Tragic Age of the Greeks*, Sean Kirkland
Nietzsche's *Unfashionable Observations*, Jeffrey Church
Nietzsche's *Human, All Too Human*, Ruth Abbey
Nietzsche's *Dawn*, Katrina Mitcheson
Nietzsche's *Gay Science*, Robert Miner
Nietzsche's *Thus Spoke Zarathustra*, Charles Bambach
Nietzsche's *Beyond Good and Evil*, Daniel Conway
Nietzsche's *On the Genealogy of Morality*, Robert Guay
Nietzsche's *The Case of Wagner and Nietzsche Contra Wagner*, Ryan Harvey and Aaron Ridley
Nietzsche's *Twilight of the Idols*, Vanessa Lemm
Nietzsche's *The Anti-Christ*, Paul Bishop
Nietzsche's *Ecce Homo*, Matthew Meyer
Nietzsche's *Late Notebooks*, Alan Schrift

Visit our website at edinburghuniversitypress.com/series-edinburgh-critical-guides-to-nietzsche to find out more

Nietzsche's *The Case of Wagner* and *Nietzsche Contra Wagner*

A Critical Introduction and Guide

Ryan Harvey and Aaron Ridley

EDINBURGH
University Press

Edinburgh University Press is one of the leading university presses in the UK. We publish academic books and journals in our selected subject areas across the humanities and social sciences, combining cutting-edge scholarship with high editorial and production values to produce academic works of lasting importance. For more information visit our website: edinburghuniversitypress.com

© Ryan Harvey and Aaron Ridley, 2022

Edinburgh University Press Ltd
The Tun – Holyrood Road
12(2f) Jackson's Entry
Edinburgh EH8 8PJ

Typeset in 11/13 Bembo by
IDSUK (DataConnection) Ltd

A CIP record for this book is available from the British Library

ISBN 978 1 4744 5939 6 (hardback)
ISBN 978 1 4744 6138 2 (webready PDF)
ISBN 978 1 4744 6136 8 (paperback)
ISBN 978 1 4744 6137 5 (epub)

The right of Ryan Harvey and Aaron Ridley to be identified as the authors of this work has been asserted in accordance with the Copyright, Designs and Patents Act 1988, and the Copyright and Related Rights Regulations 2003 (SI No. 2498).

Contents

Acknowledgements	vii
Chronology	viii
Primary Sources and Abbreviations	xi
Introduction: The Case of Wagner	1
1. The Artwork of the Future: A Prelude to the Philosophy of the Future	14
The artwork of the future	14
'Athenian self-dissection' and the decline of culture at the hands of science	18
Science, redeemed by her defeat, reaches out to her acknowledged victor: art	22
Vitalism and art	24
The Birth of Tragedy and the 'music-making Socrates'	26
Socrates, make music!	28
Knocking at the portals of the present and the future	32
We must now consider similar phenomena in the present	33
2. The Pessimism of Strength: An Attempt to Revise the Socratic and Tragic Cultures	41
The essence of tragic culture	41
An attempt to self-criticise	43
To 'make music' from the materials of life	48
The twilight of an idol	53
The uniting and dividing point of two cultures	59

3. Music in the Microcosm and the Macrocosm	64
Becoming the legitimate heir and successor to the pre-Socratics	64
Human, All Too Human and the beginning of Nietzsche's post-Wagnerian confrontation	67
Dawn on the horizon	71
The Gay Science	75
Beyond Good and Evil: prelude to a philosophy of the future	81
Ecce Homo	87
4. Music as the Late Fruit of Every Culture	98
The Case of Wagner	98
The preface	101
The charges	107
Sections 1–2	108
Section 3	111
Sections 4–5	115
Section 6	124
Sections 7–8	149
Sections 9–10	164
Sections 11–12	174
5. The Case of Nietzsche; or, How to Become More Wagnerian than Wagner	184
First postscript	184
Second postscript and epilogue	211
Conclusion	229
Coming full circle	229
A dangerous game	232
Glossary of Key Terms	240
Guide to Further Reading on *The Case of Wagner* and *Nietzsche Contra Wagner*	245
Bibliography	247
Index	253

Acknowledgements

We would like to thank Dan Conway and Keith Ansell-Pearson for inviting our contribution to the present series. Without their encouragement and support, this work would not have been possible. We also wish to thank two anonymous reviewers of our preliminary proposal for both the generosity they showed towards our initial project as well as the insightful commentary they provided in terms of how we might improve it.

Special thanks are also due to Marco Murelli and James McGuiggan, both of whom read through early drafts of the manuscript, either in whole or in part, and provided invaluable feedback from their unique specialities and perspectives.

Chronology

1844	Friedrich Wilhelm Nietzsche is born on 15 October in Röcken, Saxony.
1849	Nietzsche's father Ludwig, a Protestant minister, dies of 'softening of the brain'.
1850	Nietzsche's younger brother, Joseph, dies, and the family moves to Naumburg.
1858–64	He attends the elite boarding school Schulpforta on a full scholarship that he received as the orphan of a minister.
1864	Enrols at the University of Bonn to study theology, although he no longer plans to become a minister. He joins a fraternity, but resigns soon after.
1865	Follows the philologist Professor Albrecht Ritschl to the University of Leipzig. He buys a copy of Schopenhauer's *World as Will and Representation* in his landlord's shop.
1865	Refuses to take Communion during his Easter visit home to Naumburg.
1866	Publishes an essay on Theognis in a philological journal edited by Ritschl.
1867	Enlists in an artillery regiment after managing to pass a physical exam.
1868	Injures himself while riding. Reads Kuno Fischer's book on Kant. Meets Richard Wagner in a café in Leipzig, through the mediation of Mrs Ritschl. After

	his 24th birthday becomes emancipated from his guardian.
1869	Appointed Extraordinary Professor of Classical Philology in Basel on Ritschl's recommendation. Renounces Prussian citizenship. Begins frequent visits to Wagner in nearby Tribschen.
1870	Volunteers as a medical orderly in the Franco-Prussian War, but after two months becomes ill with dysentery and diphtheria.
1872	Publishes his first, controversial book, *The Birth of Tragedy out of the Spirit of Music*. Accompanies Wagner to Bayreuth for the laying of the foundation stone for the new opera house.
1873	Meets Paul Rée in Basel.
1873–75	Publishes *Unfashionable Observations*. Relationship with Wagner begins to sour.
1876	Begins working with Peter Gast, who takes dictation for an essay on Wagner. Visits the Bayreuth Festival and sees Wagner for the last time in Sorrento.
1878	Publishes the first part of *Human, All Too Human*.
1879	Publishes the two additions to *Human, All Too Human*. Resigns from Basel with a small pension. Begins a long period of wandering, mostly through Italy and Switzerland, staying in off-season boarding houses.
1881	Publishes *Daybreak*.
1882	His friendship with Paul Rée ends. Publishes the first edition of *The Gay Science*. In April travels to Rome, meets Lou Salomé, and proposes marriage to her. She declines and the relationship ends badly.
1883–84	Publishes *Thus Spoke Zarathustra*.
1884	Breaks with his sister Elisabeth over her fiancé's anti-Semitism.
1886	Publishes *Beyond Good and Evil*. Plans new editions of previous works, for which he writes five new prefaces, among other material.
1887	Writes *On the Genealogy of Morality* in July and August. It is published in November in an edition of 600 copies. He pays for the printing himself.

1888	Publishes *The Case of Wagner*. Writes *The Anti-Christ, Ecce Homo, Nietzsche Contra Wagner* and *Twilight of the Idols*.
1889	Suffers a breakdown and collapses in Turin, after writing megalomaniacal postcards to many friends and celebrities. He is retrieved by his friend Franz Overbeck, who takes him to Basel. Nietzsche's mother then takes him to an asylum in Jena.
1890	Nietzsche is moved to his mother's apartment in Jena, and then to Naumburg. His sister Elisabeth returns to Germany from Paraguay. She later takes control of her brother's literary estate.
1894	Elisabeth founds the Nietzsche Archive, which houses Nietzsche and his papers.
1896	Elisabeth moves Nietzsche and the Archive to Weimar.
1900	Dies in Weimar on 25 August.

Primary Sources and Abbreviations

Nietzsche

AT *Attempt at a Self-Criticism*, in Nietzsche 1993
BGE *Beyond Good and Evil*, Nietzsche 2014
BT *The Birth of Tragedy*, Nietzsche 1993
CW *The Case of Wagner*, Nietzsche 1967
D *Dawn*, Nietzsche 2011
DS 'David Strauss, Confessor and Writer', in Nietzsche 1995b
EH *Ecce Homo*, Nietzsche 1989
GM *On the Genealogy of Morality*, Nietzsche 1998
GS *Gay Science*, Nietzsche 1974
HAH1 *Human, All Too Human*, Nietzsche 1995a
HAH2 *Assorted Opinions and Maxims / The Wanderer and his Shadow*, Nietzsche 2013
HL 'On the Utility and Liability of History for Life', in Nietzsche 1995b
KSB *Kritische Studienausgabe, Sämtliche Briefe*, Nietzsche 1986
NCW *Nietzsche Contra Wagner*, Nietzsche 2005
SE 'Schopenhauer as Educator', in Nietzsche 1995b
SL *Selected Letters of Friedrich Nietzsche*, Nietzsche 1969, 1985
TI *Twilight of the Idols*, Nietzsche 1968
TSZ *Thus Spake Zarathustra*, Nietzsche 1933
UF *Unpublished Fragments and Notebooks*, Nietzsche 1999, 2009, 2013, 2019

WB 'Richard Wagner in Bayreuth', in Nietzsche 1995b

Textual references are followed by the section number and section name when necessary. Nietzsche's notebook entries (as UF) are followed by notebook entry reference and date of entry. For Nietzsche's selected letters in English (as SL), we specify the date of publication and page number, but we also include the corresponding reference for the letters in German (as KSB), which cite the volume number and page, and include the addressee and letter date.

Schopenhauer

BM 'On the Basis of Morality', in Schopenhauer 2009
FW 'Prize Essay on the Freedom of the Will', in Schopenhauer 2009
PP 1 *Parerga and Paralipomena*, vol. 1, Schopenhauer 2014
PP 2 *Parerga and Paralipomena*, vol. 2, Schopenhauer 2015
WWR 1 *The World as Will and Representation*, vol. 1, Schopenhauer 2014
WWR 2 *The World as Will and Representation*, vol. 2, Schopenhauer 1966

Textual references are followed by section or chapter number and name as necessary. With the exception of WWR 2, we have relied on the *Cambridge Edition of Schopenhauer's Works*.

Cosima Wagner

CWD 1 *Cosima Wagner's Diaries*, vol. 1, Wagner 1978/1980
CWD 2 *Cosima Wagner's Diaries*, vol. 2, Wagner 1978/1980
DBCW 1 *Die Briefe Cosima Wagners an Friedrich Nietzsche*, vol. 1, Wagner 1938–40
DBCW 2 *Die Briefe Cosima Wagners an Friedrich Nietzsche*, vol. 2, Wagner 1938–40

Textual references to CWD are followed by the page and date of entry. For Cosima's letters to Nietzsche (as DBCW), which only exist in the German original, textual references are followed by the page and letter date.

Richard Wagner

BB *Richard Wagner's Diaries*, aka the *'Brown Book'*, Wagner 1980
PW *Prose Works in 8 Volumes*, Wagner 1893–97
SLRW *Selected Letters of Richard Wagner*, Wagner 1987

Textual references to PW are followed by the volume number and page. For Wagner's selected letters in English (as SLRW), textual references are followed by the page number and include the addressee and letter date. Textual references to BB are followed by the page number and date of entry.

Introduction: The Case of Wagner

> He has wounded me, the one who awakened me.
>
> UF 28[6], spring–summer 1878

Of all the books that Nietzsche produced during the final year of his productive life, *The Case of Wagner* is the only one that was published during those closing months of 1888 – indeed it was rushed to be so. Why? Considering that the book itself runs to hardly sixty pages in the German original and *prima facie* seems to be just another attack on Wagner and his music, *The Case of Wagner* today tends to be lumped into that larger mass of the much more familiar and distinguished collection of books that Nietzsche produced that year, including *The Anti-Christ, Twilight of the Idols* and *Ecce Homo*, and so is typically passed over by anthologists as being, on the whole, inconsequential to his philosophy more generally.

Indeed, as it presently stands, the majority of Nietzsche's commentators have not been terribly interested in his relationship with Wagner: they have been inclined to regard Nietzsche's obsession with him as a biographical quirk, and have ignored his last and most substantial discussion of Wagner as a result. Yet Nietzsche's preoccupation with Wagner was indeed a *lifelong obsession*. No other topic or figure more consistently and persistently shows up in Nietzsche's books from beginning to end as does Wagner and his theories. Nietzsche not only felt strongly enough about Wagner to write a book about him and then to anthologise many of his earlier remarks in his *Nietzsche Contra Wagner*, he also turned to a discussion of Wagner – sometimes at length, sometimes disguised as 'the artist' – in every single book that he ever wrote. It is this that makes the scholarly neglect of *The Case of Wagner* so surprising.

At the same time, and yet outside of the traditional scholarship on Nietzsche, *The Case of Wagner* is not by any means a new subject matter of philosophical debate. In some respects, it has taken on a life of its own. But in this case one might wonder why it has the status of a philosophical problem at all. What does Wagner have to do with philosophy more broadly, and why is there a 'case' against him? Why have philosophers since the time of Nietzsche found it necessary to take him on? These become very interesting questions in their own right, for what they seem to suggest is that Wagner's art, not only as a creative deed, but also in terms of the historical and philosophical exegesis in which he contextualised it, really might have exposed some kind of raw nerve when it came to the relationship between philosophy and art. One need only point out that some of the most enduring charges against Wagner have been made by thinkers or philosophers who were artists themselves. This fact alone suggests – and it is certainly the case in the historical lineage of Wagner criticism from Nietzsche to Mann to Heidegger to Adorno – that taking on Wagner has been motivated in large part by an ambivalent kind of admiration for him.[1] In this sense the intellectual tradition of taking on Wagner, or what amounts to 'the case of Wagner as a genre', has been marked, at least since the time of Nietzsche, by artists who are philosophers (or philosophers who are artists) to once again set the relationship between philosophy and art to rights, however they happen to see that right.

So how then should we understand Nietzsche's case of Wagner? On the one hand, the mere fact that the case of Wagner persists to the present day and is taken up by a number of modern thinkers under the banner of Wagner criticism does surprisingly little to clarify this point. On the other hand, if the case of Wagner does not simply or exclusively refer to a circumscribed event in the history

---

[1] This is never truer than with Adorno (1981), whose 'case' against Wagner is significant, in Tanner's own estimation, for demonstrating 'how a thinker of genius can be led by reacting to Wagner's art into wild postures of rejection, and sneaking admiration' (1996: 225).

of ideas inaugurated by Nietzsche in the last year of his productive life, then the question that we should really ask is the one that attempts to clarify precisely this point; namely, what do we mean by the case of Wagner? Are we referring to the case of Wagner as Nietzsche initiated it and so understood it, or are we referring to the case of Wagner as some kind of ideological genre? These are very important questions to consider in their own right, for when it comes to understanding what the case of Wagner actually signifies for philosophy, there is no question that Nietzsche plays a unique and critical role in determining it, both in terms of how that case arose as well as the charges in which that case consists. And yet Nietzsche's case of Wagner is, in both its origins and its intentions, hardly clear at all.

Meanwhile for those commentators who have ventured to write about, or at least touch upon, Nietzsche's now infamous polemic against Wagner, the vast majority have stopped dissatisfyingly short of explaining what the case of Wagner actually is and why it matters for philosophy, and instead remain more or less content with acknowledging that the case itself has its origins in *some* kind of influence that Wagner exerted on Nietzsche.[2] But in order for this kind of truism to explain what the case of Wagner is and why it matters for philosophy, we would have to go far beyond the mere fact *that* the influence existed, and investigate instead *what* the nature of that influence was. If we discount from our tally the mere fact that the influence existed, most of the literature written about the two has done very little to actually analyse it.[3]

It is also unfortunate that, in general, Nietzsche's commentators have shown far less familiarity with Wagner than the latter's

---

[2] Even Bryan Magee's more or less pioneering work in this area, titled *Wagner and Philosophy* (2000), gets nowhere near the mark in this respect.

[3] As far as Nietzsche's biographers are concerned, Julian Young's more recent philosophical biography (Young 2010) is about as well researched and thoroughly detailed as one could desire in a work of this kind, and yet despite his comprehensive treatment of Nietzsche's life, for the most part he steers clear of the philosophical connections between the two. Again, we are not concerned with the mere fact *that* the history occurred, but rather *what* that history *signifies* in so occurring.

commentators have with Nietzsche. For instance, even though Nietzsche plays a minor role in what is an otherwise incredibly detailed study of Wagner, Westernhagen's biography (1981) demonstrates considerable understanding of the dynamics between the two men. The same can be said for Geck's more recent exceptional treatment of Wagner (Geck 2013), which highlights just how closely art and life were merged for Wagner – the very themes indeed that preoccupied Nietzsche throughout his entire productive life. Perhaps, however, it is Borchmeyer's study which shows the most impressive acquaintance with Nietzsche's thought and the influence that both Wagner and his prose works exerted on it. Yet despite how obvious the influence is here, Nietzsche's commentators are virtually silent. In this respect, it would seem that the traditional portrait that Nietzsche scholars have been trying to paint of Nietzsche and his philosophy for the past half century or so would just as soon prefer that Wagner's influence not exist, or what is effectively the same thing, that it be reduced to one that is essentially negligible to the total value of Nietzsche's philosophy.

There are, however, precedents for perspective, and in many respects the pioneering scholarship of Nietzsche's first modern-day champion, Walter Kaufmann, has unfortunately set the tone for this preconception. In fact, nowhere is the nature of this one-sided partiality so conspicuously on display than in the footnote Kaufmann rather presumptuously adds to the end of section 15 of his groundbreaking translation of *The Birth of Tragedy* in which he proclaims that

> the book might well end at this point . . . the discussion of the birth and death of tragedy is finished in the main, and the following celebration of the rebirth of tragedy [in the ten-section panegyric of Wagner] weakens the book and was shortly regretted by Nietzsche himself.
> (Nietzsche 1967: 98n)

As Michael Tanner commented in his introduction to the Whiteside translation, Kaufmann's statement 'is written from the standpoint of someone who not only had no interest in Wagner, but who wished Nietzsche never had either' (Nietzsche 1993: xi). Yet despite his partisanship, Kaufmann's knowledge of Nietzsche was extensive, and so he surely must have known that Nietzsche *himself* had acknowledged that the essay had been modelled on Wagner's essay 'The Destiny of Opera',[4] and that its metaphysical themes of 'illusion' and 'reality' are virtually identical with those found in Wagner's 'Beethoven' essay, which itself had relied on Schopenhauer's claim that the art of music accesses the noumenal order most directly in order to argue that the musical genius alone has access to a reality that is far more invariant than the shifting, illusory 'light-world' before our eyes.[5]

Indeed, as is well known, Wagner's own meditations on the philosophy of Advaita Vedanta had exposed him to the notion that reality in the absolute sense is predicated only of that which is self-existent, and that all else that exists by reason of its inherence in something other must be deemed Māyā in the metaphysical sense.[6] Thus from the standpoint of the immutable and self-existent, the 'light-world before our eyes' can only ever be a comparative dualism, a dream world or a Māyā in the metaphysical sense.[7] The analogy here is pregnant, for much like dreaming, we fail to realise while in the midst of it that we are in truth the cogniser, the cognised and the cognition; yet until we awaken, we believe that our subjectivity is bound by the forms of experience that govern the dream world instead of recognising that both they and

---

[4] 'Well then, the design is settled – to be modelled on Wagner's *The Destiny of Opera* – rejoice with me!' SL (1969: 82 [KSB 3: 243]), letter to Carl von Gersdorff, 18 November 1871.

[5] Both Borchmeyer (1991: 110–12, 169–70) and Köhler (2004: 517–21), another Wagner commentator, seem to recognise this thesis, albeit with varying degrees of insight.

[6] That the universe as a whole is a Māyā is not to deny that it possesses a relative reality, only that it is *not* self-existent. This is a subtlety in Indian philosophy that Nietzsche never grasped.

[7] Although he clearly amalgamates the terminology of Buddhist and Vedantic thought, an early note in Wagner's diary, known as the *Brown Book*, clearly reveals the themes he would later try to expound in his 'Beethoven' essay, and which we later find, quite obviously, in *The Birth of Tragedy*:
'Truth = nirvana = night
Music = Brahman = twilight
Poetry = samsara = day' BB 148 (18 May 1868).

the judgements of reality we make in accordance with them are valid *only* for the dream world. Hence the implications here for Wagner's own arguments were quite significant, for if the common denominator of both the dream world and the waking world lay in the subject or self as different orders of conscious reality that we *can* and *do* experience and cross-correlate, then there must be by analogy still more invariant, fundamental orders of conscious reality with which subjectivity is unified as well. It is the unique role of the musical genius, Wagner maintained, to apprehend these more invariant orders – in his case, to behold the will-to-life as the abstract form or Idea of the world – in order to give it both representation and expression for the 'light-world' before our eyes and the 'sound-world' before our ears (PW 5: 65–72, 'Beethoven'). For if 'I AM' the universal subject – the true zero-point of all subjectivity – and therefore the fulcrum from which even the most universal form of world-reality depends, then this notion, in which all that is created is 'art' and therefore 'illusion', was cast into the more acceptable 'classical' dichotomy between the Apollonian and Dionysian as a means to explain the genesis of Greek tragedy and the apogee of its culture and is, for better or worse, the real key to the metaphysical theses found in *The Birth of Tragedy*.[8]

Yet this says nothing at all about the arguments we find in the essay about culture, which heavily depend on Wagner's Zurich essays, especially 'The Artwork of the Future'. This latter essay is central not only to Nietzsche's entire discussion of the birth and death of tragedy, but likewise, Wagner's arguments that connect life and art as the *conditio sine qua non* of a flourishing culture and thus make the creative deed the genuine metaphysical activity of human beings, is found to be at the very core of Nietzsche's case of Wagner.

---

[8] For Wagner's explanation of the compromise between the Apollonian and Dionysian elements in Greek tragedy, see his essay 'The Destiny of Opera' (PW 5: 138–9). On the connection between transcendent fatalism, transcendental idealism and the dream-like nature of our existence, see Schopenhauer's essay 'On the Transcendent Speculation on the Apparent Deliberateness in the Fate of the Individual' in PP 1, especially pp. 191–7, which quite vividly lays out the epistemological and metaphysical backdrop for *The Birth of Tragedy*.

Suffice it to say, then, that our purpose in this volume is to try to move Nietzsche's engagement with Wagner back to centre stage, where it belongs. And since the nature of our inquiry is concerned with interpreting *The Case of Wagner* as a text, it follows that the primary object of our inquiry must be to demonstrate the nature and extent of Wagner's intellectual influence on Nietzsche precisely in order to unravel the logic behind Nietzsche's enigmatic case of Wagner. After all, it is the nature of this influence that drives Nietzsche's case of Wagner in the first place. This inquiry will in turn help us to address the auxiliary question that is invariably bound up with the nature of that influence; namely, in what sense does Nietzsche's case of Wagner become a matter for philosophy?

In order to do justice to the arguments and to make sense of the challenge that Nietzsche fashions against Wagner, it will be necessary to attend to some of the personal and intellectual dimensions of Nietzsche's relationship with Wagner which inform the narrative context of the claims we encounter in the text itself. It is our contention that Wagner and his theories dominated Nietzsche's intellectual life, and that *The Case of Wagner* as a text must be seen, at least from Nietzsche's perspective, as a very real duel with Wagner over the final meaning of culture. Without attending to this background about how Wagner's influence informed Nietzsche's final position as a philosopher, *The Case of Wagner* can be seen as little more than a curiosity, since the fundamental issues at stake – including why Wagner and his theories were important enough for Nietzsche to return to again and again, and therefore *why* it matters for philosophy – will remain perpetually overlooked.

Our approach to the interpretation of both *The Case of Wagner* and *Nietzsche Contra Wagner* will permit us to identify and define the trajectory of a number of overarching themes in Nietzsche's work as a whole, and to demonstrate how they crystallise into his final and most substantial discussion of Wagner as a result. In this respect, our approach is especially relevant when we come to consider *Nietzsche Contra Wagner*, for as it stands, the latter is essentially an anthology of Nietzsche's earlier remarks about Wagner taken from his previous books, but what little original material it does contain presupposes a direct acquaintance with his relationship with Wagner. Without this contextual backdrop, the book itself is – and will remain – utterly enigmatic. Taken as a whole then, our intention here is meant not only to guide, but to educate, Nietzsche's readers about why Wagner mattered so much to him.

The object of our investigation will be partitioned roughly into three phases. The first is concerned with establishing the nature of Wagner's intellectual influence on Nietzsche, which culminates not merely in the production of *The Birth of Tragedy*, but beyond it to a handful of philosophical commitments about the creative deed and its connection with a flourishing culture. While the circumstances that surround *The Birth of Tragedy* are generally seen as the time of Nietzsche's greatest intellectual convergence with Wagner and the height of his 'pro-Wagnerian' position, our concern here is to explain what it is in particular about his early 'pro-Wagnerian' position that permanently conditioned Nietzsche's approach to art and life, as these commitments will become highly relevant for his eventual case against Wagner. The second phase is concerned with examining these philosophical commitments in light of what might be called Nietzsche's 'post' or 'contra-Wagnerian' position. Here we find, as a text, Nietzsche's *Attempt at a Self-Criticism* to be especially significant in framing the nature of this contrast.[9] The *Attempt* functions both as a preamble and a postscript to *The Birth of Tragedy*, and in doing so, binds the discourse between forward and backward by reclaiming what had passed for the culture of the present up until then (namely Wagner) into an expectation of what is to come for the future (namely Nietzsche). Penned only two years before *The Case of Wagner* itself, the *Attempt* records some of Nietzsche's most relevant philosophical objections against Wagner by emphasising, on the one hand, the substance and continuity of his earlier 'pro-Wagnerian' commitments in the context of his present philosophical project, while on the other, untethering them from

---

[9] The *Attempt* was written in 1886, fourteen years after the original publication of *The Birth of Tragedy*, and was appended to the edition of BT that was issued that year.

Schopenhauer and Wagner, the heroes of the original essay. In this sense, there is perhaps no better hermeneutic focal point for analysing the contrast between his 'pro' and 'contra Wagnerian' positions than the *Attempt*. We then turn to a focused, diachronic examination of Nietzsche's post-Wagnerian works, which allows us to trace this contrast, and indeed to articulate in precisely what sense Nietzsche's philosophical commitments towards the creative deed and its connection with a flourishing culture – the very presuppositions central to his 'pro-Wagnerian' position of culture – become the basis for the case he builds against Wagner and his art. Once we have established the theoretical framework on which Nietzsche's case of Wagner is built and through which his personal challenge to Wagner derives its meaning, we will be prepared to inaugurate the third phase of our investigation through the formal analysis of *The Case of Wagner*.

Structurally, we begin in Chapter 1 by examining one of Wagner's most important and philosophically significant essays from his Zurich period, 'The Artwork of the Future'. The reason we begin our analysis with this essay will become apparent in the sequel, but suffice it to say that 'The Artwork of the Future' is remarkable for its philosophical commitment to what we call the ontology of vitalism, and for the role it plays, both diagnostically and prescriptively, in explaining the decline of art as culture from the time of the ancients, as well as the conditions that might bring about its rebirth. The essay is also noteworthy for fingering the origins of this decline in the ancient world through what Wagner had identified as 'Athenian self-dissection'. In this sense, 'The Artwork of the Future' presents us with one of Wagner's most explicit arguments about the connection between life and art on the one hand, and the so-called 'decline of art at the hands of science' on the other. Finally, but perhaps no less significantly, the essay opines, with Wagner largely speaking for himself, that only when the conditions that brought about tragedy in the ancient world had been seeded – that is, only when art and life were reunited through the universal art forms of poetry and drama – would the 'artist of the future' be at hand. Needless to say, the significance of the 'artist of the future' and its relationship to the decline and rebirth of cultures is very clearly laid out.

Looking then towards *The Birth of Tragedy*, it is an easy matter to demonstrate that Nietzsche marshalled what amounts to Wagnerian theses from first to last by arguing that the so-called Socratic culture, which had destroyed the culture of vitalism on which the tragedy of the ancient world had been built, should itself be seen in its final death throes, while by contrast the vitalism inherent in both Schopenhauer's philosophy and Wagner's music dramas signifies the tangible promise for the rebirth of a new European culture. In this respect, we will show that Nietzsche's earliest meditations on the problem of culture were completely dominated by the problems introduced by Wagner's aesthetics and the promise that he himself represented for the rebirth of a new European culture. It is in this context that we grapple with the symbol of what Nietzsche had then called the 'music-making Socrates', which, as far as we know, has never been sufficiently analysed by the secondary literature on Nietzsche. Yet we maintain that *this* symbol, which specifically designates the *form of a culture*, and which initially represented Wagner and his music as the fulfilment of that culture, ultimately came to signify what Nietzsche sought for himself *contra* Wagner. Therefore the symbol of the 'music-making Socrates', and what later came to be more broadly associated with the idea of the 'philosopher who practices music', holds the key to why Nietzsche's case of Wagner becomes a matter for philosophy.

By utilising a close textual analysis in *The Birth of Tragedy*, we point out that the most fundamental problem at stake in fomenting the 'music-making Socrates' as a cultural form is the question of whether Socratism and art in their present forms are polar opposites. At the core of this examination, however, and guided once again by the steady hand of Wagner, Nietzsche's intention here is to point out that, in the first place, Socratic culture, which has both inherited and incorporated a very long tradition of the rational as first presented by the figure of Socrates, and thus has historically overemphasised rationality at the expense of creativity in accordance with his precedent, is actually (and quite ironically) indebted to the creative vision of Plato and his artistic depiction of Socrates. After all, it is the Socrates of Plato (not the Socrates of Xenophon) through whom we have moulded our history of the rational, and yet this depiction of rationality is embedded in an incredibly rich work of art, and so implicitly relies on the deed of Plato. Through his Dialogues, which signify the artistic deed as such, it is Plato and not Socrates who proves *de facto* that such a fusion between life, science and art was actually possible. Thus, in the context of regenerating a declining and moribund Western culture which had had its origins in the 'devitalizing nature' of Greek science, the primary thesis we find in *The Birth of Tragedy* is that life and art are at the basis of even the Socratic culture itself — that alleged enemy of all art — and that consequently rationality and vitality in the Western canon should have never been divorced from one another. Consequently, the 'music-making Socrates' as we find it in *The Birth of Tragedy* signifies a cultural form in which rationality and creativity must reunite for the purposes of art and life.

In light of these developments, the central issue that we examine in Chapter 2 is how this cultural form changed after Nietzsche had broken away from Wagner. In this sense, Nietzsche's *Attempt* provides us with some very important clues as to the nature of his 'post-Wagnerian' position, and in particular, the rival conception of culture that by that time he had worked out to counter Wagner. As we will show, the basis of this rivalry lay in Nietzsche's desire to fuse the disciplines of philosophy and music for the purposes of life and thus to embody the cultural form of the 'philosopher who practices music' *contra* Wagner. In the context of the *Attempt*, this forces Nietzsche to take up the very models of philosophical and artistic vitalism, and thus the 'heroes' of the original essay pointing towards the rebirth of culture — Schopenhauer and Wagner — specifically in order to refute them. By maintaining, in the first place, that the true ethical implication of Schopenhauer's vitalism entails the unconditional assertion, not the negation, of the will for life, and that affirmation itself is necessary for the purpose of life, Nietzsche contends here that the original 'heroes' in actuality represent the very antitheses of philosophical and artistic vitalism, and that contrary to the bombastic, 'totally German' and 'un-Greek' culture that Wagnerism had come to signify, Nietzsche's challenge to Wagner lay precisely in his attempt to philosophically and artistically resolve the problem of culture at the individual level.

Given that affirmation, not negation, is entailed by the philosophy of vitalism and that Nietzsche's concern is to resolve the problem of culture at the individual level *contra* Wagner, we explore what this means in greater detail in Chapter 3 by using a cross-section of excerpts drawn from Nietzsche's 'post-Wagnerian' writings to illustrate how this rival conception of culture was at pains to compete with Wagner and Wagnerism over the cultural form of the 'philosopher who practices music', and that this competition culminates in his *Zarathustra* as the deed that proved (in Nietzsche's frame of reference) that he had, in effect, achieved precisely what Wagner could not. In the meantime, we note that Nietzsche takes full advantage of the fact that Wagner and Wagnerism had come to signify decline, and moreover for precisely those reasons that Wagner himself had identified in his 'Artwork of the Future'.

By the time we begin our formal analysis of *The Case of Wagner*, which is the object of Chapters 4 and 5, it will be clear that Nietzsche's case of Wagner indisputably possesses an underlying structure to it in which Nietzsche simply holds Wagner to account for his theoretical arguments about the connection between vitalism and art on the one hand, and its relationship to the decline of culture on the other. By appealing to Wagner's own theory about the conditions that govern the decline and rebirth of culture, as well as his 'failure' to live up to it in his final works, Nietzsche simply held Wagner and his 'artwork of the future' to account in order to become a foil for his *Zarathustra*. Once Nietzsche could convince his readers that Wagner's art had fallen victim to his own theories about what governs the decline and rebirth of culture, it followed that Nietzsche could declare himself to be the true 'philosopher who practices music' with his *Zarathustra*, and therefore the true heir of the tragic culture in perfect consistency with his 'pro-Wagnerian' period. In light of these presuppositions, it becomes far easier to grasp the principal 'charges' that make up *The Case of Wagner*, and both our detailed analysis and subsequent discussion of the text itself will reflect this.

Looked at in this way, we argue that Nietzsche's case of Wagner is a case of psychological hegemony in which Nietzsche's personal challenge to Wagner had come to be grafted on to Wagner's own arguments about the organic logic that governs the decline and rebirth of culture, and was then used as the backdrop for his war against Wagner over the meaning of the 'philosopher who practices music' for culture. In light of these conclusions, we offer our final perspective on Nietzsche's case of Wagner by observing that he plays a very dangerous game in his stated task of 'overcoming' Wagner, precisely because the case he makes against Wagner is completely bound up with the case he makes for himself. These final observations in turn provide us with some very suggestive notions about *Nietzsche's* case of Wagner, and how it is fundamentally different from the so-called 'case of Wagner as a genre'. In order then to examine just how pervasive this influence was – in fact to prove that Nietzsche was under the influence of Wagner, and that Wagner was on his agenda from *The Birth of Tragedy* to *The Case of Wagner* – let us get down to particulars.

1
The Artwork of the Future: A Prelude to the Philosophy of the Future

The artwork of the future

In 1849, shortly after Wagner had settled in Zurich as a political exile after his role in the Dresden uprising, he sat down to, in his words, 'pour my heart out to the world'.[1] His chief concern was to 'come to a precise understanding of the issues involved' in his more immediate artistic creations for all those who supported him. Otherwise, Wagner opined, 'we shall all spend the rest of our lives groping around in a loathsome world of half-lit forms . . . in which the benighted traveller can see nothing at all but where he continues to clutch desperately and piously at long familiar objects to guide him on his way'.[2] The result was his essay 'The Artwork of the Future', and the consequence for much that follows was, as we shall see, decisive.

The chief concerns of Wagner's essay are twofold. On the one hand, the essay is concerned with analysing the art forms of modernity and then explaining their deterioration from earlier, more integrated forms. On the other hand, it is concerned with creating and sustaining works of art that possess the features of those earlier, more integrated forms as a means to achieve a kind of radical rebirth of culture.

In order to ground his genealogical analysis of art and culture, Wagner frames his discussion of humanity and nature and their

---

[1] SLRW: 177, letter to Ferdinand Heine, 19 November 1849.
[2] SLRW: 176, letter to Theodor Uhlig, 16 September 1849.

relationship to one another by first appealing to a philosophical orientation that is best captured by the term *vitalism*. As this orientation is central not only to Wagner's analysis of art and culture more generally but to his philosophy as a whole, it is important to grasp the meaning of this term in order to facilitate much of what follows. Vitalism, especially in the Wagnerian sense, should be understood as a philosophical orientation that gives the category of life ontological priority over the categories of mind or intellect, and that points to an existence or reality that can never be known in the exclusively conceptual sense. In this respect, vitalism maintains that the category of life is not only fundamental and original, but that it pervades the category of mind or intellect, which are regarded as secondary and derivative. In this sense, then, mind and nature, Wagner maintains, are not ultimate terms in dialectical tension, but are in reality comprehended by a category that embraces them both: life. But as the principle of intellect is derived from that of life and attains its clearest and most precise focus within the consciousness of man, the fundamental problem, Wagner argued, is that man's identity with life became progressively restricted to the self-conscious focal point of one's own egoistic 'I' as an entity that was separate and apart from nature.[3] As a consequence, nature itself soon came to be regarded as a term that was foreign to man's own essence – an 'object' separate and apart from man himself. To remedy this severance, man soon developed science in order to delve into nature, and by dissecting, analysing and systematising his observations, slowly learned to aid his understanding about the essence of both nature and themselves.

Yet as science clarifies the essence of both man and nature and their relationship to one another, this clarification in the end can only ever point back to the principle of life itself – the source indeed from which both man and nature spring. It is this clarifying power of science, Wagner argues, that teaches man not only to understand and recognise the cyclical necessity that attaches to all mineral, vegetable, animal and human manifestations on

---

[3] For simplicity's sake we have followed the translation of Wagner's essays in using 'man' to convey the idea of humanity and the human being in the abstract.

earth, the totality of which flourish and pass away on a planet that is itself governed by cyclical revolutions; it is the recognition of cyclical necessity as a fundamental law of life in nature that will finally bring man over to art, for it is only through art that a comprehensive vision of life can be depicted which in some measure represents the necessary truths of man and nature in their relationship to life itself.[4]

Wagner goes on to argue that man will never be that which he can and should be 'until his Life is a true mirror of nature' (PW 1: 71) – in other words, until man recognises the necessity of life within himself as the only real power. Until then only arbitrary powers, not necessary ones, will hold sway over the psyche of man in the form of dogmas – religious, scientific or otherwise – or those of patriotism and other nationalistic prejudices. Therefore modern man, according to Wagner, must advance his knowledge past the dialectical tension that exists between mind and nature in order to firmly establish it in the recognition that he and nature are truly one as a conscious, experiential fact. Only in this way can art as culture be born again. Wagner summarises

---

[4] In the very first section of his essay, Wagner summarises this monumental teleology as plainly as can be: 'From the moment when man perceived the difference between himself and nature, and thus commenced his own development as *man*, by breaking loose from the unconsciousness of natural animal life and passing over into conscious life – when he thus first looked at nature in the face and from the first feelings of his dependency on her, thereby aroused, evolved the faculty of thought – from that moment did error begin, as the earliest utterance of consciousness. But error is the mother of knowledge; and the history of the birth of knowledge out of error is the history of the human race, from the myths of primal ages down to the present day . . . Through this knowledge does nature grow conscious of herself; and verily by man himself, who only through discriminating between himself and nature has attained that point where he can apprehend her, by making her his "object". But this distinction is merged once more, when man recognizes the essence of nature as his very own, and perceives the same necessity in all the elements and lives around him, and therefore in his own existence no less than in nature's being; thus not only recognizing the mutual bond of union between all natural phenomena, but also his own community with nature. If nature then, by her solidarity with man, attains *in* man her consciousness, and if man's life is the very activation of this consciousness . . . so does man's life itself gain understanding by means of science, which makes this human life in turn an object of experience. But the activation of the consciousness attained by science, the portrayal of the Life that it has learnt to know, the impress of this life's necessity and truth, is – *Art*' (PW 1: 70–1).

this thesis with well-nigh perfect precision on the following page of his essay when he states that

> The path of science lies from error to knowledge, from fancy to reality, from religion to nature. In the beginning of science, therefore, man stands toward Life in the same relation as he stood toward the phenomena of Nature when he first commenced to part his life from hers. Science takes over the arbitrary concepts of the human brain, in their totality; while, by her side, Life follows in its totality the instinctive evolution of Necessity. Science thus bears the burden of the sins of Life, and expiates them by her own self-abrogation; she ends in her direct antithesis, in the knowledge of Nature, in the recognition of the unconscious, instinctive, and therefore real, inevitable, and physical. The character of science is therefore finite: that of Life, unending; just as error is of time, but Truth eternal . . . The end of science is the justifying of the unconscious, the giving of self-consciousness to Life, the re-instatement of the senses in their perceptive rights, the sinking of caprice in the world-Will of Necessity. Science is therefore the vehicle of knowledge, her procedure mediate, her goal an intermediation; but Life is the great ultimate, a law unto itself. As science melts away into the recognition of the ultimate and self-determinate reality, of actual Life itself: so does this avowal win its frankest, most direct expression in art, or rather in the *work of art* . . . The art-work, thus conceived as an immediate vital act, is therewith the perfect reconcilement of science with Life, the laurel-wreath which the vanquished, redeemed by her defeat, reaches in joyous homage to her acknowledged victor. (PW 1: 72–3)

From this excerpt we are provided with a vivid conceptual schema of the unfolding of man and nature for conscious life. The intellect, which had once been severed from life to look upon nature as its object, evolved into the faculty of self-conscious reason. And through the clarifying power of science as its highest achievement, reason in man has recognised that it is in truth identical with life itself, and so consciously returns to the source from which both reason and nature sprang in order to reflect back to nature the principle of life as 'the great ultimate', and to consecrate this knowledge in the immediate vital act that is the work of art. The implication of Wagner's thesis can hardly be skirted: art is the truly metaphysical activity of man.

'Athenian self-dissection' and the decline of culture at the hands of science

As we can see, the principle of life is for Wagner the ultimate ontological category: it is the source from which both humanity and nature spring as well as the depths into which both are resolved. But for Wagner, there is a very big difference between what he deems 'an unconscious life-pulse' which follows the instinctual necessity of nature, and the recognition of this necessity as a conscious, experiential fact. The former is necessarily collective, because the unconscious life-pulse at the basis of manifestation has yet to attain the stamp of self-conscious cognition through individualised expression. Indeed 'the folk', Wagner tells us, is the essence of all those 'who feel a common and collective want', but do so only dimly and instinctually, for they have yet to cognise this 'want of necessity' apart from the collective (PW 1: 75). But when individual cognition attains conscious identification with the instinctual necessity of nature, and then strives as a consequence to bring forth this vital force to conscious expression in the work of art, only then does the light of cognition 'uphold to life the picture of its own existence, and lift unconscious life to conscious knowledge of itself' (PW 1: 197). Thus we find that the genuinely expressive or creative act is driven by this 'want of necessity' and that it arises organically from within the collective womb of 'the folk'; but only the artist qua genius is capable of bringing forth this unconscious life-pulse to concrete expression in the work of art.

Having argued up to this point in the essay that the need for art is no arbitrary matter, Wagner then singles out the one example of an art form whose 'glorious fruits' had arisen from the unconscious depths of the folk: 'Before what phenomenon', Wagner asks us, 'do we stand with more humiliating sense of the impotence of our frivolous culture, than before the art of the *Hellenes*?' (PW 1: 89). In the context of Wagner's essay the nature of this question is significant, for Wagner's case study of Greek tragedy from this point forward functions both diagnostically and prescriptively in the arguments about culture that ensue. Now, before we consider the nature of his arguments, we should point out that it is immaterial whether or not the art of tragedy arose in the manner specified by Wagner. What *is* important is that Greek tragedy signified a historical art form that could accommodate the philosophical framework Wagner had applied to it, in which art as culture could be defined and deduced.

According to Wagner, Greek tragedy attained the summit of artistic perfection in its portrayal of life, for by its poetry, music, symbol and mime, Greek tragedy had been able to depict the great truth that life in nature is cyclical, as both man and nature are equally subject to its necessity, and that the element of vital time, therefore, is tragic.[5] In this regard, Greek tragedy had been the only art form of antiquity to have plumbed the depths of life in order to 'uphold to life the picture of its own existence'; and as this insight and portrayal of life is precisely the object of art according to Wagner's thesis, art in this sense would be synonymous with culture.

Using the music drama of Greek antiquity as the prototype of an earlier, more integrated form of art, Wagner begins by sketching out a genealogical analysis of the art forms that have since come down to modernity, tracing their separation from the Greek prototype, and explaining the nature of that separation almost exclusively in terms of a vitalistic cause. In particular, Wagner argues that the forms of art that we now possess have long since bifurcated the 'total man' into forms that address themselves either to the 'inner' or 'outer' man, but not both, as was once the case for the music drama of Greek antiquity.

---

[5] It is important to note why we describe time here as 'vital', as there is an implicit distinction between the notion of 'vital' as opposed to 'quantifiable' or 'mathematical time'. While the essence of vital or living time is *irreversible* and therefore tragic, quantifiable or mathematical time is clearly reversible.

To explain what he means by the 'inner' and 'outer' man, Wagner begins by telling us that the faculty of vision is the strongest sense organ corresponding to man's outward nature. Vision is the faculty responsible, in effect, for man's perception of individuation, and supports all intellectual judgements rooted in distinction and difference. Conversely, however, the faculty of hearing is the strongest sense organ corresponding to man's inward nature, and especially through the art of music, undergirds all judgements rooted in unity and sameness. Yet from this bifurcation of the total man, we have art forms that have come down to the present day which address themselves almost exclusively to the 'outer man' (namely, the plastic arts of architecture, sculpture and painting) or to the 'inner man' (namely, the humanistic arts of dance, poetry and music), and they do so, Wagner argues, not out of any real necessity, but out of what he calls 'egoistic excess'. And while it is never directly stated, it nonetheless seems clear that the fragmented nature of the art forms now in existence in every way reflect humanity's own fragmented psyche in its separation from nature, and it is this relationship to nature that is responsible for, and that conditions, the splintered, fractured and decadent art forms as they presently stand.

What is especially noteworthy for our purposes is that Wagner traces the original splintering of the art forms to a singular ground or cause which, in his framework, has *vital* ramifications. In particular, Wagner tells us that

> Tragedy flourished for just so long as it was inspired by the spirit of the folk . . . but when the national brotherhood of the Folk was shivered into fragments, when the common bond of its religion and primeval customs was pierced and severed by the sophist needles of the egoistic spirit of Athenian self-dissection – then the folk's artwork also ceased: then did the professors and the doctors of the literary guilds inherit the ruins of the fallen edifice, and delved among its beams and stones to pry, to ponder, and to re-arrange its members. With the laughter of Aristophanes, the folk relinquished to these learned insects the refuse of its meal, threw art upon one side for

two millennia, and fashioned of its innermost necessity the history of the world; all while those scholars cobbled up their tiresome history of literature, by order of the supreme court of Alexander. (PW 1: 136)

Indeed, as Wagner goes on to explain, once tragedy had been rent asunder, the art of poetry no longer prophesied, 'but only *described*' (PW 1: 137). It was not long afterwards that poetry turned to science, and soon after to philosophy (PW 1: 139). In other words, 'the egoistic spirit of Athenian self-dissection' ushered in the event of science at the very moment that the ancient music drama was flowering on Greek soil, thereby severing man from himself, and in turn, the unconscious life-pulse at the basis of all manifestation. Tragedy was destroyed, and in its stead we were left with a 2,000-year-old record that testifies to the decline of art at the hands of science – a trend that has culminated in the creations of modern art, 'the sexless, barren child of this dream' (PW 1: 74).

If, therefore, we consider his thesis seriously, the *diagnostic* aspect to Wagner's case study of Greek tragedy signified an art form in which the emphasis on the rational or logical aspect in man had not yet created a schism between himself and nature, and consequently the 'unconscious life-pulse' at the basis of manifestation. One's identity had not yet been bound up with, and restricted to, the self-conscious focal point of one's egoistic 'I' as that alone which is exclusively rational, and so had not yet estranged itself from nature to look upon her as an object separate and apart from oneself. Art, and therefore religion, were still possible, for reason was still rooted in the principle of life, allowing the artist to depict a total vision of the nature of existence. This is what gave the ancient music drama its terrible and profound insight into existence as a whole, for here was a wisdom that arose from the unconscious depths of life and was then symbolised, artistically, through the beat, the rhythm and the periodicity of poetry, music and mime in the Greek chorus as the truest expression of the 'unconscious life force' of folk. But this all changed when 'the egoistic spirit of Athenian self-dissection' came on the scene.

Science, redeemed by her defeat, reaches out to her acknowledged victor: art

In Wagner's estimation, the very existence of an art form that had reached a high degree of synthesis in antiquity, and from which the decline of the arts into their present forms could be traced, provided in some sense its own justification. At the same time, the diagnostic aspect of Wagner's case study is central to his thesis about the philosophical significance of art, and lays the foundations for his subsequent criticism of the art forms of modernity. In this respect, then, Wagner's case study of the ancient music drama also functioned prescriptively as a blueprint for how culture could be revitalised, and throughout the body of his essay Wagner provides us with clues as to how the artwork of the future would be achieved.

We need only consider Wagner's comments about the 'artwork of the future' in the section of his essay titled 'The Artist of the Future'. It is here that we get perhaps the most fruitful comments regarding the prescriptive nature of the music drama as a blueprint for how art as culture could be revitalised. The declarations that Wagner makes here are the culmination of his compelling but tortuous meditations on the decline of art since the time of the ancient Greeks, and in spirit accentuate the ontological commitment to vitalism at the base of his entire argument about culture. In this section, Wagner begins by asking what the present-day life conditions must be in order for the separate art branches that have come down to modernity to be reunited in the artwork of the future. As each branch of art has its own specialised artist, the artist of the future would have to be, at least in principle, one who specialises in as many of the present-day art forms as possible. At the same time, the artwork of the future cannot be created according to an arbitrary canon, for only comparatively few art forms are grounded in the immediate conditions of life. Therefore to determine who the artist of the future will be, Wagner tells us that we must first trace back his appearance to the art forms that are grounded in the immediate conditions of life from which the artwork of the future would arise. As we might expect, the art forms in question are poetry and drama. So when it comes to the question of who will become the artist of the future, Wagner tells us that it will be 'Without a doubt, the poet. But *who* will be the poet? Indisputably the *performer.* Yet *who*, again, will be the performer? Necessarily, the *fellowship of all the artists*' (PW 1: 195–6).[6]

Wagner goes on to tell us that 'the Artwork of the Future is an associate work, and only an associate demand can call it forth' (PW 1: 196). And while Wagner's 'fellowship of artists' implies a *communal* effort in which the folk would once again become the creative force from which the innovation of all genuine art would be made possible, it seems hardly worth mentioning that Wagner, with his own distinct specialities as both a librettist and a musician, was really nominating himself.[7]

The nature of dramatic action, Wagner reiterates, borrows all its materials from the concrete particularities of life, while the dramatic art itself acts as a mirror to life by upholding to it 'a picture of its own existence'. Drama is therefore the consummate art form of the 'outer man' and forms the intelligible bond that directly links art with life.[8] At the same time only music – or 'tone poetry' in Wagner's nomenclature – directly accesses the feeling nature of the 'inner man', for it is immediate and irrefutable.[9] Therefore by bringing together music and drama – and, in a manner of speaking, Wagner's own genius for these two art forms – the inner and outer man would be reunified once again and the artwork of the future would be achieved.

---

[6] In identifying poetry as one of the principal art forms of the artist of the future, Wagner himself hastens to footnote the word 'poet', noting that the term itself should not be restricted to its more traditional literary sense, but that it should be sufficiently broad to include the notion of tone poetry (that is, music) as well (PW 1: 196 note 38).

[7] This is especially clear when we consider Wagner's explanation of the artist and his relationship to the folk, as well as how he uses both Beethoven and Shakespeare in his essay as the two examples whose universalising genius in the separate domains of music and drama prefigure (to Wagner) Wagner's *own* totalising art as symbols of the tendency towards which the artwork of the future was pointing.

[8] Compare PW 1: 196–7.

[9] As Wagner remarks much earlier in the essay, 'the inner man can only find direct communication through the ear, and that by means of voice's tone. Tone is the immediate utterance of feeling and has its physical seat within the heart, whence start and whither flow the waves of life-blood. Through the sense of hearing, tone urges forth from the feeling of one heart to the feeling of its fellow' (PW 1: 91).

Vitalism and art

At this point, we can bring a couple of very important points into focus regarding Wagner's prescriptive blueprint for how art as culture should be revitalised. First, as we have already pointed out, the principle of life is the fundamental ontological category for Wagner, and this ontology unquestionably points to a worldview that is grounded in what we called vitalism. From this philosophical orientation, one very important consequence for Wagnerian aesthetics follows: if the category of life has priority over the categories of mind or intellect, then it follows that all conceptual constructions which are not rooted in a creative source can only possess instrumental, not absolute, values for life and thought. For Wagner, the essence of life is fundamentally creative, and that implies that all genuine conception is *generative*, not discursive.[10] This is perhaps most convincingly illustrated by the fact that science, in Wagner's analysis, will never know or discover anything other than the principle of life itself – the very principle that the artist instinctively recognises and, in the total work of art, depicts (PW 1: 139).

Second, and perhaps more importantly, Wagner's theses unequivocally imply that the artist of the future must be by turns both a philosopher and an artist. Philosophically, the individual artist must recognise the periodicity of nature and the necessity of its cycles, and so must perceive that the unfolding of man, and the evolution of his faculties, are, as a microcosm of nature, governed by that very same periodicity and necessity. Accordingly, the faculty of reason, through which nature 'has attained her consciousness in man', will finally lead reason back to a conscious recognition that she and nature are identical, and through nature, to the grounding that comprehends them both: to 'life as the great ultimate'.

---

[10] In this connection, it is noteworthy to point out that the ancients themselves called the creative force in nature the λόγος σπερματικός (*logos spermatikos*). Hence the very idea that the creative activity of the intellect is totally non-discursive, and becomes aware of its object in a way that has nothing in common with reasoning from premises to conclusions, is fundamental to the activity of the genius that Wagner so prized.

Artistically, however, the individual philosopher must tap into the same creative source out of which both man and nature are derived in order to hold up to life, through the mirror of art, the innermost kernel of the world, the necessary truths of life itself. Because all genuine conception is deemed to be creative or generative, the inescapable consequence is that the philosophical and artistic drives must be united as a precondition for a flourishing culture. Only then can the artwork of the future be achieved. Furthermore, if the role of both philosopher and artist is to bring this 'unconscious life-pulse' to conscious expression in the work of art, then the artist of the future is in some manner a progenitor in his or her capacity to realise both the elements of wisdom and the expression of that wisdom from out of the collective womb of the folk.

Third and finally, it should be clear that Wagner's position on cultures in general and flourishing ones in particular is that they are always rooted in the presuppositions of vitalism. As a consequence, there is a relationship between the strength and flourishing of a given culture and the emphasis that that culture places on the categories of life and instinct over the categories of mind and intellect. The more a given culture emphasises and accentuates the categories of mind or intellect over those of will and life, the more anaemic, enervated and decadent that culture has become. This is, in point of fact, the *raison d'être* of Wagner's entire genealogical analysis of the arts that have come down to the present day from the time of the ancients.

Taken together, then, we are now able to recognise how Wagner's case study of the ancient Greeks functions both diagnostically and prescriptively in his attempts to address the problem of culture and to clear the way for the artwork of the future. Diagnostically, the decline of the arts from the more integrated ancient forms was due almost entirely to a declining form of life in which the categories of mind or intellect superseded those of man's unconscious instincts for life. This led to an increasingly fractured sense of self estranged from nature, and eventually in turn from man's own instincts for life. As we now know, the death of the tragic concept began with the 'egoistic spirit of Athenian self-dissection'. Yet just as the death of vitalism as a world-view had been responsible for the death of all genuine art as culture, so too would its rebirth be the precondition of the rebirth of art as culture. Therefore, prescriptively, Wagner's case study of the ancients is concerned, plainly and simply, with the conditions according to which the rebirth of culture might be achieved.

The Birth of Tragedy and the 'music-making Socrates'

Having examined Wagner's essay in some depth, it is important that we turn our attention briefly to *The Birth of Tragedy*, Nietzsche's first published work, and the essay that formally established his alliance with Wagner as the artist of the future. The nature of this investigation is highly significant, for as we shall see, the idea behind the 'philosopher who practices music' – or what Nietzsche calls here in *The Birth of Tragedy* the 'music-making Socrates' – not only designates the form of a culture and thus the 'turning point' to bring about the rebirth of art as culture, much as Wagner's essay had done; it is also the central symbol around which Nietzsche's subsequent 'war in aesthetics' with Wagner revolves. By recognising the value of this symbol through the analysis that we provide, we will finally be able to grasp the theoretical foundations that animate the case of Wagner and from which the terms of Nietzsche's dispute with him derive their chief thrust and significance.

There are three sections in *The Birth of Tragedy* that allude to the figure of the 'music-making Socrates', and it is important to point out that all three either directly prefigure Nietzsche's extended panegyric to Wagner (§§14 and 15) or are part and parcel with it (§17). Superficially at least, the historical figure of Socrates and the 'music-making Socrates' possess very different valuations in *The Birth of Tragedy*, so it is important to grasp how these two figures are related to one another and in what sense the 'music-making Socrates' in particular becomes necessary for the rebirth of tragic culture.

While BT 12 has been singled out by countless commentators as the definitive section in which Nietzsche pins responsibility on the historical figure of Socrates for having destroyed Greek tragedy, we can now affirm that this censure has its origins in Wagner's essay from more than twenty years previously. But what makes this censure particularly significant is that, much like Wagner's treatment of the problem in his own essay, Nietzsche understands the historical figure of Socrates as part of a larger trend, that is, as a symbol of the tendency or direction towards which the tragic culture was heading. In BT 14, Nietzsche tells us that the anti-Dionysiac tendency towards tragedy, as typified by the optimistic element of dialectic, had been around and at work destroying the roots of the chorus 'with the rod of its syllogisms' already in the time of Sophocles, and that the figure of Socrates 'was simply its most magnificent expression'.

As he pursues the thread of this argument into section 15, it is clear that Nietzsche views the historical appearance of Socrates, more than anything else, as the prototype of an instinct that ran counter to the creative instincts that conceived the tragic culture; namely, 'the prototype of *theoretical man*' (BT 15). Through the historical figure of Socrates, this new instinct found expression in the idea that 'rational thought, guided by causality, can penetrate to the depths of being, and that it is capable not only of knowing but even of *correcting* being' (BT 15). Yet this new instinct, which saw error as the embodiment of evil, was itself (to Nietzsche) rooted in error, precisely because it was uprooted from the principle of life.[11] What followed from the 'inverted instincts' of Socrates was the rise of modern 'theoretical man' and, in effect, the decline of culture at the hands of science. Thus, when Nietzsche tells us, as he does towards the close of BT 14, that we 'must not shirk the question of where such a phenomenon as Socrates was pointing' in the midst of this anti-Dionysiac tendency, we can be certain that it was not the mere historical

---

[11] Note that what is especially outrageous to Nietzsche is that the value of the concept has been inverted in the person of Socrates to that which distinguishes, defines, analyses, criticises and, in general, discursively reasons from premises to conclusions. In other words, the concept no longer *generates*, so that what had once been seen as primary and original (that is, life itself) is now regarded through the concept as somehow secondary and derivative. As Nietzsche notes in BT 13, Socrates' instinct for life, and 'the tremendous driving-wheel of logical Socratism' behind him was inverted and antipodal.

figure of Socrates that was problematic for the tragic culture, but rather what his appearance signified by so emerging.

As far as Nietzsche's arguments are concerned in BT 15, which on the whole attempt to connect the significance of Socrates with the advent of modern theoretical man, Nietzsche flatly tells us that 'we cannot help but see Socrates as the turning point, the vortex of world history' (BT 15). In other words, the historical figure of Socrates is the most magnificent expression of a culture committed to the idea that rationality must be divorced from the creative instincts for life – an instinct that, as we know from Wagner's analysis, runs counter to the tragic age of the Greeks.

Socrates, make music!

While the 'immediate effect of the Socratic impulse led inexorably to the dissolution of Dionysiac tragedy' (BT 14), Nietzsche acknowledges at the same time that the phenomenon of Socrates cannot be regarded as an altogether 'negative agent of destruction' (BT 14), and he supports this contention by appealing to the nature of the Platonic dialogues as a whole. Now the question of course becomes, why? The answer to this question is critical, for in what immediately follows, it soon becomes clear that the nature of the dialogues themselves is intimately bound up with the question of whether Socratism and art are the polar opposites that they at first seem to be, and whether they were seen to be so even in the time of Socrates himself. By appealing to Plato's depiction of the final moments in the life of Socrates, Nietzsche's endeavour here is to test, at least in part, the rigidity of this opposition, for it is precisely at this point in BT 14 that we encounter, for the first time, the question of whether the 'artistic' or 'music-making Socrates' is a contradiction in terms, and whether the appearance of such a phenomenon becomes necessary for the rebirth of culture. In this respect, it is essential for us to grasp how the Platonic dialogues function in the arguments that ensue, and what their relationship is to the nature of the 'music-making Socrates' for culture.

In order to test this opposition, Nietzsche begins by recounting an anecdote given in Plato's *Phaedo*. The scene is Socrates' cell on the day of his execution. His friends enter to visit him one last time and Socrates is soon asked why, when he had never written a single line of poetry, he was now composing a hymn to Apollo and putting some of Aesop's fables into verse. In response, Socrates tells his friends that he had often had a dream in which he was told to 'make and cultivate music', but he had always thought that his dream was bidding him do what he was doing already, which was the study of philosophy. Doubts, however, had crept in, and according to Nietzsche, these doubts were indicative of a very real deficiency in Socrates' approach to philosophy, for as Nietzsche goes on to tell us

> Where art was concerned, the despotic logician had the sense of a lacuna, a void, something of a reproach, of a possibly neglected duty . . . Until shortly before his death, he drew comfort from the idea that his philosophy was the highest of the arts, spurning the notion that a deity might remind him of 'vulgar, popular music.' To salve his conscience entirely, he finally resolved in prison to make the very art he held in such low esteem. And with this attitude he wrote a hymn to Apollo and put some Aesopian fables into verse . . . This voice of the Socratic dream vision is *the only indication that he ever gave any consideration to the limitations of logic.* He was obliged to ask: 'Is that which is unintelligible to me necessarily unintelligent? Might there be a realm of wisdom from which the logician is excluded? *Might art even be a necessary correlative and supplement to science?*' (BT 14, our emphasis)

When we examine Nietzsche's interpretation of this anecdote, its most outwardly apparent feature is that it introduces an element of ambiguity as to whether the 'despotic logician' might have recognised the limitations of logic in the final moments of his life. However, the rhetorical effect of this tension, which Nietzsche introduces but leaves us to resolve, is deliberate, for if the 'despotic logician' might have doubted the totalising nature of logic during the final moments of his life, it follows that the nature of this ambiguity might very well open up a further uncertainty as to whether, in fact, there *are* limitations to logic of which modern theoretical man should be apprised. In other words, Nietzsche's interpretation of the anecdote is specifically framed in order to test a point of Wagnerian propaganda regarding the limitations of science, and how those limits, once recognised, might bring forth the genuine work of art.[12]

In light of these statements, Nietzsche's interpretation of the anecdote in the *Phaedo* now becomes clear. According to Nietzsche, Socrates had simply been misinterpreting his divine sign all along, but it was only during the final moments of his life that a genuine afflatus walked in on the maieutic master: here, just hours before his death, Socrates was made to realise that there *is* a somewhat that is more fundamental than reason, or at the very least correlative to it, and that music does, in fact, speak to it. 'After all', Socrates reasoned, 'music is certainly intelligible, so perhaps *my* logic for what is intelligible is simply the definition of what is intelligible from the limitation of my own point of view.' The logical consequence of this realisation, Nietzsche implies, is that Socrates had only practised one part of the great art, but not the great art in its entirety, and during the final moments of his life his divine sign had made this perfectly clear.

Yet notwithstanding, we are still left wondering what this anecdote implies about the 'music-making Socrates' as a cultural form and how it is connected with the rebirth of culture. Accordingly it is here that we encounter what one might call a meta-narrative problem connected with our understanding of 'modern theoretical man'. While there is no question that the Platonic dialogues as a whole have been indispensable in shaping the notion of what is rational right down to the present day, there is at the same time one critical insight that is perpetually overlooked in tracing this narrative history of 'the rational' back to the historical Socrates as the prototype of modern theoretical man: to see Socrates as the symbol of rationality who routinely triumphs over his vanquished and exhausted foes with the oft-repeated formula that only what is rational is beautiful, and whose singular insistence on this equation

---

[12] Compare PW 1: 72–3, 'Artwork of the Future'.

soon became the intellectual imperative of science, is to completely disregard the fact that this is a *depiction of the rational as a world-view*, and it is a depiction moreover that has been built upon art as the immediate vital act of life – Plato's in particular. There is no question that the dialogues themselves are concerned with cultivating our own understanding, but it is also true that as the image of dialectical intelligibility, Socrates himself has been presented to us as a work of art, and it is precisely this image of Socrates that Plato created and embedded within an incredibly rich artistic presentation.[13]

Thus when we consider the symbol of the dying Socrates, so filled with dramatic life and so rich in invention, a symbol so powerful that the image itself soon became the emblem over the portals of science symbolising its own 'inverted instincts' towards life (according to Nietzsche's arguments), we must also recognise in the same moment that this archetypal depiction of rationality was created by none other than Plato – that same Plato who, in his early youth, had written tragedies, epigrams and dithyrambs before he had 'burnt his writings in order to become a pupil of Socrates' (BT 14). Plato may have ardently desired to reveal the dialectical greatness of his master to the world, and yet '*from complete artistic necessity he had to create an art form* that was related on a deep level to the art forms already in existence, which he repudiated' (BT 14, our emphasis). Indeed, Nietzsche points out that the Platonic dialogues as a whole are a mixture of all available styles, which almost seem as if 'tragedy had absorbed all earlier genres within itself' to find itself 'hovering somewhere between narrative, lyric poetry and drama, between prose and poetry' (BT 14), and perhaps, indeed, music besides.[14]

What, then, are we to make of these claims? Very simply, Nietzsche's arguments imply that for all of his professed devotion to the dialectic method, Plato had to resort to his *creative*

---

[13] Compare Schopenhauer's thoughts on the Socrates of Plato as opposed to that of Xenophon in PP 1, 'Fragments for the History of Philosophy', 3.

[14] In his essay 'The Destiny of Opera', Wagner notes that Plato was the first to unify myth, epic and dramatic invention in his dialogues in order to set 'philosophic theses in a quasi-popular light', and for which his principal teachings are consciously formulated and embedded within 'directly witnessed scenes from life' (PW 6: 138).

instinct after all. Plato's instinct for tragedy finally triumphed over his newly found 'rational' love for dialectics, so that when it came to composing his dialogues, it was the fusion of these two elements – rationality and creativity – that produced not only the totalising and comprehensive world-view of science as given through the figure of Socrates, but also an entirely new genre of art in the process, for in his wake, Nietzsche reminds us, 'Plato gave posterity the model for a new art form – the novel' (BT 14).

The moral of the story, of course, is that rationality cannot be divorced from the creative instincts for life, which is the very urge or desire to which music speaks, but it is Plato and *not* Socrates who ultimately furnishes us with this insight. And when we examine the Platonic dialogues as a whole, it quickly becomes apparent that these two elements are not divorced from one another, but are on the contrary in perfect harmony.

Knocking at the portals of the present and the future

Through our analysis of BT 14, we discovered that the cultural form of the 'music-making Socrates' implies the fusion of the rational and creative elements of consciousness, a phenomenon that is especially marked in the figure of Plato. But in the context of Nietzsche's arguments here, what does the advocacy of this position mean for the decline and rebirth of art as culture as we find them in BT 15, shortly before he appeals to the figure of the 'music-making Socrates' for the second time? The principal meaning is that we must come to recognise that art is the immediate vital act of life, for once we do (according to the Wagnerian thesis), it 'becomes the perfect reconcilement of science with life, the laurel-wreath which the vanquished, redeemed by her defeat, reaches out in homage to her acknowledged victor' (PW 1: 73, 'Artwork of the Future').

In other words, once science 'melts away' into the recognition of life as the 'ultimate self-determinate reality' (PW 1: 73), we shall see 'the insatiable, optimistic zest for knowledge, exemplified in the figure of Socrates, transformed into tragic resignation and a need for art' (BT 15). It is this imminent decline of the Socratic culture that leads Nietzsche to 'knock agitatedly at the portals of the present and the future' at the climax of BT 15 in favour of a new cultural 'transformation'; for only when rationality is united to the creative instincts for life will it 'lead to ever-new configurations of genius, and particularly that of the *music-making Socrates*' (BT 15). To be perfectly clear, the new form of culture must unite the philosophical and artistic drives (as Wagner had claimed was necessary), for only this 'configuration' would lead to the rebirth of tragic knowledge.

We must now consider similar phenomena in the present

Knowing as we do now that the historical Socrates and the 'music-making Socrates' symbolise two totally different valuations, and that the latter in particular is intimately bound up with Wagner's prescriptive thesis for how the rebirth of culture might be achieved, we can hardly be surprised at what Nietzsche tells us next at the beginning of BT 16. Specifically, he informs us that the nature of this example is meant 'to explain how tragedy perishes when deprived of the spirit of music *just as sure as it can be born only of that spirit*' (BT 16, our emphasis), and the value of this explanation, as Nietzsche plainly states here, is meant for us 'frankly' to 'consider similar phenomena in the present' (BT 16). In other words, the reason Nietzsche appeals to the decline of Greek tragedy as well as the conditions that might vindicate its rebirth is precisely in order to highlight the organic and dynamic similarities between the conditions of the past and those of the present.

While the specific metaphysical claims that follow are outside the immediate scope of this book, the discussion of culture that ensues makes it clear that the philosophy of Schopenhauer and the music dramas of Wagner are promoted as the necessary ingredients for the rebirth of the tragic spirit, and that they are in some manner analogous to the early tragic philosophies of the pre-Socratics and the dawn of tragedy in the person of Aeschylus before it succumbed to the dialectical impulse of syllogistic thought and an optimistic faith in the explicability of nature. By marking out the problem of modern Socratic culture in terms that are antithetical to the spirit of tragedy — and by extension Wagner's art — it is clear that Nietzsche defines their relationship as one of opposing tendencies in dialectical tension. It is in this spirit that we encounter Nietzsche's final allusion to the figure of the 'music-making Socrates' in section 17 of *The Birth of Tragedy*.

Given the emphasis we have placed on grasping the conceptual framework of Wagner's arguments about the decline and rebirth of culture that are at work in *The Birth of Tragedy*, it is worth reproducing the relevant passage in its entirety.

> Here we are concerned with the question of whether the opposing power to which tragedy succumbed will always have the strength to obstruct the artistic reawakening of tragedy and the tragic philosophy. If the tragedy of the ancients was diverted from its course by the dialectical impulse towards knowledge and scientific optimism, we might conclude from this that there is a never-ending struggle between the theoretical and the tragic philosophies. And only after the scientific spirit has been taken to its limits, and had been forced by the demonstration of those limits to renounce its claim to universal validity, can we hope for a rebirth of tragedy. We might employ the symbol of the *music-making Socrates*, in the sense discussed earlier, to describe that cultural form. (BT 17)

Once again, the parallels with the Wagnerian thesis are unmistakable, and from this passage we can finally fashion the argument's overall structure. According to the tenor of the general argument, Greek tragedy, which had succumbed to the 'Athenian self-dissection' of Socratic culture, had, at the same time, severed humanity from themselves and from their creative instincts for life. Consequently the nature of music, which is the consummate art form of the inner man, disappeared from the drama once the category of reason superseded that of life itself, and this in turn led to the 'decline of art at the hands of science'. But as the 'deepest and most universal science can know nothing else but life itself', science 'can only gain her perfect confirmation in the work of art' (PW 1: 139). In other words, only when 'science melts away into the recognition of the ultimate self-determinate reality, of actual life itself' (PW 1: 73) will the scientific spirit be taken to its limits, and only then can we hope to win this acknowledgement through the work of art. Once this happens, the severed art forms of music and drama will once more be unified, and only then will 'inner' and 'outer man', the will and its representation, the Dionysian and the Apollonian, find themselves in harmony once again. This is the formula for the artwork of the future and, as Nietzsche acknowledges, the symbol of the 'music-making Socrates' describes this cultural form.

Yet in order to pave the way for the rebirth of tragedy, the teleology of the 'music-making Socrates' must combat the 'anti-Dionysiac tendency' of 'blind science' and 'knowledge at all costs' by restoring the relationship between art and life. This implies that the teleology of the 'music-making Socrates' is utterly antipodal to the teleology of the historical Socrates and his school, an instinct that completely 'negates culture' (UF 21[11], summer 1872–early 1873). And if these two phenomena stand in an antipodal relationship to one another, then the phenomenon of Socrates on the one hand and the 'philosopher who speaks music' on the other represents the dividing and uniting point of two cultural tendencies in antithetical tension. Figure 1 helps us to envision how this organic form to art as culture is structured. With this diagram before us, we are in a much better position to grasp the significance of what usually passes for Wagnerian propaganda in the remaining sections of *The Birth of Tragedy*. As far as both thinkers are concerned, modernity had reached the bottommost point of the downward swing in a declining culture, and the solution, in the form of an extended panegyric to Wagner, is precisely what *The Birth of Tragedy* purports to provide: the 'philosopher who speaks music' must materialise in order to restore the relationship between art and life.

As we can see, between the emerging Socratic culture and the precipitous decline of the tragic culture in the ancient world, the figure of Socrates stood as the destructive force behind one

Reason <u>divorced</u>
from the creative instincts for life =
'Socrates'

<u>**The Rebirth of Culture**</u>　　　　　　　　<u>**The Decline of Culture**</u>

The birth of tragedy　　　　　　　　　　　　The death of tragedy

Dionysian culture　　　　　　　　　　　　　Socratic culture

Tragic knowledge　　　　　　　　　　　　　Egoistic knowledge

Unity of drives　　　　　　　　　　　　　　Fragmentation of drives

Pre-Socratics : Aeschylus ::　　　　　　　　　Socrates : Euripides ::
Schopenhauer : Wagner　　　　　　　　　　Socratic culture : Opera

Rationality <u>fused</u> to the
creative instincts for life =
'Music-making Socrates'
Philosopher Who Speaks Music

Figure 1.1 Nietzsche's 'pro-Wagnerian' conception of culture

world-view and yet the progenitor of another, thereby symbolising the dividing and uniting point of two cultures in contradictory or antithetical tension. Indeed, we know according to Nietzsche's own diagnosis that 'the decline of Greek tragedy seems necessarily to have been the result of a curious dissociation of the two primal artistic drives, a process that went hand in hand with a degeneration and transformation of the character of the Greek people' (BT 23). Poetry and music were transformed into science and philosophy,[15] and the most 'magnificent expression' of this anti-Dionysiac instinct was the historical figure of Socrates. Yet based on our analysis of Wagner's 'Artwork of the Future' as well as the rebirth of the tragic concept as it occurs in *The Birth of Tragedy*, we

---

[15] With the decline of tragedy, 'poetry turned to science, to philosophy' (PW 1: 139, 'Artwork of the Future').

can now see that the figure of the 'music-making Socrates', which specifically designates the form of a culture, occupies in every way the same kind of privileged position between the Socratic and tragic cultures, whose world-views are in direct conflict with one another, and in this very important respect it too symbolises the dividing and uniting point of two cultures in contradictory or antithetical tension. Hence the aim of *The Birth of Tragedy*, which is in *this* sense Wagnerian propaganda through and through, is to argue, convince and persuade us as readers that Socratic culture had long ago reached the apogee of its evolution, but that the inner logic of its world-view is now exhausted, and has reached the bottommost point of its devolvement as a cultural form. The 'scientific spirit', which is the very essence of Socratic culture, has devolved into a boundless and desperate search for knowledge at any cost, and the once naive delight in the 'scientific spirit' of an emerging culture has changed to weariness, exhaustion and the eradication of the instincts.

On the other hand, the rebirth of the tragic concept, which would see its oracle fulfilled in Germany through the music dramas of Wagner, depends on the fusion of these once dissociated drives, and therefore regenerates an entirely new cultural expression. As Nietzsche explains, the beginning of this regeneration lies principally in recognising how

> through Kant and Schopenhauer the spirit *of German philosophy*, which flows from the same sources, was able to destroy scientific Socratism's complacent delight in existence by demonstrating its limitations, and how it thus introduced an infinitely more profound and serious consideration of ethical questions and art, which we might almost describe as *Dionysiac wisdom* in conceptualized form. Whither does the mystery of the union of German music and German philosophy point, if not to a new mode of existence of which we can only gain an inkling through Greek analogies? (BT 19)

As we can plainly see, Nietzsche's appeal here to 'Greek analogies' functions both diagnostically and prescriptively, just as Wagner's essay had done twenty-three years earlier. Yet the figure at the centre of this cultural rebirth, and therefore the new turning point or vortex of world history, is the 'philosopher who speaks music' and, in this early work in particular, the 'music-making Socrates' who is called to unify philosophy and art for the purposes of culture.

With this preliminary explanation, a very important question still remains: even if we assume this depiction to be true, what would make the upward swing towards the rebirth of culture different from what it had been in the ancient world? There is one critical difference, and given the significance of the pre-Socratics and the role Nietzsche claims they played in the birth of tragedy, it is worth quoting Nietzsche's first entry to notebook 23 from his 'philosophers book' to get a concrete sense of how all of these analogical elements fit together.

> In order to understand them as wholes, one must recognize in them the first outline and germ of the Greek *reformer*; their purpose was to pave the way for him [i.e., the artist], they were supposed to precede him as the dawn precedes the rising sun. But the sun did not rise, the reformer failed: hence the dawn remained nothing but a ghostly apparition. However, the simultaneous emergence of tragedy demonstrates that something new was in the air; but the philosopher and legislator who would have comprehended tragedy never appeared, and hence this art died again and the Greek reformation became forever impossible. It is not possible to think of Empedocles without a sense of profound sadness; he came the closest to filling the role of that reformer. That he also failed at this and soon disappeared – following who knows what horrible experiences and what hopelessness – was a pan-Hellenic catastrophe. His soul had a greater capacity for empathy than any other Greek soul; and yet perhaps not enough, for all in all, the Greeks are deficient in this quality. And it was precisely the tyrannical element in their blood that prevented the great philosophers from attaining the profound insight and sweeping vision that Schopenhauer possessed. (UF 23[1], winter 1872–73)

As Nietzsche makes very clear here, the upward swing towards the birth of culture, at least in the ancient world, possessed all the necessary ingredients that would have established the tragic world-view as an enduring philosophical and artistic outlook except perhaps for the one essential and decisive catalyst: *the philosopher and legislator who would have comprehended the depiction of tragedy as an art form never appeared*. But in paving the way for the rebirth of the tragic concept, the important and critical difference is that this time there *is* a philosopher who is able to grasp the artistic depiction of tragedy and who can foment the tragic world-view as an enduring philosophical and artistic outlook. In other words, the critical difference is that there is now a 'philosopher who speaks music' to cross-pollinate philosophy in both its rational and creative tendencies. Looking at the so-called 'problem of culture' from the standpoint of Nietzsche's 'pro-Wagnerian' writings, we are poised for this 'German reformation of culture', and from the 'Strauss' essay to 'Richard Wagner in Bayreuth', this is precisely what Nietzsche's four *Unfashionable Observations* represent. What Schopenhauer had begun would be carried on by Nietzsche, and here we have the deeper and more symbolic reason why Schopenhauer is invoked time and again by him, for the artistic mission of Wagner's music dramas is contextualised within Schopenhauer's sweeping vision of existence, and is therefore morphologically equivalent to the culture of the pre-Socratics as contemporaries to the tragedies of Aeschylus.[16] We can see the completion of the circle, the 'upward swing', when Nietzsche remarks in a note from 1874 that

> [Schopenhauer's] greatness is extraordinary, to have once again peered into the heart of existence, without scholarly digressions, without tiresome lingering and entanglement in philosophical scholasticism. The study of the one-quarter-philosophers who followed him is attractive for the sole purpose of seeing how they immediately arrive at the place where scholarly pro and con,

---

[16] It is a well-known fact that Wagner believed himself to be a disciple of Aeschylus.

brooding, contradiction, but nothing more is permitted – and where, above all, one is not permitted to *live*. He demolishes secularization, but likewise the barbarizing power of the sciences; he arouses the most enormous need, just as Socrates was an arouser of such need. People have forgotten what religion was, as they have the significance that art has for life. Schopenhauer stands in contradiction with everything that today passes for culture: Plato with everything that *was* culture in Greece at that time. Schopenhauer was catapulted ahead of his time. (UF 35[11], spring–summer 1874)

When we consider the content of this note alongside the content of note 1 from notebook 23, it becomes quite clear that the critical difference between the incipient rise of culture in fifth-century Athens and the German reformation of culture as given by *The Birth of Tragedy* is the fact that this time there is finally on hand a 'philosopher who speaks music' to foment the rebirth of the tragic concept as an enduring cultural form.

Now as far as the claims of *The Birth of Tragedy* are concerned, surely the figure to recognise the limits of the scientific spirit, and the call to renounce its claims at the threshold of those limits, sounds suspiciously like Wagner's self-nomination from twenty-three years earlier. At the same time, however, our work has analysed precisely what the symbol of the 'music-making Socrates' signifies as a cultural form. For while it is commonly accepted that Nietzsche's preoccupation with the philosopher as a cultural diagnostician intensified over the course of his productive life, especially following his break with Wagner, what is routinely overlooked is that running alongside Nietzsche's cultural criticism of Wagner are his exhortations for the philosopher to make and cultivate his own music. And now that we have deciphered the cultural significance of the 'music-making Socrates' as the symbol of both the critical and creative drives, or rationality united to the creative instincts for life, it will become increasingly clear, as we move into an analysis of Nietzsche's writings against Wagner, that not only did Nietzsche never abandon this symbol, but it is at the foundation of his cultural war against Wagner. It is to this problem that we now turn.

2
The Pessimism of Strength: An Attempt to Revise the Socratic and Tragic Cultures

The essence of tragic culture

The groundwork that we established in Chapter 1 is significant for what now follows, for as we begin to examine Nietzsche's later writings, and what is taken to be his final position against Wagner, it will become increasingly clear that not only do the principles of vitalism continue to play a key role in explaining the decline and rebirth of art as culture, precisely as they do in Wagner's own theoretical arguments about it, but that they continue to condition Nietzsche's own thought about the problem of culture, and ultimately the cultural war he wages against Wagner. In this connection, Nietzsche's belated postscript to *The Birth of Tragedy* – his *Attempt at a Self-Criticism* – is highly relevant, since the *Attempt* tries to clarify the critical and essential features of both the Socratic and tragic cultures in the first instance, and by doing so categorise in what sense Wagner and his art belong, no longer to the tragic, but now to the Socratic culture. Yet the nature of this clarification has one other surprising result: by trying to reclassify Wagner and his art as predominantly 'Socratic', Nietzsche's argument expressly entails that Wagner's privileged position in the overall organic and dynamic unfolding of art as culture has shifted from being a symbol of rebirth to one of decline. Finally, since the 'music-making Socrates' – or 'the philosopher who practices music' – remains the central symbol around which the rebirth of art as culture is effected, our analysis here will show that, as Nietzsche saw this role as increasingly filled by himself, the

Attempt itself becomes, in a very real sense, a referendum on the heroes of the original essay in terms of their ability to prefigure the 'philosopher who practices music' for culture.

Before we can appreciate in what respects the nature of this central symbol had undergone a transformation in the intervening years, it will benefit our analysis to briefly highlight a couple of important thematic consistencies between *The Birth of Tragedy* and the *Attempt*. First, in both the original essay and in the postscript, pessimism remains the inescapable consequence of those who experience the burden and weight of existence. Indeed, *The Birth of Tragedy* makes it clear that there is an intimate connection between the depth with which such 'noble spirits' confront the burden and weight of existence and the form of culture that results from it.

Second, there is the deeply seated concern that some cultures face the burden and weight of existence more or less directly than do others, and in the course of the original essay, Nietzsche had identified three archetypal cultures based on the world-view that each one (more or less) adopts or assumes to confront existence.[1] All three of these cultures are 'illusory' or 'Apollonian' inasmuch as they offer up a totalising, overarching depiction of existence as a means to help stimulate people's engagement with life as such. At the same time, however, the more a given culture is forced to veil or obscure the inescapable consequence of pessimism in its depiction of existence, the greater the degree of that culture's entanglement in illusory thinking about it. Indeed, the 'three levels of illusion' that we find in BT 18 correspond to these three *archetypes* of culture, and were Nietzsche's rough attempt to stratify the degree to which each culture had found it necessary to veil the inescapable consequence of pessimism. According to

---

[1] For the 'Socratic culture', the burden and weight of existence is confronted by a belief in the value of knowledge, and in particular 'the delusion that it might heal the eternal wound of existence'. For the 'Hellenic culture', on the other hand, the burden and weight of existence is confronted by a belief in the value of depiction, representation and portrayal, and so is 'caught up in the seductive veil of beauty and art that floats before his eyes'. Finally, the 'Brahmanic culture' confronts the burden and weight of existence through its knowledge of the cyclical nature of life itself; namely that 'beneath the whirlpool of phenomena eternal life flows indestructibly onwards' (see BT 18).

Nietzsche's 'three levels of illusion', the Brahmanic culture veils its picture the least, while the Socratic culture veils its picture the most. In this respect, then, there is one common denominator or fundamental principle which unites the original essay with the *Attempt*: the basis of all cultural expression, and therefore the form of culture itself, is built upon a totalising or 'macrocosmic' depiction of what life and existence is, but such depictions in turn are ultimately derived from *individual* 'noble spirits' who confront the burden and weight of existence most directly. The more direct the depiction of existence is, the more 'truthful' it is, and this in turn means that those who conceived it can handle the burden and weight of existence without needing to 'sweeten' or 'falsify' it.[2] With this exposition, we are now in a position to analyse the significance of Nietzsche's *Attempt* and to explain its significance for his post-Wagnerian philosophical project.

An attempt to self-criticise

By all accounts, the ostensible purpose of Nietzsche's *Attempt at a Self-Criticism* was to distil a handful of themes that had first appeared in *The Birth of Tragedy* but that still retained philosophical significance when viewed through the lens of his present philosophical project. Yet in the fourteen years that had intervened, the nature of the 'music-making Socrates' and what it signified for the rebirth of art as culture had undergone a significant transformation. No longer was the meaning of culture bound up with the ambitious plans for a new Europe that would be reborn by appealing to, and advocating for, the wider popularity and acceptance of Wagner's music and Schopenhauer's philosophy in a kind of totalising 'macrocosmic' approach to the problem of culture. On the contrary, the problem of culture would find its meaning or significance at the individual level, and would therefore be bound up with the idea of becoming *oneself* that cultural expression. Hence, the critical difference that we find in Nietzsche's post-Wagnerian writings more generally,

---

[2] Compare especially BGE 39 on this point.

including what we find here in the *Attempt*, is what we call, following Nietzsche, a 'microcosmic' approach to the problem of culture.³

At the basis of his 're-evaluation' was Nietzsche's insistence that the origins of culture begin at the individual level with the courage to accept and embrace existence in an unqualified and uncompromising way. Nietzsche called this new re-evaluation 'the pessimism of strength'. Consequently the true meaning of his original essay (according to Nietzsche) was just this ability of the ancients to confront the burden and weight of existence and its relationship to the culture that they produced. By contrast, the essay was manifestly not a case study meant to examine 'similar phenomena in the present' (that is, the philosophy of Schopenhauer and the music of Wagner) (BT 16).

Viewing the ancients through the lens of his new re-evaluation, Nietzsche frames this interpretation very early on in section 1 when he asks whether pessimism is '*inevitably* the sign of decline', or whether by contrast there is such a thing as 'a pessimism of *strength*' that is akin to the tragic concept. After all, if there is such a thing as the 'intellectual predilection for what is hard, terrible, evil, problematic in existence', which arises 'from well-being, overflowing health, the *abundance* of existence' (AT 1) then it follows that pessimism *per se* is not invariably linked with 'enfeebled instincts' and thus declining cultures. The implication, then, is that there is more than one species of pessimism, and so by teasing out its critical and essential features, we might distinguish that species of pessimism that is intimately bound up with 'enfeebled instincts' and declining cultures as opposed to the pessimism which foments the tragic concept.

---

³ This distinction between the two kinds of cultures and its connection with the individual as a musical expression first appears in *Human, All Too Human*, and is based in large part on Schopenhauer's analogy between the metaphysics of music and the scale for the objectivation of the will in nature in both the microcosm and macrocosm. For this conception, see an especially revealing passage in WWR 1, 52, as well as PP 1, 'Fragments for the History of Philosophy', 2, which clearly lays out that music allows its listeners to both *feel* its innermost message with certainty as well to *cognise this feeling* in its abstract universality, for the very form of music is built upon the apogee of a priori logic and rationality: number. Outside of Wagner himself, no one else (as far as we know) has grasped the depth of Schopenhauer's insight on these points.

To draw out this contrast, Nietzsche begins by revisiting the distinctions he had made years before between the widely divergent cultural forms that resulted from the pre-Socratics and those that followed in the wake of Socrates. Once again, Nietzsche confirms that while the form and expression of Hellenic culture flowered with the birth of the tragic myth, the Socratic culture by contrast flowered with the belief in reason and the systematic pursuit of knowledge as a consequence. Yet now there is one very important caveat to these observations: the cultural form that followed in the wake of Socrates – that which brought about the death of tragedy through the 'Socratism of morality' and 'the cheerfulness of theoretical man' – was based on an orientation towards life that was *already* depleted and exhausted.[4] In other words Socratic culture, and its depiction of existence in particular, was derived from *degenerating instincts*. In this admission then, what we find is an explicit connection between affirmation and conception, and thus the relationship that exists between the former and the form of culture that is conceived as a consequence.

This is precisely the issue that Nietzsche seems to be probing when he presses the practical consequences of the Socratic culture more generally, and in particular, the *motive* for science as a way of life; namely that as a 'symptom' of life, the 'scientific approach' might be nothing other than the 'flight from pessimism', and therefore a 'subtle form of self-defence against – *the truth*'. Rather than confront the burden and weight of existence 'honestly', we have something like 'cowardice and falsehood' instead. In this respect, then, science and the scientific world-view may have emerged as a means to combat the distress of life itself, and would therefore be, in a manner of speaking, a systematic attempt to *escape* from the inescapable conclusion of pessimism. It is *this*, Nietzsche goes on to suggest, that constitutes the ultimate Socratic irony (AT 1).

---

[4] 'What is the meaning, for those Greeks of the best, strongest, most courageous age, of the *tragic* myth? . . . And of the tragedy that was born from it? And on the other hand, that which brought about the death of tragedy: the Socratism of morality, the dialectics, modesty and cheerfulness of theoretical man – could not that very Socratism be a symptom of decline, fatigue, infection, and anarchical dissolution of the instincts? And might the "Greek cheerfulness" of the later Greeks be nothing but the glow of the sunset?' (AT 1).

But to be clear, this is *not* the species of pessimism on which the tragic myth as a cultural form was based. The latter was forged through the pessimism of strength following the pre-Socratics, and as Nietzsche tells us in sections 4–5, the characteristic mark of the pessimism of strength is the good, rigid resolve to accept and affirm the image of 'everything terrible, evil, cryptic, destructive and deadly underlying existence' (AT 4), without resorting to 'the *moral* interpretation and significance of existence' (AT 5). The pessimism of strength 'dares to demote morality and locate it in the phenomenal world, and not only among the "phenomena" ... but among its "deceptions", as illusion, delusion, error, interpretation, artifice, art' (AT 5). In fact, this is what Nietzsche claims he meant by the purely aesthetic interpretation and justification of the world imparted in the original essay: 'the existence of the world is *justified* only as an aesthetic phenomenon' (AT 5). In the absence of morality being able to justify its meaning, Nietzsche contends that only the representation, its totalising picture of existence, can justify it. So even though they were pessimists, the pre-Socratics had the will to tragedy, and to that extent the origins of tragedy, at least according to Nietzsche's conjectures here, really could have been 'joy, strength, overflowing health, and excessive abundance' (AT 4) – in a word, Dionysian.

All of this, however, is made to contrast with the Greeks who followed in the wake of Socrates and who, 'precisely at the point of their dissolution and weakness' in confronting the burden and weight of existence, 'became ever more optimistic, superficial, theatrical', and in turn 'more and more ardent' for a 'logical interpretation of the world'. It is this modern victory of optimism, Nietzsche goes on to suggest, that is 'a symptom of waning power, of approaching senescence, of physiological fatigue', and *not* pessimism *per se* (AT 4). With this contrast between the two cultures, Nietzsche is quite clear that the element responsible for a declining culture is an orientation towards life characterised by senescence, physiological fatigue and, in a phrase, degenerating instincts. And if science and the scientific approach to life really did emerge from the post-Socratics as a way to confront the distress of life itself, then it follows that senescence, physiological fatigue and the degenerating instincts for life had found their most crystallised expression in the scientific approach to life as a cultural form. Therefore if pessimism is responsible for a declining culture, then it is grounded *only* in that species of pessimism which is derived from a depleted, exhausted and devitalised orientation to the problem of existence. This is the *pessimism of degenerating instincts*, and the cultural form derived from it is the Socratic.

By distinguishing between these two cultural forms, and especially by suggesting how the forms of a culture are connected to the ability (or inability) of a given people to affirm the nature of existence, Nietzsche raises the issue, much as Wagner had done in his own essay, of how 'vital' a given people are, and how that vitality expresses itself in the cultural forms that result. So once again, pessimism remains the inescapable consequence of confronting existence in both the original essay and in the *Attempt*, for the more a given culture has to veil or obscure the inescapable consequence of pessimism, the greater the degree of that culture's entanglement in illusory thinking about the nature of existence.

But while all cultural forms are in some measure 'illusory' or 'Apollonian', that does not mean that all cultures are steeped in illusion to the same degree. By reiterating, as Nietzsche does here, that the forms of a culture are connected to the ability (or inability) to 'confront' and thus 'affirm' the nature of existence most directly, the implication is that those cultures that derive abstractions that either stray too far, or are completely divorced from, the immediacy of life itself have formed a culture that has somehow co-opted or usurped the vitality of the given folk to which it belongs. Hence those forms that refuse to affirm the tragedy of living time and the pessimism of sentient life are actually, paradoxically, more pessimistic than those that give form and expression to it, since they are by definition failing to affirm life. Such cultural forms, which include the Socratic above all, are trying to find 'escape routes' by appealing to the 'moral interpretation and significance of existence', or by insisting that there be a visible bond between virtue and knowledge, truth and morality. In this sense, however, they are really 'falsifying life' the most as a conceptual construct. The scientific approach to life is a pessimistic world-view that refuses to admit that it is pessimistic, because (as Nietzsche said many years earlier in a draft version of the essay) it cannot look at facts squarely in the face and affirm life without 'deceptively glamorous names in order to be able to live' (UF 10[1], January 1871). It is *this* 'entanglement in illusory thinking' about the nature of existence – this relationship between the vital principle and the concept derived from it – that is responsible for the so-called 'degenerating instincts' towards life. As we will soon discover, the vitalism entailed in Nietzsche's thought goes far beyond that of either Schopenhauer or Wagner, and is in some measure responsible for his final position against them.

To 'make music' from the materials of life

At this point, it should be fairly clear that Nietzsche's *Attempt* is principally concerned with revising the optics of *The Birth of Tragedy*, and his explanation of the origins of the tragic culture is at the same time a referendum on the heroes of the original essay in terms of how to confront the problem of existence at the individual level. Indeed, if the first problem for the promise of an emerging culture is how to confront the problem of existence at the individual level, and therefore how to accept the inescapable conclusion of pessimism without recourse to Apollonian 'stimulants' or conceptual-ideological intoxicants, then such a claim necessarily includes the ones he believed he had endorsed in the original essay – Schopenhauer's deliverance from the will and Wagner's music as a catalyst for that deliverance.

In the first place, then, Nietzsche's insistence here on the pessimism of strength becomes the formula through which he not only attempts to pivot his position against Schopenhauer and Wagner, but also to resolve the 'problem of culture' at the individual level. In other words, it is bound up with the idea of becoming *oneself* the expression of culture. But in the second place, if the pessimism of strength is the very essence of the tragic culture, as well as the new framework through which to test his insistence that the origins of culture begin at the individual level, what Nietzsche is actually claiming is to have derived a far more consistent ethical principle from vitalism than either of the heroes of the original essay, for in its most uncompromising sense, the ethics of vitalism entails the *unconditional assertion*, not the negation, of the will for life. As we shall see, these two ideas dovetail into how the individual begins to 'make music' from the materials of life. Finally and most notably, the historical Socrates continues to symbolise the dividing and uniting point of two cultures in antithetical tension, but now Schopenhauer and Wagner are no longer seen as symbols prefiguring the rebirth of art as culture, but have shifted in valuation to become symbols of decline.

To be sure, the politics of Nietzsche's revolt here is significant, for when it comes to the idea of 'making music' from the materials of life, there is no question that Schopenhauer himself had already laid the groundwork between vitalism, the nature of music and an ethical doctrine that was continuous with nature using none other than the figure of Socrates as the uniting and dividing point of what philosophy had been as well as what it became. In section 52 of his well-known treatise on music and its connection with the will, Schopenhauer tells us that

> a mere moral philosophy without an explanation of nature, such as Socrates tried to introduce, is entirely analogous to a melody without harmony ... and that conversely a mere physics and metaphysics without an ethics would correspond to a mere harmony without melody. (WWR 1, 52)

Complementing these thoughts in his chapter *On Ethics*, Schopenhauer goes on to tell us that

> Since Socrates, the problem of philosophy has been to connect the force which produces the phenomenon of the world and in consequence determines its nature, with the morality of the disposition or character, and thus to demonstrate a *moral* world order as the basis of the *physical* ... but I have shown ... that the force working and operating in nature is identical with the *will* in ourselves. In this way, the *moral* world-order actually enters into direct connexion [sic] with the force that produces the phenomenon of the world ... Consequently, the problem raised since the time of Socrates is now already solved for the first time, and the demand of our thinking reason, that is directed to what is moral, is satisfied. (WWR 2, ch. 47)

In other words, if, as Schopenhauer claims, the force operating in nature is identical with the will in ourselves, then there is an ostensible connection between one's individual disposition or character and the force that produces the phenomenal appearance of the world. Furthermore, since harmony and melody when taken together are entirely analogous to the connection between a metaphysical conception and its ethical corollary in action, it follows that the force that produces the phenomenal appearance of the world corresponds with the potential *harmonies* found in the will's objectivation in nature, while that which is expressed through the character of a specific individual entirely corresponds with a given *melody* (WWR 1, 52). The inescapable conclusion of this figure, then, is that the action of the individual, and the particular melody he expresses, must labour to resonate with the manifold harmonies found in the will's objectivation of nature, and that the individual interacting with the world as such must 'make his own music' out of life. Here is an ethical teaching that is *immanent*, not transcendent, and one that in actuality complements Schopenhauer's metaphysical conception, which is likewise immanent. Therefore as far as the concept of the philosopher as a species is concerned, this would render the very different types of philosophers found in the world as being, in *senso proprio*, instruments who sing a particular music of life by allowing, as Nietzsche had once remarked, 'all the tones of the world to resonate within him and to project the tonality of this sound outside himself by means of concepts [that is, their teachings]' (UF 19[71], summer 1872–early 1873).

Now, if this is the true ethical corollary of Schopenhauer's own metaphysical conception, then at what point does the *resignation* of will appear within us, if indeed it is the same expression of the force operating in nature? And what is its relation to Greek tragedy in particular? This is the central point at issue that Nietzsche takes up against Schopenhauer in section 6 of the *Attempt* and, after having quoted Schopenhauer's opinion of our relation to tragedy,[5] Nietzsche tells us point blank about 'how differently Dionysus

---

[5] For the opinion Nietzsche references here, compare WWR 2, ch. 37.

spoke to me! How far I was then from all that resignationism!' (AT 6) – Naturally, Nietzsche claims, for resignation of will is an ethical teaching of Christianity and is therefore inconsistent with the ethical implications of vitalism. This is a point that Nietzsche never tires of telling his readers when it comes to Schopenhauer's solution, namely that it was a 'Christian' solution – 'hasty, youthful, only a compromise, a way of remaining – remaining stuck – in precisely those Christian-ascetic moral perspectives'.[6] Therefore when we read this critique of Schopenhauer, we must understand, above all, that Nietzsche is assailing what he believes to be an inconsistency – indeed a lack of harmony – between Schopenhauer's metaphysical conception and his ethics. To accept will and not reason as more fundamental is to commit to the unconditional assertion, not the negation, of the principle of life. This is precisely the charge that Nietzsche brings against Schopenhauer, and it is what legitimises Nietzsche's claims of 'succession' over Schopenhauer as the philosopher of the tragic concept here in the *Attempt*.

And yet, according to Nietzsche, 'the book contains something far worse' than having tried to articulate Dionysian intimations with Schopenhauerian formulae. After all, what did the world of Greek tragedy have to do with contemporary German music? Here, Nietzsche confesses, 'I *spoiled* the grandiose *Greek problem*, as I saw it, by adulterating it with the most modern ideas!' (AT 6). As Nietzsche goes on to tell us, contemporary German music – by which he really means Wagner's music – is 'romantic through and through, and the most un-Greek of all possible art forms', but it is also 'a narcotic of the worst kind . . . with its dual properties of being both an intoxicating and a befogging narcotic' (AT 6).

Unfortunately this attack on Wagner's music relies on the implicit assumption that Nietzsche had somehow resolved the question of 'what is Dionysian?' in the interim – a question that had *never* found a satisfactory answer in the original essay – and in this important respect he begs the entire question. In particular, Nietzsche assumes on the one hand that his 'authority' for the Dionysian has been established merely by presupposing as true

---

[6] Compare GS 357.

what he believes the original essay actually is (namely 'music'), while at the same time he leverages this as a conclusion in order to dissociate the 'Dionysian' from whatever prior associations it may have had with Wagner's music – the very phenomenon whose panegyrics the original essay was purported to herald. Already in section 3, Nietzsche tells us that even though he finds the original essay today an 'impossible book', nevertheless it is

> a book for initiates, 'music' for those who have been baptized in the name of music and who are related from the first by their common and rare experiences of art . . . a book which, as its impact has shown and continues to show, has a strange knack of seeking out its fellow-revellers and enticing them on to new secret paths and dancing-places. What found expression here . . . was a *strange* voice . . . to which the name of Dionysus was appended as yet another question mark. (AT 3)

And so with the 'music' of this book, Nietzsche tells us that his affirmative instinct for life 'turned *against* morality and invented a fundamentally opposite doctrine and valuation of life, purely artistic and *anti-Christian*' (AT 5) over and against the heroes of the original essay, and that he baptised this instinct as 'Dionysiac' or 'Dionysian'. Accordingly, by distinguishing the species of pessimism that *is* responsible for declining cultures, Nietzsche is letting us know that the erstwhile heroes of the original essay had succumbed to 'anti-Dionysian' tendencies, and should now be viewed as additional victims of Socratic culture and the pessimism of degenerating instincts – Schopenhauer with his 'Christian' solution to the will, and Wagner, whose whole art 'wants to present itself as a companion piece and supplement to Schopenhauer's philosophy' (GS 99), a decaying and despairing decadent himself, who 'sank down helpless and shattered before the Christian cross' with his final music drama *Parsifal* (NCW 'How I Broke Away from Wagner' 1). Therefore by arguing that the pessimism of strength is the very essence of the tragic culture, while the pessimism of degenerating instincts is, by contrast, the very essence of the Socratic, of which Schopenhauer and Wagner are merely the latest, most modern symptoms, Nietzsche in effect aligns *himself* as the 'legitimate successor' and heir of the pre-Socratics, and by extension the sole figure (of the original triumvirate) to grasp the inner meaning and significance of the tragic culture of the Greeks. While Schopenhauer and Wagner, like the Greeks from Socrates onwards, had all fallen prey to the pessimism of degenerating instincts, only Nietzsche remains as the exclusive authority to speak of 'what is Dionysian'. As the original bifurcation leading up to *The Birth of Tragedy* had once been Schopenhauer, Wagner and the pre-Socratics in opposition to Socrates and the problem of modernity, with his revision of pessimism, especially as it is given in the *Attempt*, it seems indisputable that the bifurcation Nietzsche now wants us to acknowledge is Nietzsche and the pre-Socratics in opposition to Socrates, Schopenhauer, Wagner and the problem of modernity.

The twilight of an idol

In coming to a preliminary statement about Nietzsche's relationship to Wagner in his post-Wagnerian works, it should now be clear that Nietzsche still endorses Wagner's theoretical arguments about culture in which the principles of vitalism play a key role in explaining the decline and rebirth of art as culture, and that he never really abandoned the Wagnerian thesis that Socrates signified the degeneration of the Greek instincts for life, and thus destroyed art as culture. As is evident from our analysis of Nietzsche's 'pro-Wagner' position as well as the posture he assumes in the *Attempt*, not only did Socrates usher in the degeneration of the Greek instinct for life in terms of his more immediate effects, he also became the archetype of modern theoretical man with his ever more ardent desire for logic and his more cheerful, optimistic, scientific approach to life. Nowhere is the connection between these two events made any clearer than in section 4 of the *Attempt*, where Nietzsche notes that science and the scientific approach to life really did emerge as a cultural form characterised by senescence, physiological fatigue and the degenerating instincts for life, and that as the vital principle diminished, the Greek mind increasingly compensated for it by appealing to a superficial, theoretical optimism about life rooted in the logical interpretation of the world (AT 4). So while the historical Socrates remains the archetypal villain who ushered in this decline, it seems fairly clear that Nietzsche is eager to take credit for the very same questions that Wagner had originally raised in relation to the problem of culture.

At the same time, however, Nietzsche's ambition to become the 'music-making Socrates' seems to suggest, at the outset, an affinity for the figure of Socrates, and at the very least it creates confusion when set side by side with his critique of Socrates as a historical figure. In the light of our analysis, however, we now know that this is a plain misreading, for it is not the mere figure of Socrates himself that is important, but rather what he *signifies* for culture. From the standpoint of both Nietzsche's 'pro-' and 'contra-Wagnerian' positions, the historical Socrates is seen to have acted in precisely the same way that the 'music-making Socrates' is supposed to act in reforming the excesses of his society, and in this respect, both figures symbolise the uniting and dividing point of two cultures in antithetical tension, since they are themselves catalysts for the widely divergent cultural forms that exist prior to their appearance with those that follow in their wake. In other words, both the figure of Socrates and the 'philosopher who practices music' play the same functional relationship *within* the whole; but as concern for the whole pertains (at least in Nietzsche's eyes) to the consequences for art as culture, the meaning of that relationship, and therefore their position in relation to the decline and rebirth of art as culture, ensures that the two figures remain utter antipodes.

By analysing these significances properly in the overall structure of Nietzsche's 'pro-' and 'contra-Wagnerian' positions, it should be clear that there is a very real difference between this critique of Socrates as the progenitor of cultural decline and that of the 'philosopher who practices music' as the progenitor of cultural rebirth. Indeed, it is the 'philosopher who practices music' of his 'post-Wagnerian' writings that remains the central symbol around which the rebirth of art as culture is achieved. Yet as Nietzsche saw the latter role as increasingly filled by himself, the implication is that the original elements of his 'pro-Wagnerian' position would have to shift in light of his 'contra-Wagnerian' project and its consequences for culture. As we will shortly discover, it is this shift and its consequences for culture which form the backdrop of Nietzsche's 'contra-Wagnerian' position and the 'war on culture' that he wages against Wagner.

For the present, however, it is important to show that Nietzsche's critique of Socrates as an element of cultural destruction remains relatively fixed across both his 'pro-' and 'contra-Wagnerian' positions, and to do so, we need only turn to his last and most significant statements about Socrates as they occur in *Twilight of the Idols*. In doing so, two points will become abundantly clear: 1) the excesses of Western culture were never pinned on anyone or anything other than the 'anti-Dionysiac' tendency of Socratic eudaemonism; and 2) there is a critical distinction between Socrates as the physician of decadence and therefore 'declining life', and Nietzsche as the physician of instincts and 'ascending life'. Both points closely follow the Wagnerian thesis about life and its relationship to the decline and rebirth of art as culture, as well as who was responsible for the decline of the tragic culture. The analysis we provide will help to clarify in what sense Nietzsche is challenging Wagner's hegemony by not only assuming Wagner's cultural criticisms, but by positioning himself as the *de facto* solution to them.

In section 2 of 'The Problem of Socrates', Nietzsche tells us that *he* had recognised Socrates and Plato as 'declining types', as symptoms of decay, as early as *The Birth of Tragedy*. Yet what is pertinent to this section is that Nietzsche attempts to obviate the value judgements of the *consensus sapientium*, which includes above all the wisdom of Plato and Socrates that life is worthless, by noting that

> *the value of life* [either for or against] *cannot be estimated*. Not by a living man, because he is a party to the dispute, indeed its object, and not the judge of it; not by a dead one, for another reason. – For a philosopher to see a problem in the *value* of life thus even constitutes an objection to him, a questionmark to his wisdom, a piece of unwisdom. (TI 'The Problem of Socrates' 2)

The nature of these points is extremely important for all that follows, for what Nietzsche essentially says is that the value judgement of the whole cannot be mounted from within the whole. To pass judgement on the value of life is ultimately superfluous, since life itself, in the first place, is the very matrix in which judgements about life, whether for or against, ultimately inhere, while in the second place, the very activity of living presupposes its value as a necessity. So here we see right at the start that Nietzsche's commitment to vitalism asserts itself with a vengeance.

In the following section, Nietzsche relates the storied ugliness that attaches to the physiognomy of the historical Socrates and intimates that this ugliness is an index of his character.[7] The claim advanced here, which flowers in the following section, is that, while the historical Socrates was the physical embodiment of one who had succumbed to the dissoluteness and anarchy of his instincts, he was exceptional in that not only did he recognise the anarchy of his instincts, he also found a weapon to combat them: his 'superfetation of the logical', which, according to Nietzsche, culminated in that 'bizzarest of equations and one which has in particular all the instincts of the older Hellenes against it', namely, 'reason = virtue = happiness' (TI 'The Problem of Socrates' 4).

As we move into section 5, Nietzsche then submits the methodology of dialectic to a withering critique, noting that the older cultural forms (that is, before Socrates) regarded dialectics as bad manners, as those who thought it necessary to present 'reasons' for what is otherwise presupposed and given – in this case, life itself – were regarded with mistrust. Since only those with no other expedient gave themselves up to dialectics, Nietzsche then points out in section 6 that dialectics should only be regarded as 'a *last ditch weapon* in the hands of those who have no other weapon left' (TI 'The Problem of Socrates' 6). Yet by far the most important consequence of engaging in dialectics is that the 'dialectician *devitalizes* his opponent's intellect' (TI 'The Problem of Socrates' 7). Thus the true hallmark of dialectics is the exhaustion and enfeeblement of the intellectual instincts.[8]

---

[7] TI 'The Problem of Socrates' 3. The subtext here also alludes to the idea that Socrates himself was not really 'Greek', since the Hellenic culture more generally 'worshipped the seductive veil of beauty' while Socrates and the Socratics 'sat amid a sea of beauty' and had 'either a hostile or a theoretical attitude toward art'. See, for instance, BT 18 and UF 19[70], summer 1872–early 1873.

[8] On these points, compare PP 1, 'Fragments for the History of Philosophy', 3.

With this deduction in hand, we are led to the climax in section 9, where Nietzsche observes that the historical Socrates at once 'grasped *his* case'. He realised that 'the same kind of degeneration was everywhere silently preparing itself: the old Athens was coming to an end', and so 'Socrates understood that all the world had need of him'. It was at precisely this point, Nietzsche claims, that Socrates realised his solution; that is, if the 'instincts want to play the tyrant; we must devise a *counter-tyrant* who is stronger' (TI 'The Problem of Socrates' 9). Socrates, who was himself 'the extreme case' of these mutually antagonistic and degenerating instincts, had found a way to become master of himself, and seeing his solution, almost as though it were the product of a vision, he soon enthroned reason to tyrannise over the instincts. Reason became the *counter-tyrant* to the instincts, forcing them either to submit to dialectics or to perish out of irrationality. In other words, what we find here is that the historical Socrates acted *in precisely the same way* that the 'philosopher who speaks music' is supposed to act in comprehending the tendencies of his society and then reforming its excesses by providing physic to it. Unfortunately, there is one very important difference: by making such a 'tyrant of *reason*, as Socrates did', the one great problem that followed from that point forward was that rationality and vitality became permanently bifurcated. 'The moralism of the Greek philosophers from Plato downwards is pathologically conditioned', Nietzsche tells us in section 10, in which 'reason = virtue = happiness means merely: one must imitate Socrates and counter the dark desires by producing a permanent *daylight* – the daylight of reason' (TI 'The Problem of Socrates' 10).

So Socrates may have saved the Greek world from perishing through his personal art of self-preservation, but at what cost? It is here in section 11 that we find Nietzsche's final judgement on the historical Socrates – a judgement that agrees in all respects with the Wagnerian thesis he laid down in his earliest works.

> I have intimated the way in which Socrates exercised fascination: he seemed to be a physician, a saviour. Is it necessary to go on to point out the error which lay in his faith in

'rationality at any cost'? – It is self-deception on the part of philosophers and moralists to imagine that by making war on *décadence* they therewith elude *décadence* themselves ... The harshest daylight, rationality at any cost, life bright, cold, circumspect, conscious, without instinct, in opposition to the instincts, has itself been no more than a form of sickness, another form of sickness – and by no means a way back to 'virtue', to 'health', to happiness ... To *have* to combat one's instincts – that is the formula for *décadence*: as long as life is *ascending*, happiness and instinct are one. (TI 'The Problem of Socrates' 11)

As we can see, the moral of Nietzsche's depiction here is that while Socrates may have been a physician in the sense that he had comprehended the specific tendencies of his milieu and then reformed its excesses by prescribing reason to counter-tyrannise the instincts, he was a physician of *décadence*, of *degenerating instincts*. Battling the instincts goes against life, and is therefore associated with a descending or declining type of life, for as long as life is ascending, so Nietzsche tells us, happiness and instinct are one. The conclusion we must draw, therefore, is that Socrates was no true physician of culture.

And so here again we find, in Nietzsche's 'final' position, that the teleology of the 'philosopher who speaks music' is diametrically opposed to the teleology of Socrates and his school, since it is the latter who completely 'negates culture' (UF 21[11], summer 1872–beginning 1873). The true philosopher as the physician of culture must be above all consistent with the ethical implications of vitalism: such a one must not go beyond the possibility of experience by appealing to the 'moral interpretation of existence', as did the historical Socrates. On the contrary, such a one is required to embody the pessimism of strength by finding a way to affirm all that is hard, terrible, evil and problematic in existence out of overflowing health and the abundance of life, not out of its impoverishment. It is in this very real sense that the philosopher as physician of culture must find a way to 'make music' out of life, and why, in Nietzsche's estimation, it is *he* and not Wagner who embodies this ideal.

The uniting and dividing point of two cultures

Although we have shown that Nietzsche's critique of Socrates as an element of cultural destruction remains fixed across both his 'pro-' and 'contra-Wagnerian' positions, it should now be clear that so too did his 'antipode': indeed the very fact that these two parameters for culture remain constant across both his 'pro-' and 'contra-Wagnerian' positions is precisely what allows Nietzsche to classify Wagner and his art as symptoms of the degenerating instincts for life as part of his 'contra-Wagnerian' project.

To be clear, we have seen that the 'music-making Socrates' of *The Birth of Tragedy* specifically referred to the form of a culture in which rationality is reunited with vitality in order to procreate the *rebirth* of art as culture. And although we know that this designation originally applied to Wagner and his art, once Nietzsche began to see the role of the 'philosopher who speaks music' as increasingly filled by himself, it followed that he would have every reason to insist that Wagner and *his* music were no longer capable of filling it.

Indeed, our analysis of the *Attempt* has shown that the entire *raison d'être* for Nietzsche's return to *The Birth of Tragedy* fourteen years after it was originally penned was precisely in order to bifurcate himself from the heroes of the original essay in light of his present philosophical project. By distinguishing the species of pessimism that belonged to the tragic culture, Nietzsche in one sense derived an ethical doctrine that was far more consistent with the ontology of vitalism, and in the process, this distinction became a referendum on the heroes of the original essay in terms of their *own* ontological commitments to vitalism. In Nietzsche's eyes both Schopenhauer and Wagner had, unforgivably, advocated for some form of the 'moral interpretation and significance of existence'. But as this 'solution' to the problem of life was exactly what Nietzsche reaffirms here to have been symptomatic of the Socratic culture, it is this feature of their respective works that puts both Schopenhauer and Wagner in propinquity with the Socratic, not the tragic, culture. Consequently Schopenhauer and Wagner become pessimists of a very different stamp: by having appealed to the 'moral interpretation and significance of existence', Schopenhauer and

Wagner had shown themselves to be, in reality, 'devitalized rationalists'; and so, much like the Greeks from Socrates onwards, they had succumbed to the pessimism of degenerating instincts, and in consequence shift from being symbols for the rebirth of culture to become instead additional victims of its decline.

From the standpoint of Nietzsche's 'contra-Wagnerian' project more generally and of *The Case of Wagner* in particular, the implication of all of this, of course, is that Wagner and his music had *never* embodied the essence of tragedy that might otherwise inaugurate such an epoch-making turning point as originally laid down in *The Birth of Tragedy*. It is precisely in this sense that Nietzsche steps into the role that both Schopenhauer and Wagner had 'prepared' in order to become their 'heir'.[9]

In this very important respect, then, it is paramount that we recognise not only how these two cultural forms and the parameters that define them remain fixed across both his 'pro-' and 'contra-Wagnerian' positions, but how they function against both Schopenhauer and Wagner in Nietzsche's 'contra-Wagnerian' position.

First we have already shown that both the figure of Socrates and the 'philosopher who speaks music' function as catalytic agents for culture: both hasten the downfall of the cultural form that existed prior to their appearance while at the same time they procreate an entirely new cultural form that follows in their wake. It is in this sense that we maintain that they both symbolise the uniting and dividing point of two cultures in antithetical tension.

But while Socrates and the 'philosopher who speaks music' play the same functional relationship *within* the whole, they do not at all possess the same meaning *to* the whole. And as the

---

[9] Both Young (2010) and Conway (2012) have emphasised, quite rightly, that Nietzsche's fundamental allegiances to Wagner, both in terms of the Wagnerian ideal of 'self-discipline' and, in Young's words, 'the original Wagnerian programme' to redeem 'Western culture through the rebirth of "the Greek"' (Young 2010: 360) are central to Nietzsche becoming Wagner's 'heir'. What we have shown, however, is that Nietzsche's endeavour to overcome Wagner and, even more significantly, his self-proclaimed 'success' in so doing, are deeply embedded within, and depend upon, the fundamental assumptions that connect vitalism with art and their relationship to the decline and rebirth of art as culture as an overall pattern in history – something which we will see come to a head in *The Case of Wagner* itself.

Reason **divorced**
from the creative instincts for life =
'Socrates'

Rebirth of Culture		**Decline of Culture**
The birth of tragedy		The death of tragedy
Dionysian culture		Socratic culture
Tragic knowledge		Egoistic knowledge
The pessimism of strength		The pessimism of degenerating instincts
Pre-Socratics : Aeschylus :: Nietzsche : Zarathustra		Socrates : Euripides :: Schopenhauer : Wagner

Rationality **fused** to the
creative instincts for life =
'Music-making Socrates'
Philosopher Who Speaks Music

Figure 2.2 Nietzsche's 'contra-Wagnerian' conception of culture

'whole' for Nietzsche concerns the rebirth of art as culture, it is apparent that one symbolises a cultural form that destroys art as culture, while the other symbolises a cultural form that revitalises it. In this important sense, each figure and the cultural form they represent remain in diametrical opposition to one another in terms of the decline and rebirth of art as culture, as we can see in Nietzsche's 'contra-Wagnerian' conception of culture in Figure 2. With this 'revision' to the organic form of art as culture, what we have here in effect is Nietzsche taking over Wagner's theoretical explanation about the 'sophist needles of Athenian self-dissection' that had led to the decline of tragedy, in order to illustrate, as we shall see in the sequel, that Wagner's art failed to live up to its own principles. Moreover it is this 'revision' that embeds the charges we find in *The Case of Wagner*. Thus, if there is any 'similarity' between Nietzsche and the figure of Socrates, it is a purely analogical one, as both the figure of Socrates and the 'philosopher who speaks music' represent this uniting and dividing point of two cultures in antithetical tension. That, however, is where the 'similarity' ends, for the one constant that bifurcates the 'ascent' or 'decline' of art as culture across his 'pro-' and 'contra-Wagnerian' positions is the schism or division between vitalists and 'devitalized rationalists'.

It is the failure to appreciate this distinction, incidentally, that makes Nehamas's otherwise influential reading of Nietzsche's relationship to Socrates so erroneous, for even in the very notebook where Nietzsche confesses his 'closeness' to him,[10] what we find by contrast is that every other note in the exact same notebook testifies to the claim that the appearance of Socrates destroyed Greek culture,[11] and that what governed this destruction was the emergence of the so-called 'moral interpretation and significance of existence'. This is especially true in note 25, where Nietzsche tells us that 'the Greeks were well on the way to *correctly assessing* human existence, its irrationality, its suffering, *but they never reached this*, thanks to Socrates'. Instead, we find that 'an unbiased view of men is missing in all the Socratics, who have terrible abstractions, "the good, the just", in their heads' (UF 6[25], summer 1875).

Again in note 14, we find Nietzsche articulating precisely what we have described as his early 'pro-Wagnerian' conception of culture, of which Schopenhauer and Wagner are seen as elements that are analogous to the pre-Socratics and Aeschylus in terms of their cultural significance, and thereby stand *opposed* to the influence of Socrates on the other. In particular, Nietzsche tells us that early Greek philosophy 'was *throughout* a philosophy of *statesmen*', and that this is the 'greatest difference' between the pre- and post-Socratics.

---

[10] 'I must confess that *Socrates* is so close to me that I am almost always fighting a battle with him' (UF 6[3], summer 1875; compare Nehamas 2000: 132).

[11] See, for instance, UF 6[4]: the results of Socratism were, above all, 'damage to science and ethical living'; UF 6[7]: 'Socrates *knocks everything over* at the moment when it has approached the truth *most closely*; this is particularly *ironic*.'

Among them one does not find the "revolting claim to happiness", as one does from Socrates onward. Not everything revolves around the condition of their soul ... I will add Schopenhauer, Wagner, and early Greek culture together: this presents a view of a magnificent culture. (UF 6[14], summer 1875)

Here again the bifurcation is evident, but the reason for this attitude should now be clear, since the bifurcation Nietzsche finds between Schopenhauer, Wagner and the pre-Socratics on the one hand, and Socrates and the post-Socratics on the other, is grounded in the fact that the former are exemplars of vitalism, whereas Socrates and the post-Socratics are exemplars of 'devitalized rationalists' who usher in concern for their soul and its 'revolting claim to happiness'. Therefore if there is any truth in the claim about Nietzsche's proximity to Socrates, we must conclude that it is a proximity derived from Nietzsche's stated task of comprehending '*the inner coherence and the necessity of every true culture*' (UF 19[33], summer 1872–early 1873), for the nature of these notes, when taken together, clearly reveals that Nietzsche's interest is completely bound up with recognising the *catalytic agency* of Socrates for culture, with his attitude being hostility and antagonism at worst, and ambivalence at best. Now, as these notes were penned in 1875, what is perhaps most significant about them for our purposes is that Nietzsche's 'pro-Wagnerian' conception of culture remained intact against the Socratic culture, and only shifted over into a symptom of 'devitalization' and 'decline' after his official break with Wagner in 1876. Thus the fundamental question to ask regarding *The Case of Wagner* in particular is: how did Nietzsche's conception of the 'philosopher who practices music' change *after he had broken away from Wagner*? This is the central issue.

3
Music in the Microcosm and the Macrocosm

Becoming the legitimate heir and successor to the pre-Socratics

In the preceding chapter, we argued that there are two very important elements relevant to Nietzsche's 'post-Wagnerian' philosophical project, and ultimately what is at stake in *The Case of Wagner*. In this connection we examined Nietzsche's *Attempt*, since it is specifically here that Nietzsche endeavours to re-examine the critical and essential features of both the Socratic and tragic cultures in light of the heroes of *The Birth of Tragedy*.

In particular, our analysis of the *Attempt* confirmed that during the fourteen years that had elapsed, Nietzsche's provisional solution for culture had shifted away from one bound up with the macrocosmic giganticism of Wagner in Bayreuth to one that would find its meaning and significance at the individual level, and therefore with the idea of becoming *oneself* a fundamental unit of cultural expression. For if the contention is that the basis of all cultural expression is ultimately derived from how a given people confront the nature of existence, then it follows that the origins of culture must begin at the individual level with the courage to accept and embrace the weight of existence first, without falsifying one's depiction of it in the process. By finding a way to affirm all that is hard, terrible and problematic in existence without depicting it in a manner that strays from, and therefore 'falsifies', its nature, the individual can affirm the total meaning and significance of existence in both their conception *of* it and their conduct *towards* it. As our analysis showed, the depiction of existence that, Nietzsche contended, least falsifies its nature is rooted in what he called the pessimism of strength, and is what he deemed to be the essence of the tragic culture.

By contrast, those cultural forms that do not express and affirm this pessimism in their depiction of existence, but try on the contrary to find 'escape routes' from it, such as uncovering the 'moral interpretation and significance of existence' or other 'Christian solutions' to the will, or perhaps even getting caught up in distractions such as the 'intoxicating and befogging narcotic' of Wagner's music, cannot be, by definition, affirming life. To require such conceptual-ideological intoxicants or other 'Apollonian stimulants' in order to be able to live is, according to Nietzsche, a symptom of the 'devitalization' and 'impoverishment' of life.

Thus, when taken together with what we called Nietzsche's 'microcosmic approach' to the problem of culture, we observed that Nietzsche had derived an ethical doctrine that was far more consistent with the metaphysical implications of vitalism than either of his great mentors, Schopenhauer and Wagner, and that when it came to re-evaluating the problem of culture, Nietzsche believed that he had surpassed them both in offering a resolution to confronting the nature of existence. In the final analysis, then, the cultural forms that remain truest to the nature of existence will be those that depict it as a vital deed. But it was precisely here, according to Nietzsche, that Schopenhauer and Wagner, like the Greeks from Socrates onwards, had faltered: they had all fallen prey to the pessimism of degenerating instincts by trying to explain away the burden and weight of existence, and the nature of suffering in particular, by appealing in some way, shape or form to the moral interpretation and significance of existence. With these distinctions in hand between himself and his two great mentors, Nietzsche effectively aligned himself as the legitimate successor and heir to the pre-Socratics, and the sole figure of the original triumvirate who best grasped the meaning and significance of the tragic culture of the Greeks.

Yet even though Nietzsche's revision of vitalism might have provided him with an opening to propose how one's duty to confront and affirm existence is connected with the creation of culture at the cellular level, the question that now presents itself is why the nature of its solution is relevant to Nietzsche's final position against Wagner. The provisional answer, of course, is that if the 'philosopher who speaks music' continues to signify a cultural form that entails a balance between the rational and creative elements of conscious life, but is now reframed *against* Wagner and the macrocosmic giganticism of Bayreuth as the duty to confront the problem of existence at the individual level, then it follows that this new cultural form must find a way to unite the rational and creative elements of conscious life by 'making music' from the crucible of existence as such. In this respect, the duty to confront existence at the individual level and the commitment to 'make music' out of that confrontation have resolved themselves into two separate but interrelated themes, which will help us in our final attempt to resolve Nietzsche's 'post-Wagnerian' philosophy, since it is the nature and meaning of this cultural form that drives Nietzsche's case against Wagner.

The first requirement of this cultural form resonates with what we will call the *what* in Nietzsche's thesis. This is the duty to confront the nature of existence, of suffering in particular, even in its most unimaginable and incomprehensible forms. To do so is tantamount to possessing the courage to accept the burden and weight of existence directly and transparently, and is, as we have seen, precisely what is entailed by the pessimism of strength. The second requirement of this cultural form, however, resonates with what we call the *how* in Nietzsche's thesis, which has to do with the nature of music itself, with its peculiar ability to convey meaning or content in an immediate and irrefutable way. With these two themes in hand, we must now examine how the latter in particular becomes the means through which the former is confronted, and how this relationship between the two is central to Nietzsche's final conception of culture.

If therefore we are to enquire into the nature of Nietzsche's *Case of Wagner*, and what animates the case in particular, we need to recognise how the duty to confront the suffering of life is connected to the philosopher's ability to transform it into a work of art – to 'make music from the materials of life' – for this conception is, on the whole, a remarkable transformation of Nietzsche's earlier solution to the problem of culture implied in his endorsement of Wagner and Bayreuth. Yet it is precisely this relationship between what we have called the *what* and the *how* that will reveal Nietzsche's final conception of culture and how he uses it to leverage his challenge against Wagner.

Human, All Too Human and the beginning of Nietzsche's post-Wagnerian confrontation

While it is not our intention to exhaustively analyse Nietzsche's post-Wagnerian writings, it is our intention to briefly illustrate the nature of this shift diachronically. For a philosopher who was especially committed to the relationship between art and life, the nature of this ideological shift formed a direct challenge to Wagner and Bayreuth that became increasingly vociferous in Nietzsche's later works, since it was principally bound up with Nietzsche himself becoming the cultural solution *contra* Wagner. To recognise, therefore, that this is the principal challenge that is presupposed in *The Case of Wagner*, we need to briefly examine the nature of this *idée fixe*, which begins with *Human, All Too Human* and storms right through to *Ecce Homo*, so that when we come to evaluate *The Case of Wagner*, our analysis will presuppose what we believe to be the most logically coherent and internally consistent structure at the basis of Nietzsche's dynamic and lifelong obsession with Wagner.

Perhaps the best summary of Nietzsche's earlier 'macrocosmic approach' to the problem of culture is captured by a passage towards the end of section 2 of his 'History' essay, published only a year after *The Birth of Tragedy*.[1] Yet only in his next essay,

---

[1] 'Suppose someone believed that no more than one hundred productive human beings, educated in working in the same spirit, would be needed to put an end to the cultivatedness that has just now become fashionable in Germany; would he not be strengthened by the recognition that the culture of the Renaissance was borne on the shoulders of just such a band of one hundred men?' (HL 2). Indeed, through the lengthy, involved and labyrinthine argument that follows, Nietzsche's thesis about precisely who can take possession of history in the service of life becomes a hardly veiled nod towards Wagner's attempt to bring German mythology alive in the form of his music dramas, pitting him against what Nietzsche sees as a wasteland culture that luxuriates in knowledge – that characteristic impulse of Socratic culture that led to the 'decline of art at the hands of science'.

'Schopenhauer as Educator', does Nietzsche make the significance of individual greatness explicit for a unified culture: because the problem of life, the value of existence, must be faced on its own terms, the courage to face it without appeal to dogmas, scientific or otherwise, requires the strength of genuine individuality. It is no mistake then that an authentic culture has always rested on the strength of genuine individuality, on the genius, which is given in the form of its highest specimens – the artists, the philosophers and the saints – and it is here that Nietzsche counsels us to develop the *Schopenhauerian human being* within us as the archetype of individual strength. The connection between this condition and its consequences for culture cannot be more apparent than in the following passage:

> I am now in a position to supply an answer to the question posed earlier: whether it is possible to get in touch with the great ideal of the Schopenhauerian human being on the basis of a regulated, self-initiated activity. One thing, above all, is certain: those new duties are not the duties of a solitary individual; on the contrary, through them one is integrated into a powerful community, one that, to be sure, is not held together by external forms and laws, but by a fundamental idea. This is the fundamental idea of *culture*, insofar as it is capable of charging each one of us with one single task: *to foster the production of philosophers, artists, and saints within us and around us, and thereby to work towards the perfection of nature*. For just as nature needs philosophers for a metaphysical purpose, so, too, it also needs artists; for the purpose of its own self-enlightenment, so that it might finally be presented with a pure and finished image of what, in the tumultuousness of its own becoming, it never has the opportunity to see clearly – in short, for the purpose of its own self-recognition. (SE 5)

Note here that the 'duties' for the creation and proliferation of a new culture 'are not the duties of a solitary individual', but rest rather on a community of like-minded individuals bound together by a 'fundamental idea'. Considering at this time that Schopenhauer and

Wagner had formed such a community of like-minded individuals and were examples of these highest specimens for culture, the beginnings of this German reformation of culture (as we emphasised in Chapter 1) had appeared over and against the decadent forms of Socratic culture.

But now beginning with *Human, All Too Human*, not only do we find dozens of aphorisms that are hypercritical of the 'artist' and all 'higher art', we find almost from the very first aphorism that the prized archetypes of genius themselves – the artist, the philosopher and the saint that had been so necessary to bring about the birth of a genuine culture – come under special attack through a method of scepticism and scientific reductionism, influenced in large part by the writings of Nietzsche's new friend, Paul Rée.[2] In the first instance, Wagner's theories and his allegiances to them are undeniably the foil for Nietzsche's new views, and Wagner himself was not slow to pick up on this – so much so that Wagner wrote two articles that appeared in the *Bayreuther Blätter* between July and October 1878[3] ridiculing Nietzsche's new take on genius as the product of biochemical phenomena. But what came in for particular scorn was Nietzsche's newly found 'scientific method', that 'latest product of the historical school of applied philosophy' which now believed it could explain all the mysteries in the life of the universe with its 'reckless claims ... in the province of biology' (PW 6: 74–5, 'Public and Popularity'). Wagner accused Nietzsche of nothing less than luxuriating in the utilitarian promise of 'pure *science* and its eternal *progress*' – in effect, succumbing to precisely one of those 'conceptual-ideological intoxicants' about life that had sent him 'spinning in a constant whirl, now flying from accepted views, then flying back again in some confusion' (PW 6: 73–4).

---

[2] Small (2005) does an excellent job of examining the relationship between these two figures.

[3] The *Bayreuther Blätter* was a periodical founded by publisher, editor, and Wagner's long-time acquaintance Hans von Wolgozen in 1878 to promote enthusiasm for Wagner's music dramas. The two articles in question here are 'Public and Popularity', published in July 1878, and 'The Public in Time and Space', published in October 1878.

Nevertheless it is here that we find Nietzsche's first attempts to respond to his own criticism of higher art by presenting his new counter-conception of culture, in which he lays increasing emphasis on the duty of the individual as an 'irreducible cultural unit' to foster a sense of culture within himself. In a section entitled 'Microcosm and Macrocosm of Culture', Nietzsche tells us that

> Human beings make the best discoveries about culture within themselves when they find two heterogeneous powers ruling there. Given someone who is as much in love with the plastic arts or music as he is enraptured by the spirit of science and who sees it as impossible to suspend this contradiction by annulling the one and completely liberating the other: the only possibility remaining for him is to shape himself into a cultural edifice big enough for both those powers to inhabit, albeit at opposite ends, while between them there reside mediating powers with sufficient strength to smooth over, if necessary, any strife that might break out. *Any such cultural edifice in a single individual, though, will have the greatest resemblance to the cultural structure of an entire era and will by analogy furnish instruction about it.* (HAH1 276, our emphasis)

From the content of this note, we get a very clear sense of what Nietzsche's new 'microcosmic approach' to culture is. While 'culture' can still be defined as the 'unity of artistic style that manifests itself throughout all the vital self-expressions of a people' (DS 1), it has now become clear with this shift towards the 'microcosm' that this 'unity of artistic style' must begin with the individual as the 'irreducible cultural unit'. In fact, Nietzsche is quite clear that this 'unity of artistic style' can only come about from the strength and authority of the individual to be able to mediate the tensions, contradictions and inconsistencies that inevitably arise in trying to accommodate and unify such seemingly disparate loves in one and the same individual. Thus, as obscure and unassuming as this aphorism seems to be on the surface, its actual implications are quite shocking when we consider where Nietzsche once stood with regard to Wagner's conception of culture; namely, so long as the individual is committed to fostering a sense of culture within himself, *a single individual will have the greatest resemblance to the cultural structure of an entire era.*

While we might easily adduce a number of additional aphorisms from the totality of *Human, All Too Human*, our purpose here is simply to discern the disjunction between the grand, sweeping, macrocosmic approach to the problem of culture and the problem of culture that begins at the *individual* level.[4] Given that the primary duty of the philosopher is to face the nature of existence without recourse to conceptual-ideological intoxicants or a minimum of 'Apollonian stimulants', Nietzsche's first public declarations against Wagner and his macrocosmic approach in *Human, All Too Human* invariably necessitate that the individual must first have the courage to confront themselves if they are to have any hope of rivalling the cultural structure of an entire era. As we will shortly discover, this idea is formulated in Nietzsche's next two works, and yet it is clear that it is already present here in its embryonic form, indicating the direction in which Nietzsche's case against Wagner is heading.

Dawn on the horizon

In *Dawn*, we find one of Nietzsche's earliest articulations of the nature and effect of all modern art set in opposition to what we have called the *what* in Nietzsche's 'post-Wagnerian' philosophy, namely the duty of the philosopher to face the nature of suffering. In section 52, titled, aptly enough, 'Where Are the New Physicians of the Soul?', Nietzsche tells us that the means of solace, of which modern art is the supreme example, are precisely what make life so full of suffering for so many; for by mistaking 'the momentarily effective, anesthetizing, and intoxicating means, the so-called consolations, for the actual remedies', people got addicted to the intoxicating effects themselves, so that 'there was

---

[4] See, for instance, HAH2 99, 'The Poet as a Signpost to the Future'; 102, 'An Excuse for Much Guilt'; 109, 'Living without Art and Wine'; 174, 'Against the Art of Artworks', just for starters.

no longer any chance for recovery'. Nietzsche then observes that while it was Schopenhauer who finally took humanity's suffering seriously again, he also wonders in the same breath who will follow Schopenhauer in finally taking the antidotes to this suffering seriously, as opposed to this 'scandalous quackery with which, under the most magnificent names, humanity has treated its diseases of the soul' (D 52). Thus from the content of this note, we witness one of Nietzsche's earliest attempts to grapple with the nature of modern art and its relationship to suffering, but especially its role in alleviating that suffering. According to Nietzsche, modern art can only ever be an ersatz antidote to the suffering found in the world precisely because of the intoxicating and befogging means with which it affects its audience. While perhaps 'momentarily effective', the spell soon wears off, leaving its audience restless, unhappy and, most importantly, ill-prepared to actually confront the very suffering from which the audience was trying to escape in the first place. Yet opposed to these 'momentarily effective, anesthetizing, and intoxicating means', Nietzsche reminds us that the true philosopher as an 'irreducible cultural unit' must be able to affirm all that is problematic in existence first if the suffering found within it is to be taken seriously again. Schopenhauer may have articulated the problem, but it will be up to Nietzsche, *not* Wagner, to furnish the solution.

In this connection, Book V of *Dawn* is especially exceptional for the manner in which Nietzsche attempts to redefine our understanding of what art is: not a momentary escape from the suffering of life, but the very activity or deed through which suffering is confronted. In particular, we are reminded that the true physician of culture must be, not so much the great synthesiser or harmoniser of tendencies or trends in a culture, as the great synthesiser or harmoniser of himself. Drawing on Schopenhauer's analogue of music with the will, the philosopher as an 'irreducible cultural unit' must first affirm all the disparate elements of living experience with its motley rhythms, tempi, timbres and dynamics in order to harmonise these elements into one single unified tonality. But it is just the nature of this tonality, whose particular expression each philosopher is, which attempts to *harmonise* 'I' with 'other', and so it is precisely here that the philosopher begins to cultivate the 'art' or 'music' of life as a means to confront suffering.

Yet for the true thinker to harmonise himself with the world as will implies that he must genuinely cultivate a music of life and not become an amorphous and anaesthetising sound wall with no character of its own. In other words, he must not become Wagner's 'endless melody'. To begin, Nietzsche tells us that nothing has been impossible for music up until now, so if we accept that premise as true, why would it not be possible for music to also find 'that brighter, more joyful, and widespread sound that corresponds to *the ideal thinker*?' After all, if the 'philosopher who speaks music' as a cultural form is to re-establish the balance between the critical and creative, and thus between rationality and vitality, then it follows that this new music must reflect that balance and that, accordingly, the ideal thinker must show that it is possible to experience, as Nietzsche suggests here, 'sublimity, deep and warm illumination, and the bliss of the highest logical consistency' in one and the same music (D 461). Again in section 531, we find Nietzsche advocating the notion that the true artist is himself his own work of art, but now with an important addendum: he now *lives* what he once desired from art (D 531).[5]

Finally, we find Nietzsche mocking the 'cheap fame of the "genius"' in section 548 by suggesting that what truly matters is whether the quantum of one's artistic genius has been overcome by 'something higher' than the energy that the 'genius' expends on his works, for in the final analysis, the works of the genius are simply spectacles designed for the consumption of the masses. In reality, the true artistic genius goes unnoticed, for the latter 'expends *not on works*, but *on himself as a work*, that is, on his own mastery, on the purification of his fantasy, on the ordering and selection of the onrushing stream of tasks and sudden insights' (D 548). This is obviously an extremely personal and exacting task, which

---

[5] Compare the preliminary draft of this aphorism: 'When one lives with profound and fructifying thoughts, one demands something completely different from art than before. That is the reason my taste in art has changed. Others demand from art the very element in which I live' (D 531, critical note 104).

explains why, according to Nietzsche, the true artistic genius's '*victory over energy* remains without eyes to see it and consequently without song and singers' (D 548). With this conclusion, we can see that the terms of Nietzsche's rivalry with Wagner are becoming increasingly clear, although not without a characteristic dose of resentment: while the requirements that Nietzsche sets forth would no doubt ensure a much sounder foundation for culture, by the same token, the nature of such an extremely personal and exacting task cannot possibly be celebrated with song and acclaim, adulation and reverence, and the fanfare associated with the 'cheap fame of the "genius"'. But that hardly stopped him from craving what he no doubt would have preferred for himself.

Before we proceed to a consideration of *The Gay Science*, which is a defining moment in the nature of Nietzsche's Wagner criticism, let us first take the opportunity to highlight a number of key themes that are already apparent in these two transitional works and that are critically important to articulating his final case against Wagner. First, we have already acknowledged that Nietzsche is especially motivated to understand the relationship between the individual and the nature and character of existence, and that the 'problem of existence' is completely bound up with the ability of the individual to face the nature of existence on its own terms. We have also acknowledged that Nietzsche's principal concern in this connection is for the individual to minimise the number of 'conceptual-ideological dogmas' to which they might appeal as a means to rationalise the nature of existence and, in effect, justify its value. Indeed, the idea that the philosopher must be strong enough to face existence without appeal to conceptual-ideological dogmas, scientific or otherwise, is the watchword of philosophical vitalism, since it is will, resolve, drive, determination and *not* reason which are argued to be more fundamental to the principle of life.

Second, with Nietzsche's first public declarations against Wagner in both *Human, All Too Human* and *Dawn*, what we find in effect is that the beginnings of his revision of culture, and especially the philosopher's role in it that had first been articulated in 'Schopenhauer as Educator', are now more or less formally pronounced against the intoxicating bombast of Wagner and Bayreuth. In contradistinction to what Nietzsche saw as Wagner's totalising, overbearing, 'macrocosmic' approach to the problem of culture, Nietzsche's commitments here suggest that we must first have the courage to face existence on its own terms before we will have any hope of transmuting the energies of our manifest vitality into an 'irreducible cultural unit'. So the fact that there are 'escape routes' from dealing with existence, such as the 'momentarily effective, anesthetizing, and intoxicating means' found in Wagner's music, implies that Wagner's solution and therefore his 'music' is a symptom of *devitalisation* and decline.

The Gay Science

The Gay Science is literally brimming over with Wagner criticism, but the latter half of Book II, especially sections 76–107, is especially noteworthy for its sustained reflections on the problem of all 'higher culture'. In this respect, section 87 is significant, for having just laid in to the music of modern theatre as a spectacle designed to intoxicate the masses (see GS 86), Wagner's exceptionality is singled out from other artists of the theatre as one who, 'more than any other musician, is a master at discovering the tones out of the realm of suffering, depressed, tormented souls and at giving speech even to dumb animals'. When it comes to Wagner's music in particular,

> Nobody equals him in the colors of late fall, the indescribably moving happiness of the last, very last, very briefest enjoyment; he finds sounds for those secret and uncanny midnights of the soul in which cause and effect appear to be unhinged and any moment something can come into being 'out of nothing.' More happily than anyone else, he draws from the very bottom of human happiness – as it were, from its drained cup, where the bitterest and most repulsive drops have merged in the end, for better or for worse, with the sweetest. He knows how souls drag themselves along when they can no longer leap and fly, nor even walk; his is the shy glance of concealed pain, of understanding without comfort, of farewells without confessions. (GS 87)

Yet what is most exceptional about Wagner is not simply that his music comprehends the realm of suffering, but that he is 'the master of the very small'. This is truly a peculiar charge, for according to Nietzsche, being the master of the very small 'is not what [Wagner] *wants* to be. His character prefers large walls and audacious frescoes' (GS 87). It soon becomes clear that what Nietzsche means here is that Wagner's art is at its best when it too centres on the intensely personal and thus the 'microcosmic'. But since his character prefers 'large walls and audacious frescoes' – in other words, the gigantic – Wagner's art is at its best precisely when he himself is *least* aware of it.

> He fails to see that his spirit has a different taste and urge and likes best of all to sit quietly in the nooks of houses that have collapsed; there, concealed from himself, he paints his real masterpieces all of which are very short, often only a single measure in length; there he becomes wholly good, great, and perfect – perhaps only there. – But he does not know it. He is too vain to know it. (GS 87)[6]

Of course, there are a number of implications that might be drawn from this final accusation, but perhaps the most fundamental one of all – and the one that, as we will see, is a direct challenge to Wagner himself – is that there is still a chasm to be found between Wagner the artist and Wagner's art. After all, how can the true artistic genius, who expends his energy '*not on works*, but *on himself as a work*, that is, on his own mastery' (D 548), exhibit such blind spots in his own self-awareness for that which he creates?[7]

---

[6] Compare NCW 'Where I Admire'.

[7] As interesting as this accusation might be, when we read this section in *Nietzsche Contra Wagner*, one will note that the last two lines, and therefore the final accusation about Wagner being 'too vain to know it', have been omitted, and in its place we find Nietzsche making the following confession: 'Wagner is someone who has suffered deeply – his *superiority* to other musicians. – I admire Wagner wherever he has set *himself* to music' (NCW 'Where I Admire'). In other words, what is most remarkable about the final form of this section is Nietzsche's admission that Wagner may have understood the intimate connection between suffering and music after all. This indeed is 'where he admires', for Nietzsche knew perfectly well that Wagner was his most formidable opponent in bringing to light the very conception of culture that he was trying to establish independently of him; that is, the duty to confront suffering by 'making music' out of life.

Given the importance we have attached so far to the notion of 'music' in the more comprehensive sense, and especially as it relates to what we have called the *how* in Nietzsche's 'post-Wagnerian' works, here we find at the climax to Book II perhaps one of the most revealing sections of all dealing with the power of music to convey meaning or content in an immediate and irrefutable way. In this connection, section 106 ('Music as an Advocate') is worth quoting in its entirety:

> 'I am thirsting for a composer,' said an innovator to his disciple, 'who would learn my ideas from me and transpose them into his language; that way, I should reach men's ears and hearts far better. With music one can seduce men to every error and every truth: who could refute a tone?' – 'Then you would like to be considered irrefutable?' said his disciple.
> The innovator replied: 'I wish for the seedling to become a tree. For a doctrine to become a tree, it has to be believed for a good while; for it to be believed, it has to be considered irrefutable. The tree needs storms, doubts, worms, and nastiness to reveal the nature and the strength of the seedling; let it break if it is not strong enough. But a seedling can only be destroyed – not refuted.'
> When he had said that, his disciple cried impetuously: 'But I believe in your cause and consider it so strong that I shall say everything, everything that I still have in my mind against it.'
> The innovator laughed in his heart and wagged a finger at him. 'This kind of discipleship,' he said then, 'is the best; but it is also the most dangerous, and not every kind of doctrine can endure it.' (GS 106)

Laying aside what is perhaps the most autobiographical feature of this dialogue, which is that it sounds suspiciously similar to one that had occurred between Wagner and Nietzsche – one in which Nietzsche had found himself 'with my pen in hand and my notebook before me' ready to jot down 'something of which

I have never thought, something that I wish to impress upon my mind'[8] – it is evident from the content that the 'innovator' ought to be capable of 'making music' even out of one's ideas, one's doctrines, one's philosophy of life with the intent of communicating their value in an immediate and irrefutable way. And with Nietzsche aspiring to become the master at the time *The Gay Science* was written, this section reveals perhaps the single best glimpse into the world of Wagnerian propaedeutics and the nature of the master–disciple relationship that was bound by it.

To begin, not only are rhythm and beat, as the fundamental aspects of music, ultimately reducible to numerical relationships subject to our sensed experience of time, so too are its melodic and harmonic fruits. To recognise this truth about music is to recognise at the same time that the exact same features have their analogue in the nature of language itself, especially the prosodic features of a language. The concatenation of individual phonetic segments that make up the fixable signs of a language are its sounds as speech. These sounds, which convey the expressive connotation of a language through its syntactical and grammatical system, including tone, stress, intonation and rhythm, impart meaning and significance to the utterance that go beyond the 'dictionary definition' of the word. These significances, which tap into the 'emotions of the inner man', and which correspond to the primeval idea of music as Wagner had once observed (PW 1: 91, 'Artwork of the Future'), convey both abstract rational as well as creative and generative values of reason associated with them. Accordingly, to 'make music' through the medium of language imbues that language with a privileged epistemic access to the hearts and minds of the listener, ensuring that it will be heard, assimilated, and perhaps even believed. Thus what we read the innovator say to his disciple at the beginning of this section is extremely important to our overall understanding of Nietzsche's competition with

---

[8] SL (1969: 118 [KSB 4: 144–5]), letter to Richard Wagner, 18 April 1873.

Wagner: we must convey meaning and content as 'music', for after all, it is not possible to *refute* a tone.[9]

In fact in an earlier section, Nietzsche frankly admits this very point when charting out, not only the storied history attached to the utility of rhythm among the ancients in effecting compulsion, but also that such a fundamental feeling can never be entirely erased (GS 84). The principal thrust, of course, is that, if not exactly an unconscious exercise in metaphysics, rhythm at the very least is an unconscious exercise in hypnotics in which the mind does not know that it is being mesmerised, and it is section 106, by way of section 84, that brings this 'lesson' out in full force.[10]

At the same time, creating a musical language to convey one's philosophical notions is just one emanation of what the 'philosopher who practices music' does, and what he must do, moreover, to rival Wagner. Therefore, in a very important section towards the end of Book V, we find out why poetry, artistry and cultivating the music of life are so important for the philosopher.[11] In section 372 Nietzsche notes that, formerly, philosophers denied life in favour of embracing their 'cold realm of "ideas"'; that indeed, 'Having "wax in one's ears" was then almost a condition of philosophizing; a real philosopher no longer listened to life insofar as

---

[9] Lou Salomé, who was Nietzsche's intellectual companion and unrequited love interest in the early 1880s, once remarked to their mutual friend Paul Rée about the contrast in their respective writing styles. 'Your style', she told Rée, 'wants to convince the reader's *head* and is therefore scientifically clear and rigorous, setting aside all emotion. N. wants to convince the whole person, he wants to reach into the heart with his word and overturn what is innermost; he wants not to *teach* but to *convert*.' See Small (2005: 41).

[10] In his discussion of the uniqueness of music, Schopenhauer reminds us that philosophy is 'nothing other than a complete and correct repetition and expression of the essence of the world in very general concepts', and that music 'uses a highly universal language to express the inner essence, the in-itself of the world ... and does so in a distinctive material, namely pure tones, and with the greatest determinateness and truth'. Accordingly, this led him to parody the original saying of Leibniz that 'music is an unconscious exercise in arithmetic in which the mind does not know it is counting' to 'music is an unconscious exercise in metaphysics, in which one does not know it is philosophizing' (WWR 1, 52). So once again, we can see that by advocating for the 'philosopher who practices music' Nietzsche is deducing an ethical practice that follows much more consistently from Schopenhauer's metaphysics.

[11] For this perspective, see also GS 290 and GS 299.

life is music; he *denied* the music of life – it is an ancient philosopher's superstition that all music is sirens' music' (GS 372).

Yet philosophy, Nietzsche exhorts us here, is much more than abstract propositions that reason from premises to conclusions; it is also the very activity of living itself. That is why, in opposition to the ancient prejudice that all music is sirens' music,

> We today are inclined to make the opposite judgment . . . namely that *ideas* are worse seductresses than our senses, for all their cold and anemic appearance, and now even in spite of this appearance: they have always lived on the 'blood' of the philosopher, they always consumed his senses and even, if you will believe, his 'heart.' These old philosophers were heartless; philosophizing was always a kind of vampirism. (GS 372)

The rhetorical analogy that we find here which likens the 'rational' philosopher to a vampire could not underscore any better the idea that what is rational in human beings not only subsists by virtue of what is vital in them, but that the age-old prejudice of the 'rational' philosopher and his 'ideas' continues to accentuate the disjunction between the two. Like any other parasitic being, the 'rational' philosopher and the vampire can only subsist by feeding off the vitality of other beings. The 'rational' philosopher and his realm of 'ideas' are so seductive that they tyrannise even the philosopher's own vitality, leading to a philosophical outlook that is lifeless, stiffened, mummified, and all the other dysphemisms that we might marshal to suggest the notion that what is produced is secondary and derivative, and does not account for the facts of life as such.

By contrast, what Nietzsche advocates here, as the true successor of Schopenhauer, is a valuation that cultivates the inverse; namely, accentuating what is vital in humanity as primary and original, and therefore more fundamental than the realm of abstract 'ideas'. Accordingly, the claim here is that the modern philosopher should dispense with the age-old assumption that what is rational is separate and apart from what is vital, and with it the attendant prejudice of denying the 'music of life' in favour of the realm of abstraction. This is precisely what the 'philosopher who speaks music' is trying to remedy as a cultural form. Thus 'music' in the sense we continue to expound here suggests a discipline that is at once both the apogee of logic and rationality, and yet reaches us in an immediate and irrefutable way. In any case it is the intention of the 'philosopher who speaks or practices music' to consciously fuse these two elements, and to bring together what have historically been regarded as disjunctive and mutually exclusive elements since at least the time of Socrates. It should be increasingly clear, based on our survey of Nietzsche's 'transitional' works, that he sees himself playing this role, and playing it *contra* Wagner.

Beyond Good and Evil: prelude to a philosophy of the future

As we saw in *The Gay Science*, Nietzsche's attempt to articulate his own counter-conception of culture was to some extent on equal footing with his criticisms of Wagner, but with *Beyond Good and Evil*, Nietzsche's attacks on Wagner and the Wagnerism that had sprouted in his wake become far more targeted than previously.

Beginning with section 28, the music of one's language – or lack thereof – is brought back into focus, especially as it features in the philosophy of the 'free spirit' on the one hand and in contrast with the peoples of the 'fatherland' on the other. Here in particular, Nietzsche tells us that what translates worst from one language to another is 'the *tempo* of its style'; and this is true for the simple reason that all language has its origins in the character of those who use it, and that this must be gradually cultivated into a unity of style and expression among the life-pulse of a given people, or what Nietzsche calls in this section, 'the average tempo of its "metabolism"'. The literary discussion that ensues becomes a convenient pretext for Nietzsche to echo Schopenhauer's reproof of the Germans for what he considers their dull, languid and lifeless tempo, and consequently, their boring, tedious and unwieldy style.[12] Truly, they could hardly

---

[12] Compare PP 2, 'On Writing and Style', 287.

be the folk dreamed about in Wagner's 'Artwork of the Future'. 'The Germans', Nietzsche relates,

> are practically incapable of a *presto* in their language: and thus, it is fair to conclude, also incapable of many of the most delightful and daring nuances of the free, free-spirited thought . . . Everything ponderous, lethargic and pompously awkward, all wordy and boring genres of style are developed with excessive diversity in Germans. . . (BGE 28)

Yet Nietzsche's ire over the careless and slovenly style of the Germans reaches the pinnacle of exasperation in section 246, in which he accuses the Germans not only of not knowing how to write, but also of not knowing how to read. The indignation here is significant, for when we consider that Nietzsche believed that in creating his *Zarathustra*, he had given the Germans 'the profoundest work in the German tongue, also the most perfect in its language',[13] the inability of the Germans to write, much less read, simply proved to him that they had no talent for rhythm, much less the ability to 'make music' out of life.

> What torture are books written in German for someone who has a *third* ear! How reluctantly he stands beside the slowly revolving swamp of sounds that do not sound, of rhythms without dance that pass for a 'book' among Germans! And how especially the German who reads books! How lazily, how reluctantly, how badly he reads! How many Germans know and demand it of themselves to know that there is *art* in every good sentence – art that wants to be figured out insofar as the sentence wants to be understood! A misunderstanding about its tempo, for instance: and the sentence itself is misunderstood! To not be in doubt about the rhythmically decisive syllables, to feel the break with the all-too-rigid symmetry as

---

[13] SL (1969: 299 [KSB 8: 340]), letter to Karl Knortz, 21 July 1888.

deliberate and attractive, to hold up a subtle and patient ear to every *staccato* and *rubato*, to guess the meaning in the sequence of vowels and diphthongs and how tenderly and richly they can color and recolor each other in succession: who among book-reading Germans has enough good will to acknowledge duties and demands such as these and to listen carefully for so much art and intention in language? In the end people simply do not 'have the ear for it': and so the strongest contrasts of style go unheard and the finest artistry is wasted on the deaf. (BGE 246)

This section is significant for a number of reasons, but chief among them is the main 'lesson' we should have learned by now from section 106 of *The Gay Science*: that music is indeed an 'advocate', as is once again presupposed here in Nietzsche's confrontation with the Germans.

Only those who recognise the nature of what music truly is can appreciate the expressive and communicative intent of the individual's language and the individual life at the basis of those expressions. All the staccato and rubato that colours and recolours the thought through the word, or the stress, intonation and rhythm that are found in the concatenation of phonemes, impart meaning and significance that go beyond the 'dictionary definition' of the word and tap into the 'emotions of the inner man', because they, like music, convey both abstract rational as well as creative and generative values for reason which are immediate and irrefutable. All of these values, however, are lost on the Germans. If, then, style in language has its origins in the character of a culture's life-pulse or vitality, that is, in 'the average tempo of its "metabolism"', and we know that the German 'metabolism' is dull, languid and lifeless, then it is hardly a wonder (according to Nietzsche's argument) that the 'German style' is precisely the same as the 'German way of life': boring, tedious and unwieldy. If anyone can refute a tone then, it would be the Germans, for only those who are deaf and atonal can be incapable of listening to the music of life. The conclusion Nietzsche wishes us to draw here, perhaps unsurprisingly, is that there are no true 'German musicians', let alone any who are capable of making music from the materials of life.[14]

But for anyone who has 'ears to hear', it is clear that Nietzsche's mockery of the Germans and their lack of musical talent is not so much directed towards Germans in general as it is towards one musician in particular, especially once we consider the opening remarks of the very next section. 'How little German style has to do with sound and with the ears', Nietzsche observes in BGE 247, 'is shown by the fact that precisely our good musicians write poorly. Germans do not read aloud, for the ear, but merely for the eyes: meanwhile they have put their ears away in a drawer.'

What is especially noteworthy about the remaining observations of this section is how Nietzsche proceeds to contrast this unfortunate decline of the 'musicality of language' in the modern world with the implicit understanding of language as music in the ancient world. In the ancient world, Nietzsche tells us, no one would have read silently to oneself, because the rules of written style were the same as those of speech. And no one speaks without employing, in addition to the words they use, quite other modes, such as gesture, intonation, rhythm and the accentuation of words in order to convey affective values not otherwise captured by the 'dictionary definition' of the words; that is to say, 'with all the swells, inflections and reversals of tone and changes in tempo in which the ancient *public* world took delight'. It is here in particular that Nietzsche tells us that

> Back then the rules of written style were the same as those of spoken style; and its rules depended in part on the amazing development and the refined requirements of the ear and the larynx, partly on the strength, endurance and power of the ancient lung. A period [that is, the punctuation mark] in the sense of the ancients is above all a physiological whole, insofar as it is encompassed in a single breath. Such periods as are found in Demosthenes and

---

[14] Compare 'I shall never admit that a German *could* know what music is' (EH 'Why I Am So Clever' 7).

Cicero, swelling twice and subsiding twice and all within a single breath: those were the pleasures for *ancient* people who knew from their own training to appreciate the rare and difficult virtue of performing such a period: – *we* really have no right to the *great* period, we moderns who are short of breath in every sense! (BGE 247)

The more immediate and philological implication of Nietzsche's criticism here is that the final form of our written language is actually 'verbal language for the eye' in which diacritical marks, and in general all punctuation, textually denote the original gesture-language of the spoken word with which it was completely bound up. Yet we as moderns, and especially as Germans, have completely disregarded this truth, since we have put our ears in a drawer when we read. The more general, philosophical implication, however, is that modernity, but most especially Wagner, has no right to pry open this great period (both as punctuation mark and as epoch) for the sake of his art.

Yet what is even more fascinating about the accusations we find in this section, and why it is an attack on Wagner's music in particular, is that the very same claim about language and its relationship to the folk comes straight out of Wagner's playbook in 'Artwork of the Future'. Indeed the notion that all spoken language must be gradually cultivated into a unity of style and expression among the life-pulse of a given people is what creates the folk as a fundamental unit of culture (PW 1: 74). In particular, what we read here is that the word by which speech seeks to communicate its expressive intent is, at the same time, a *tone* which directly expresses the general feeling with which the word is bound up (PW 1: 92); and thus only when tone and speech are united is it possible to convey the immediate affective values of one's original expressive and communicative intent through the word. By fusing both, as for example in lyric poetry, we develop a means of communication that addresses the entire being, the rational and the vital. This is precisely what makes the art of lyric poetry, and its depiction in dramatic form, the apogee of artistic expression for Wagner, for it unites what is 'logical' as speech with what is 'musical' as tone (PW 1: 104).

Now if this sounds familiar, it should, because this is exactly what we have indicated Nietzsche himself was trying to achieve in becoming the 'philosopher who speaks music'. Accordingly, when we examine the disparaging remarks that open BGE 247, we can be certain that Nietzsche's criticisms presuppose Wagner's theory about the nature and style of language, for the very principles that Wagner articulates are operative in Nietzsche's criticisms of Wagner here. When it comes to Wagner's own prose, for instance, Nietzsche tells us that Wagner the philosopher has no talent for 'music'. In fact Wagner writes horribly, and even in the essay that was ostensibly written to commemorate him, Nietzsche had to concede this point. Something of the 'repeatedly broken' and 'uneven rhythm' of Wagner's dialectic causes 'excitement and disquiet', for one is apt to find his texts 'richly swollen with superfluous words' and written 'in the style of spoken, not of written discourse' (WB 10).[15]

But the challenge to Wagner goes even further than this. By asserting that there are no true German musicians, and certainly none that are capable of listening to the music of life, Nietzsche has in effect paved the way for himself and, in particular, his *Zarathustra* as the legitimate counter-offer to Wagner and Bayreuth. In fact, Paul Loeb's excellent study has demonstrated quite convincingly that Nietzsche's *Zarathustra* is deeply indebted to Wagner's own *Ring* cycle as a whole,[16] while Lesley Chamberlain has pointed out that *Zarathustra* itself is nothing short of an out-and-out competition with Wagner and his *Ring* cycle, in which 'proposition and response are spectacular' (Chamberlain 1996: 66). *Zarathustra* is the spiritual antithesis of the dull, heavy and ponderous German typified by Wagner's music, with teachings that signify instead the metaphor of 'dance' – a graceful flexibility that moves on light feet and is the key to self-surmounting, while structurally the musicality of *Zarathustra*'s language is the symphonic form flowing beneath the quasi-mythical narrative of Zarathustra's

---

[15] Compare UF 32[30], beginning 1874–spring 1874.
[16] Paul Loeb's outstanding and impressively detailed study of Nietzsche's *Zarathustra* (2010) illustrates just how pervasive the Wagnerian vision and logic were on Nietzsche's philosophy.

teachings and the Songs of Zarathustra. The condensed imagery and symbolism of Zarathustra's teachings effectively function as cellular leitmotifs that organise the narrative content, and are draped against the background of a lyrical hero wandering from adventure to adventure in order to convey his 'teachings'. Like Wagner's *Ring* cycle, *Zarathustra* offers us no shortage of serpents, forest murmurs, singing birds, dwarves, riddles and itinerant shepherds. But in contrast to Wagner's 'excessive use' of triplets and five- and seven-beat phrases,[17] the sound pattern of the prose is proportioned and symmetrical, hence 'classical'; while at the same time, Nietzsche's use of the aria and chorus as operatic devices is emphasised over the Wagnerian 'endless melody'.[18]

Thus when we examine the criticisms that Nietzsche levels against Wagner and his music, we must recognise that they are increasingly aimed at discrediting Wagner as someone who does not measure up to the principles he had laid down about music either as a formal musician or a thinker in the so-called art as culture that he had been responsible for creating. In the meantime, Nietzsche had continued to embark on a far more aggressive promotional and marketing campaign of his own to be recognised as the 'philosopher who speaks music' – a position that we will finally see brought to fruition in our formal analysis of the text.

Ecce Homo

Outside of *The Case of Wagner*, nowhere does Nietzsche's challenge to Wagner come to a head more perfectly than in *Ecce Homo*, and in this respect the individual threads we have been weaving so far between the *what* and the *how* in Nietzsche's 'post-Wagnerian' conception of culture become evident. At this point, then, we will try to bring together the strands of our discussion in anticipation of the final denouement, for once we recognise that Nietzsche's philosophy, and especially his achievement in 'composing Zarathustra', are

---

[17] See SL (1969: 162 [KSB 5: 261]), letter to Carl Fuchs, end of July, 1877.
[18] Compare HAH2 134, 'How the Soul Should Be Moved According to Modern Music', and NCW 'Wagner as a Danger' 1.

a direct challenge to Wagner and Bayreuth, we will at once appreciate the significance of his parable in telling us that the first part of his masterpiece *Zarathustra* 'was finished exactly in that sacred hour in which Richard Wagner died in Venice' (EH 'Why I Write Good Books' TSZ 1).

To begin, let us briefly recap what Nietzsche's provisional solution to the problem of culture had become following his break with Wagner. As we have noted, the solution no longer resided in the 'macrocosmic' approach to the problem of culture, in which Wagner's totalising project at Bayreuth and all its attendant ills had turned out to be nothing at all like the 'rebirth of culture out of the spirit of music' that Nietzsche had envisioned from the time of his earliest association with Wagner.[19] Instead the approach, as we have now seen, shifted towards the 'microcosmic', in which the individual was now deemed to be the fundamental or 'irreducible cultural unit' of the larger culture by definition. Thus when it came to the problem of revitalising that larger culture, the responsibility would ultimately inhere in the individual as that 'irreducible cultural unit' to transform or recreate themselves first. This requirement necessitated a 'unity of artistic style', which could only come about through individual strength and, in particular, a tautening of the individual's duty to mediate the tensions, contradictions and inconsistences that inevitably arise in the course of trying to unify such seemingly disparate directions in one and the same person. In this respect, the creative urge of the artist would have to be directed back towards themselves, for only through one's attempt to create oneself do the artist and the work of art become one and the same object. The fundamental problem, however, is that the individual must work with the materials of life itself, and so must be more than a mere artist, whose sole concern is simply to beautify the real. The individual must also be a philosopher, for they

---

[19] Obviously the biographical reasons for this are varied and complex, but for an excellent, first-hand account which, in many ways, summarises in microcosm Nietzsche's pervasive disillusionment and disappointment following his break with Wagner, see Gilman (ed.) 1987: 79–80, account of Richard Reuter, summer 1876.

must be able to affirm, not simply the beautiful, the attractive and the desirable, but likewise everything questionable in existence, even if those question marks ultimately point to the illusions, delusions and deceptions of life. In other words, the individual must be strong enough to affirm the question marks of life, for this is precisely what it means to take the suffering of life seriously again. But with this turn, of course, the respective solutions of Nietzsche and Wagner in terms of *how* to take the suffering of life seriously again become perceptible; and as we have seen, it is the nature of this *how*, and the artistry at the basis of it, which forms the real conflict in Nietzsche's case against Wagner. Rather than cultivating individual strength to 'make music' from the materials of life, here we find (according to Nietzsche) only the momentarily effective, anaesthetising and intoxicating resources of all so-called 'higher culture' as a means to confront the suffering of life. In the final analysis this was a solution, not of strength, but of enervation, exhaustion and devitalisation of life. In a word, it was Wagner's art.[20]

With this brief recap, what does Nietzsche tell us in *Ecce Homo* regarding Wagner? First and above all, that they were equals, not only in terms of being the antithesis of the 'merely German' and

---

[20] Both Soll (1990) and Came (2005) maintain that Nietzsche's project is in some sense rooted in how to respond to Schopenhauer's descriptive claim that existence is invariably full of suffering. Our analysis thus far has independently confirmed this reading, since we have seen that Nietzsche's principal concern is not the mere *fact* of suffering, or what we have called the *what* of existence, but rather what to make of it and how to deal with it. This makes Nietzsche's response to Schopenhauer one that is rooted in the problem of meaning in precisely in the same way that Gemes and Sykes (2014) claim to be the case when it comes to Wagner. But where the latter authors believe that Wagner's 'solution' to the problem of meaning lay in his self-conscious attempt to construct mythological narratives in order to help us moderns affirm existence, since they stamp a kind of artificial unity on the chaos of the people that is so necessary for the flourishing of a new culture, the problem of meaning, and therefore the question of *how*, is much more *vital* than that. As we have begun to see, Nietzsche's response to Schopenhauer is rooted in the nature of music itself, with its peculiar ability to convey meaning or content in an immediate and irrefutable way. Hence *The Case of Wagner* is, as we will see, *a dispute over the nature of music itself*, and how, in Nietzsche's estimation, Wagner used and abused that privilege for the sake of his art when compared to Nietzsche's 'harmless self-artistry' and his own call to 'make music' from the materials of life.

the 'incarnate protest against all "German virtues"' (EH 'Why I Am So Clever' 4), but in one other very special sense:

> That in which we are related – that we have suffered more profoundly, also from each other, than men of this century are capable of suffering – will link our names again and again, eternally; and as certainly as Wagner is merely a misunderstanding among Germans, just as certainly I am and always will be. Two centuries of psychological and artistic discipline must come first, my dear Teutons! – But with that one does not catch up. (EH 'Why I Am So Clever' 6)

But while equals in suffering, and in the capacity for suffering, Wagner and Nietzsche are not at all equals (according to Nietzsche) when it comes to creating art as a response or an 'antidote' to this suffering. Once again it is precisely on this point of *how* that Nietzsche takes exception to Wagner. Wagner's art, Nietzsche tells us once again, is a 'toxin, a poison' designed for weary nerves, a narcotic like hashish to which one turns when 'wants to rid oneself of an unbearable pressure' (EH 'Why I Am So Clever' 6).[21] By contrast, the greatness of *Zarathustra* resides in the fact that he is the most tremendous Yes-sayer to life. So while we find that Wagner's art is a toxin designed for weary nerves, Nietzsche's *Zarathustra* is the art of one who can affirm life in a purely vitalistic way, because it teaches, out of the pessimism of strength, the philosopher's duty to confront the problem of suffering by being strong enough to 'make music' out of life. In other words, *Zarathustra* combines the philosopher's virtues of wisdom and reason with those of the artist, which are creativity and insight, and so becomes, in a manner of speaking, the final fulfilment of the 'philosopher who speaks music' as a cultural form.

That Nietzsche's *Zarathustra* is the deed that proves (to him) that the 'philosopher who speaks music' has been fulfilled as a cultural form is very important – in fact it could hardly be more important when we come to consider in what sense Nietzsche is challenging

---

[21] Compare GS 86.

Wagner. No longer did this cultural form refer to that 'richly-gifted individual' in the person of Wagner and his music which had heralded a return to life from the wearied instincts of Socratic culture through the Dionysian future of music. All Wagner's art could ever create, according to Nietzsche's account here in *Ecce Homo*, was a toxin designed for weary nerves.

By contrast, Nietzsche tells us that the achievement of his *Zarathustra* was 'the long, secret work and artistry of my instinct' (EH 'Why I Am So Clever' 9). In particular, the artistry of his instinct was the result of an 'organizing idea' which, while destined to emerge into his surface consciousness as the commanding identity, nonetheless took great affirmation of life to effect: 'slowly [the organising idea] leads us *back* from side roads and wrong roads; it prepares *single* qualities and fitnesses that will one day prove to be indispensable as means toward the whole – one by one, it trains all *subservient* capacities before giving any hint of the dominant task, "goal", "aim", or "meaning"' (EH 'Why I Am So Clever' 9).[22]

Unfortunately, Nietzsche's account of the artistry of his instinct is, as one might imagine, not the parthenogenetic birth he would have his readers believe. His capacities, in other words, did not suddenly leap forth 'in their ultimate perfection' (EH 'Why I Am So Clever' 9), as did Athena from the head of Zeus. But considering that Nietzsche's *Zarathustra* is a direct challenge to Wagner, his discussion of the artistry of his instinct has *everything* to do with Wagner. To get a sense of just how important this point

---

[22] Though Nietzsche had nothing but scorn both for the philosopher himself and for his *Philosophy of the Unconscious*, this notion is incredibly similar to the philosophy of Eduard von Hartmann, who had argued that will and reason together comprise the Unconscious. Although willing is the active element of awareness which 'breaks through to the surface', the will in striving acts on reason that is potentially present in the Unconscious, manifesting the Idea and bringing it to the surface as the expressed and no longer latent object of the will. Walter Kaufmann, in his rather immoderate hero-worship of Nietzsche, thinks that this idea, and the notion that precedes it, namely that 'consciousness is a surface', prefigures Freud. But this notion is not only explicit in Schopenhauer, of whom Kaufmann's knowledge was unpardonably anaemic, it is perhaps most consistently derived in von Hartmann, whose stated goal was to balance the insights of both Hegel and Schopenhauer.

is, it is worth noting that the same fundamental rhetoric behind Nietzsche's 'organizing idea' in *Ecce Homo* can be found fully intact in his early essay 'Richard Wagner in Bayreuth', where he reflects on the 'ruling thought' of Wagner's life (WB 8), or when he notes that 'to reflect on what *Wagner the artist is*' is tantamount to 'the cure and recovery for anyone who has thought about and suffered over *how Wagner the human being developed*' (WB 9). In fact, we find a number of telling comments about Wagner here: that, for instance, his 'appearance in the history of art is like a volcanic eruption of nature's entire, undivided artistic ability' (WB 9), or that the fearlessness with which he tackled his 'totally terrifying task shows just how powerfully he was guided by the poetic spirit, like someone who must follow regardless of where his ghostly guide takes him' (WB 9). Yet perhaps the most telling comment of all, and one that directly concerns our analysis here of Nietzsche's 'ruling thought', comes in the context of his discussion of Wagner the composer.

> In general, we can say about Wagner the *composer* that he gave a language to everything in nature that until now had not wanted to speak; he does not believe that anything must be mute. He even immerses himself in colorful dawns, forests, fog, chasms, mountainous heights, the dread of night, and moonlight and takes note of their secret desire; they too want to resound. *When the philosopher says there is one will in animate and inanimate nature that thirsts for existence, then the composer adds: and at every stage this will wants a resounding existence.* (WB 9, our emphasis)

Here, in the final clause of this excerpt, are the very words that point to the idea that the philosopher and composer must be united in one and the same being. For if music truly is an analogue for the in-itself of all appearance in which we can 'just as well call the world embodied music as embodied will' (WWR 1, 52), then it is the musician in particular who assigns all the tonalities of the world, giving language to the will in all of animate and inanimate nature. When we compare this passage against Nietzsche's 'ruling thought' in *Ecce Homo*, and how he believed the latter was instrumental to how he had become the 'philosopher who speaks music' through his *Zarathustra*, it becomes clear that Nietzsche's challenge to Wagner as we find it in *Ecce Homo* is a direct challenge vis-à-vis his two great intellectual mentors for psychological hegemony over this cultural form. This conclusion becomes almost undeniable once we consider the numerous statements Nietzsche makes to his readers in support of it, and the fact that he repeatedly takes the opportunity to point it out, not only in *Ecce Homo* but even in his private letters.

In the text of *Ecce Homo* itself, we can begin by considering why Nietzsche, according to his own account, writes such good books. Here we find in the assessment of his very first book – not only a book dedicated to Wagner, but one that we now know unquestionably drew on a number of Wagner's own ideas – Nietzsche claiming that, when it came to promoting the 'artwork of the future', or what Nietzsche calls here the 'Dionysian future of music' in the final ten sections of *The Birth of Tragedy*, what he had truly heard prefigured in Wagner's music was a vision of his *own* future:

> A psychologist might still add that what I heard as a young man listening to Wagnerian music really had nothing to do with Wagner; that when I described Dionysian music I had described what *I* had heard – that instinctively I had to transpose and transfigure everything into the new spirit that I carried in me. The proof of that, *as strong as any proof can be*, is my essay on *Wagner in Bayreuth*: in all psychologically decisive places I alone am discussed – and one need not hesitate to put down my name or the word 'Zarathustra' where the text has the word 'Wagner.' The entire picture of the dithyrambic artist is a picture of the pre-existent poet of *Zarathustra* sketched with abysmal profundity and without touching for a moment the Wagnerian reality. Wagner himself had some notion of that; he did not recognize himself in this essay.
>
> Similarly, 'the idea of Bayreuth' was transformed into something that should not puzzle those who know my *Zarathustra* . . . Wagner, Bayreuth, the whole wretched

> German pettiness are a cloud in which an infinite mirage of the future is reflected. Even psychologically all decisive traits of my own nature are projected into Wagner's ... Everything in this essay points to the future: the impending return of the Greek spirit, the necessity of counter-Alexanders who will retie the Gordian knot of Greek culture ... the absolute certainty about what I am was projected on some accidental reality [that is, Wagner and Bayreuth] – the truth about me spoke from some gruesome depth. (EH 'Why I Write Such Good Books' BT 4)

This passage is perhaps one of the most astonishing testaments to Nietzsche's competition with Wagner, and it occurs in the very essay in which Nietzsche says he had struggled over the 'meaning of Wagner' for posterity. But as Nietzsche also testifies here, the meaning of this struggle was not for Wagner, for the name 'Wagner' was nothing more than a convenient placeholder for Nietzsche's own 'organizing idea', and was thus more akin to a psychological symbol that had signposted a vision of his own future – a future moreover that included the 'impending return of the Greek spirit'. Where the real Wagner was we have no means of knowing, for as Nietzsche tells us here, Wagner 'did not recognize himself in this essay'. But if we can substitute, as Nietzsche surely claims we can, the name 'Wagner' with 'Zarathustra' as the deed that would eventually prove that philosophy and music had been fused in one and the same being, then we unquestionably find, according to Nietzsche's own account, that the promise that he had made to himself to become the 'philosopher who speaks music' from the standpoint of 'Richard Wagner in Bayreuth' had been psychologically fulfilled from the perspective of *Ecce Homo*.[23]

---

[23] Compare a notebook entry about this psychological conflict from the time Nietzsche was composing his *Zarathustra*: 'I myself have been perhaps his most generous benefactor. It is possible that in this case the image will outlive the man on which it is modeled: this has to do with the fact that there is still plenty of room in my image for a host of real Wagners: and above all for those much more richly gifted and more single-minded in purpose' (UF 7[16], spring–summer 1883).

This is just the beginning: we soon find in the context of assessing his four *Unfashionable Observations,* of which his essays on Schopenhauer and Wagner comprise half, Nietzsche making the following assertion in the very first section:

> In the *third* and *fourth* Untimely Ones, two images of the hardest self-love, self-discipline are put up against all this [that is, German 'culture'], as *pointers to a higher concept of culture, to restore the concept of culture* – untimely types *par excellence,* full of sovereign contempt for everything around them that was called 'Empire,' 'culture,' 'Christianity,' 'Bismarck,' 'success' – Schopenhauer and Wagner, *or,* in one word, Nietzsche. (EH 'The Untimely Ones' 1, our emphasis)

Here we find, as plainly as can be, Nietzsche confessing that he had distilled a psychological unity out of Schopenhauer and Wagner as types, and that as a consequence he had earned the right to inherit vis-à-vis his two great intellectual mentors the mantle of both philosopher and musician for the purposes of culture – that *he* had become the 'philosopher who speaks music'. In other words, what we find in this passage is precisely what Nietzsche had told his one serious intellectual promoter, Georg Brandes, in a letter earlier that same year.

> The two essays on Schopenhauer and Richard Wagner are, it seems to me now, confessions about myself – above all, they are avowals to myself, rather than, say, real psychological accounts of those two masters, to whom I felt as much kinship as I felt antagonism. (I was the first person to distill a sort of unity out of both of them...)[24]

Echoing these same thoughts, we find Nietzsche confessing again in section 3 that, when looking back on the two essays on Schopenhauer and Wagner, 'I do not wish to deny that at bottom

---

[24] SL (1969: 286 [KSB 8: 260]), letter to Georg Brandes, 19 February 1888.

they speak only of me. The essay *Wagner in Bayreuth* is a vision of my future, while in *Schopenhauer as Educator* my innermost history, my *becoming*, is inscribed. Above all, my promise!' (EH 'The Untimely Ones' 3). No longer do we find 'Schopenhauer as Educator', but 'Nietzsche as Educator', promising us a return to the Dionysian world-view – to the form of culture that says Yes out of suffering from the overabundance and fullness of life and to those who demand a tragic vision of life out of the pessimism of strength. Thus with 'Nietzsche as Educator' promising us the reappearance of a new tragic age, there is no question that he is also claiming to have surpassed his two great intellectual mentors in having brought it about by uniting what was best in them within himself. Psychologically in turn, there can be nowhere else for the historical actualities of Schopenhauer and Wagner to go except down, as decline, since Nietzsche must of necessity throw out the excess as psychological baggage.[25] The challenge to Wagner, and through him to Schopenhauer, has therefore been brought to a head over the right to inherit the mantle of the 'philosopher who speaks music' as a cultural form.

So as we have insisted from the very beginning, the 'music-making Socrates' and the 'philosopher who speaks music' signify not only the form of a culture that Nietzsche never really abandoned; we can now see that the form itself, in terms of its implications for the rebirth of tragedy, was at the centre of Nietzsche's 'post-Wagnerian' confrontation. It is the philosopher's duty to confront the problem of suffering (the *what*), and to do so, one must be able to 'make music' from the materials of life (the *how*). Philosophy and artistry, and by extension, rationality and creativity, must be united for the purposes of life. Thus Nietzsche's

---

[25] Conway (2012: 301) makes a very similar point in the context of Nietzsche's self-appointed task to 'overcome Wagner', but while Nietzsche's 'self-overcoming' is typically interpreted as a kind of 'recovery' from his 'pro-Wagnerian decadence', what we have shown is that 'Nietzsche's task' does not so much depend on 'recovering' from Wagner in the exclusive sense, but on superseding him. In this respect, Nietzsche's 'self-overcoming' becomes the integrating conception between 'overcoming Wagner' on the one hand and 'recovering' from him on the other, since it is primarily and fundamentally a challenge for psychological hegemony vis-à-vis his two great intellectual mentors. As we will see, this is what it means to become Wagner's (and Schopenhauer's) heir.

challenge to Wagner, especially as we find it in *Ecce Homo*, is a triumphal statement of psychological self-overcoming which recognises his claim to take over the mantle from both Schopenhauer and Wagner in resolving the problem of the *what* and the *how* for the rebirth of culture. With this move, we have finally resolved the structural foundation of Nietzsche's case against Wagner, from which the most intimate nature of the duel can finally be unravelled. These are the principal problems on which everything else rests, and it is to our formal analysis of the text, and consequently its resolution, that we now turn.

4
Music as the Late Fruit of Every Culture

The Case of Wagner

Our primary concern up to this point has been to demonstrate the nature and extent of Wagner's intellectual influence on Nietzsche, and in this respect, our fundamental objective has been to unfold the logic that exists behind Nietzsche's enigmatic *Case of Wagner*. The logic that we have unfolded so far, and that came to a climax towards the end of our last chapter, is as follows: in claiming to have distilled a 'psychological unity' out of Schopenhauer and Wagner, Nietzsche claimed, in effect, to have surpassed his two great intellectual mentors by uniting what was best in them within himself, and as a consequence, his challenge to Wagner, especially as we find it in *Ecce Homo*, is a triumphal statement of self-overcoming to the effect that he had earned the right to take over the mantle from Schopenhauer and Wagner as the philosopher and artist for the purpose of culture.

Yet in challenging Wagner to a duel over the meaning of the 'philosopher who speaks music', Nietzsche had effectively presented his readers with a dilemma for culture that entailed choosing between his 'psychological unity' on the one hand, or Schopenhauer and Wagner on the other. In other words, Nietzsche had left his readers with the choice of two alternatives for culture; and yet it was obvious, at least within the context of *Ecce Homo*, that these alternatives were mutually exclusive. With Nietzsche telling us that his *Zarathustra* was the deed that proved that he had assimilated his two great intellectual mentors into a living paradigm of philosophical and artistic unity, it was clear that his 'psychological unity' was the logical choice over Schopenhauer and Wagner, and in particular, the Wagnerian conception of culture. In the final analysis, only Nietzsche's *Zarathustra* could promise us a return to the Dionysian world-view; that is, the coming of a new tragic age, not Wagner's 'Artwork of the Future' (EH 'Why I Write Such Good Books' BT 4).

So with this rhetoric in mind, it became clear that we as Nietzsche's readers were confronted with two competing cultural forms that were mutually exclusive, since to choose one of the two alternatives for culture implies that the other is unacceptable and would have to be discarded. But at least within Nietzsche's frame of reference, we can only discard the alternative if we as readers have been convinced that it really *is* the sign of decline. This is precisely what Nietzsche is asking us to do: to discard Wagner, and through him Schopenhauer, as the signs of a declining culture. And what better way for Nietzsche to encourage his readers to discard Wagner than to tell them, by appealing to Wagner's own theories, that his art embodies the critical and essential features of a declining culture? In effect, what Nietzsche has done is turn Wagner's theoretical arguments against Wagner himself and his art in order to claim, exclusively for himself, the right to carry the mantle of the 'philosopher who speaks music' for culture, with its promise for the rebirth of a new tragic age.

Given the analysis we have presented so far, we are now in a position to demonstrate how Nietzsche's personal challenge to Wagner, and in particular his endeavour to overcome him in *The Case of Wagner*, is embedded within, and depends upon, the theoretical structure we have laid out. In this respect, the philosophical and structural invariants that originate with Wagner and Nietzsche's 'pro-Wagnerian' conception of culture, and are then used *against* Wagner during his 'post-Wagnerian' confrontation, are as follows:

1 Life, not intellect, is the ultimate ontological category. In this respect, vitalism as a world-view typifies the tragic age of the Greeks, and is what is responsible for the emergence of the tragic culture.

2. With the historical appearance of Socrates, the value of the intellect in its relationship to life is inverted: for the first time, the intellect is empowered to issue value judgements for and against life, and the prototype of a new instinct that runs counter to the one that had created tragedy emerges in which the cult of reason is enthroned over the instincts for life.
3. As life, and not intellect, is the ultimate ontological category, the strength, vitality and flourishing of a given culture is bound up with the emphasis that that culture places on the categories of life and instinct over the categories of mind and intellect. Accordingly the more a given culture emphasises the categories of the intellect over those of life, the more 'anaemic, enervated, and decadent' that culture becomes. Through this analysis, the figure of Socrates had come to symbolise the 'most magnificent expression' of a cultural form that believed rationality could be separated from its creative roots. What followed the event of Socrates was the rise of 'theoretical man' and the 'decline of culture at the hands of science'.
4. Modern culture is the direct result of this Socratic archetype which regards rationality divorced from life as the ultimate prototype of the modern human being. This explains, in brief, why there is no true modern art as culture.
5. Human beings are not simply rational beings, they are also vital beings, and therefore any attempt to bring about the rebirth of art as culture would need to account for both elements. Therefore to bring about this rebirth of culture, the solution must be, broadly speaking, the musical deed, for music is the only discipline that fuses rationality with vitality and so has the potential to effect a very real harmony of the entire human being. The implication, accordingly, is that the true physician of culture must be a 'philosopher who practices music'.

These structural invariants, as we now know, are intimately bound up with Wagner's original diagnosis of the problem of culture. But since we also know that Nietzsche's entire challenge to Wagner centres around the right to carry the mantle of the 'philosopher who practices music' for culture, it can only be meaningful if the challenge itself necessarily presupposes the validity of Wagner's overall argument about culture: on the one hand, Wagner's art would need to be defeated at the hands of his own theories, while at the same time, and on the other hand, Nietzsche could prove that he had won a victory for culture in accordance with them. This is, in point of fact, the only way Nietzsche can declare himself to be the legitimate successor of the tragic culture in perfect consistency with his pro-Wagner period. With these remarks, we can finally begin our formal analysis of *The Case of Wagner*.

The preface

Nietzsche opens his case against Wagner by framing it within what is perhaps the most important structural feature around which his arguments revolve; and in this respect, it is also the epistemological foundation from which Nietzsche's 'charges' are issued: the problem of 'ascending' and 'declining' cultures. In particular, Nietzsche must first show that Wagner and his art have succumbed to the very same features that Wagner himself had originally identified with a declining culture. And what was the single feature of the excesses of modernity which had prevented a new tragic culture from emerging? According to Wagner's own diagnosis, it was luxury (PW 1: 76–7, 'Artwork of the Future'). Yet if Wagner and his art have succumbed to the very same features that he had once identified as responsible for a declining culture, then it follows at once that he himself had succumbed to luxury; or, to use one of Nietzsche's favourite phrases, Wagner became a decadent.

At the same time, Nietzsche must show why the philosopher as the physician of culture is so necessary to his time, and therefore why he, and not Wagner, is in a unique position to recognise and thereby 'overcome' the problem of decadence. When we put these two features together, we have, in Nietzsche's own words, the following 'confession':

> What does a philosopher demand of himself first and last? To overcome his time in himself, to become 'timeless.' With what must he therefore engage in hardest combat? With whatever marks him as the child of his time. Well,

then! I am, no less than Wagner, a child of his time; that is, a decadent: but I comprehended this, I resisted it. The philosopher in me resisted. (CW Preface)

When we examine the nature of this confession, we are reminded why the philosopher as the physician of culture is so necessary to their time: only the physician of culture comprehends the direction of their time and is therefore able to pave the way for a new culture by reforming the cultural excesses that otherwise prevent a new culture from emerging. In this regard, Nietzsche is never more the physician of his culture, that is, the physician of decadence, than he is in framing *The Case of Wagner*. 'Nothing has preoccupied me more profoundly than the problem of decadence', Nietzsche tells us in the very next paragraph.

Once one has developed a keen eye for the symptoms of decline, one understands morality, too – one understands what is hiding under its most sacred names and value formulas: impoverished life, the will to the end, the great weariness. Morality negates life. (CW Preface)

Morality, after all, is a symptom of the pessimism of degenerating instincts as a result of which it became necessary for Nietzsche to 'take sides' against everything decadent in himself, including, above all, Wagner and Schopenhauer. From here it is a small step to suggest, as surely Nietzsche *is* suggesting, that it was his fate to overcome decadence and therefore Wagner. Because Nietzsche recognised his own decadence, which was at the same time the direction towards which all of modernity was tending, the claim he is specifically advocating here as the physician of his culture is that he alone was uniquely poised to overcome it, thereby paving the way for a new culture that would be, in a very real sense, post-Wagnerian.

In this connection, it is important to recognise that the substance of Nietzsche's 'confession' in this preface very aptly addresses what we have termed the *what* in Nietzsche's post-Wagnerian philosophy: because the problem of life, the value of existence, must be faced on its own terms, the courage to face it without appeal to dogmas, scientific or otherwise, requires the strength of genuine individuality. As we have already pointed out, the notion that one must be strong enough to face existence on its own terms can be traced at least as far back as Nietzsche's 'Schopenhauer as Educator' essay and the paradigm of the 'Schopenhauerian human being'. And indeed, it is a very suggestive fact that the language of Nietzsche's 'confession' here echoes a certain subjective fulfilment of the guidelines that he had first formulated for the philosopher in his relationship to culture in the earlier essay. As he then noted,

> If occupation with the histories of past or foreign peoples is of value, then it is of most value to the philosopher who seeks to pronounce a valid judgment on the entire fate of humanity . . . that is why the philosopher must evaluate his own age by contrasting it with others, and by overcoming the present for himself – even with regard to the picture he draws of life – overcome the present – that is, make it unnoticeable, paint over it, as it were. This is a difficult, indeed, scarcely achievable task. (SE 3)

When we examine this excerpt in the context of Nietzsche's assessment of the essay in *Ecce Homo*, we can see that the reality of this paradigm – being strong enough to face existence without appeal to religious or scientific dogmas, and consequently as a thoroughly vital deed – forms the very ground of his challenge to Wagner. At the same time, if the meaning of Nietzsche's duel with Wagner is rooted in the dispute over who has unified the philosophical and artistic drives for the purposes of culture, and by extension, who has the right to carry the mantle of the 'philosopher who speaks music' for culture, then being strong enough to face existence is incomplete without a final resolution about *how* this is made possible through art. In terms of Nietzsche's assertions in *Ecce Homo*, it only corresponds to one half of the 'psychological unity' with which he claims to have overcome and surpassed Wagner. Therefore what we expect in *The Case of Wagner* in particular is *a dispute over the nature of music itself,* with its peculiar ability to convey meaning or content in an immediate and irrefutable way, and how, in Nietzsche's estimation, Wagner used and abused that privilege.

What this means for our present purposes is that we are still left with the question of *how*. How is it that Nietzsche overcame his decadence, and therefore his Wagnerism, in order to pave the way for a new culture? Unfortunately, we do not find an explicit answer to this question in *The Case of Wagner* itself, but we do find one in the context of Nietzsche's discussion of decadence in *Ecce Homo*, and how he was uniquely destined to overcome it even from a physiological standpoint. Understanding how Nietzsche overcame his decadence, and therefore his Wagnerism, will allow us to examine and evaluate the epistemological pivot point from which Nietzsche's charges against Wagner are issued in the text.

According to the narrative of *Ecce Homo*, Nietzsche's genealogy was a union of both the instincts for life as well as those of sickness and decline. It was this unique constitution of both the 'ascending' and 'declining' types of life at once and in the same embodiment that had given Nietzsche, according to his own account, 'a subtler smell for the signs of ascent and decline than any other human being before me; I am the teacher *par excellence* for this – I know both, I am both' (EH 'Why I Am So Wise' 1). Continuing, he notes that

> Looking from the perspective of the sick toward *healthier* concepts and values and, conversely, looking again from the fullness and self-assurance of a *rich* life down into the secret work of the instinct for decadence – in this I have had the longest training, my truest experience; if in anything, I became master in *this*. Now I know how, have the know-how, to *reverse perspectives*: the first reason why a 'revaluation of values' is perhaps possible for me alone. (EH 'Why I Am So Wise' 1)

So despite his physiological disposition towards weakness and decline, Nietzsche had always 'instinctively chosen the *right* means against wretched states' (EH 'Why I Am So Wise' 2). Nietzsche had, in other words, instinctively inclined towards the *ascending* type of life, for only one who is healthy at bottom can make oneself healthy again. This is precisely what he tells us.

> As *summa summarum*, I was healthy; as an angle, as a speciality, I was a decadent ... I took myself in hand, I made myself healthy again: the condition for this – every physiologist would admit – is *that one be healthy at bottom*. A typically morbid being cannot become healthy, much less make itself healthy. (EH 'Why I Am So Wise' 2)

In other words, to accept decadence as an angle, as a speciality, one must be strong enough, for in that case, 'being sick can even become an energetic *stimulus* for life, for living *more*' (EH 'Why I Am So Wise' 2).[1] Here we find an explanation for why Nietzsche, in 'knowing both and in being both', could in the end overcome decline in order to transmute it into the ascending type of life. Truly what we find in *Ecce Homo* is Nietzsche telling us nothing less than that he is the very embodiment of the dividing and uniting point of decadence in history: as the actual embodiment of both the ascending and declining types of life, it was his destiny to overcome his 'timeliness', that is, his own decadence, in order to pave the way for a new culture, or what he calls here a 'revaluation of values'.

How, then, did Nietzsche turn from the declining towards the ascending type of life and overcome his decadence? Given the nature of his competition with Wagner, we should hardly be surprised to find *self-creation* at the base of how Nietzsche turned out well. For when it comes to 'making music' out of life, one must be strong enough to give style to one's character.

> That a well-turned-out person pleases our senses, that he is carved from wood that is hard, delicate, and at the same time smells good. He has a taste only for what is good for him; his pleasure, his delight cease where the measure of what is good for him is transgressed ... what does not kill

---

[1] Compare CW 5.

him makes him stronger . . . Instinctively, he collects from everything he sees, hears, lives through, *his* sum: he is a principle of selection, he discards much. He is always in his own company, whether he associates with books, human beings, or landscapes: he honors by *choosing*, by *admitting*, by *trusting* . . . He believes neither in 'misfortune' nor in 'guilt': he comes to terms with himself, with others; he knows how to *forget* – he is strong enough; hence everything *must* turn out for his best. (EH 'Why I Am So Wise' 2)

As Nietzsche acknowledges here, one can turn from the declining towards the ascending life only if the individual is strong enough to harness the materials of life for the purposes of self-creation. To have the strength to create oneself, to 'make music' out of life by facing existence on its own terms, is synonymous with the ascending life. So here we have in *Ecce Homo* Nietzsche's final resolution for how he overcame decadence through the art of self-creation and, in effect, how art makes it possible to face existence as a thoroughly vital deed.

Now it is worth pointing out that the methodology that Nietzsche offers us here once again has interesting and compelling parallels to a number of statements that we find in his earlier essay 'Richard Wagner in Bayreuth', where he tells us that the genius of Wagner's art resides in the fact that all the materials of his learning and cultivation – all philosophies, all histories, all religions – were ultimately subordinated to his 'creative power', for it is the subjective needs of the artist, as a creator of values, which dominate (WB 3).[2] Only in this respect, Nietzsche went on to note, does Wagner's art exemplify the energy and heroism of a true philosopher:

> it is precisely as a philosopher that he not only passed through the fire of many different philosophical systems without being afraid, but through the mist of knowledge and scholarship as well, and all the while he remained

---

[2] Compare PW 1: 73, 'Artwork of the Future'.

faithful to his higher self, which demanded of him *collective actions of his many voiced being*, and which commanded him to suffer and learn in order to accomplish those actions. (WB 3)

The parallels here, of course, should not be altogether surprising, for if it is true from the standpoint of *Ecce Homo* that both this essay and his essay on Schopenhauer 'speak only of me', and true again that the meaning of Nietzsche's duel with Wagner is rooted in the dispute over who has the right to become of the 'philosopher who practices music' for culture, then it is precisely this 'psychological unity' of the *what* and the *how* that becomes the very deed to overcome Wagner in *The Case of Wagner* in particular. And since only one who has recognised this declining life and overcome it is by definition rooted in the ascending type of life, it follows that Nietzsche creates his art out of the 'overfullness' of life and not its impoverishment, while conversely, Wagner's art is a late and perhaps the last fruit of a declining culture with its degenerating instincts for life (CW Preface).[3] When Nietzsche tells us that Wagner is the résumé of modernity which the philosopher and musician of today must confront for themselves (CW Preface), he is telling us, in not so many words, that the deed of his *Zarathustra* is the beginning of this 'post-Wagnerian' confrontation. With these battle lines drawn, we are unquestionably made to know who the better 'music-maker' for culture truly is. This is the epistemological foundation from which Nietzsche's charges against Wagner are issued, and which we are now ready to address in the following sections of the *Case of Wagner*.

The charges

Drafted in the form of an 'open letter' from Turin, there are twelve sections to *The Case of Wagner*, followed by two postscripts and an epilogue, all of which take up less than thirty pages. The text itself is both highly charged and extremely condensed, but by

---

[3] Compare NCW 'A Music Without a Future'.

analysing the following sections through the lens of Nietzsche's competition with Wagner, we will be able to flesh out, for the first time, the meaning of the charges he brings against Wagner. In sum, there are four principal charges, as well as a fifth and final charge which is, in some sense, the logical consequence of the previous four. The charges are as follows:

> Charge 1: Wagner's music dramas are decadent
> Charge 2: Wagner's music is flawed in various ways (that is, it is flawed rhythmically, melodically and formally)
> Charge 3: Wagner's music dramas are 'idealistic' in the pejorative sense
> Charge 4: Wagner is, above all, an 'actor' in composing them (again, in the pejorative sense)
> Charge 5: Wagner, of necessity, is 'anti-philosophical'

Sections 1–2

Nietzsche officially opens *The Case of Wagner* in a very curious way: he begins by confessing his infatuation with and zeal for Georges Bizet's opera *Carmen*, noting that he has already heard it performed twenty times. By appealing to *Carmen*, Nietzsche's ostensible intent here is to introduce a stylistic contrast between Bizet's passionate and romantic masterpiece and Wagner's turgid and ponderous music dramas. In fact all that follows in sections 1 and 2, which culminates with the proposition that 'music should be Mediterraneanized' at the beginning of section 3, is predicated on this stylistic contrast and the miserly categorical judgements of either/or that flow from it – a contrast that allows Nietzsche to draw up very neat binary statements about the style of both composers in order to push a logical evaluation that must be seen in absolute terms. The function of this stylistic contrast, at least superficially, is to establish the semantic framework for one of Nietzsche's favourite rhetorical analogies, which equates the modern, decadent and 'sick' music of Wagner with the geography of the 'north', and contrasts it with the light, passionate and 'healthy' music of the 'south'. The effect of this analogy, which becomes apparent at the beginning of section 2, is to depict the intersection of geography with culture as if it were the logical ground from which the dichotomy between Nietzsche and Wagner flows. Indeed the very fact that the text itself is written as an 'open letter' from the 'healthy south', from Turin, to those in Germany still languishing in the 'sickness' of Wagner's music is itself an ostentatious piece of literary staging. Fundamentally, however, it is important to recognise that the issue of whether music is 'healthy' or 'sick' is ultimately grounded in Nietzsche's valuation of music itself, namely that it is 'the *most vital* **art form**' (UF 7[7], spring–summer 1883). And given the emphasis we have placed on Nietzsche's competition with Wagner, we would expect that one of the most fundamental features of this stylistic contrast is to reinforce the nature of this discrepancy along categorical lines. This is exactly what we do find. In other words, the purpose of this stylistic contrast is to advance the proposition that 'better music' makes a 'better philosopher'. As music is the most vital of all the arts, Bizet's music makes Nietzsche 'fertile' for philosophy.

So how is this evaluated in section 1? Nietzsche begins by telling us that the tonality of Bizet's music is light and nimble. 'It approaches lightly, supply, politely. It is pleasant and does not *sweat*', from which follows Nietzsche's first principle of aesthetics: 'Whatever is good is light; whatever is divine moves on tender feet' (CW 1). Nietzsche goes on to tell us that Bizet's music is 'evil, subtly fatalistic' and yet at the same time it remains popular, because 'its subtlety belongs to a race, not to an individual'. Bizet's orchestration is rich and precise. 'It builds, organizes, finishes: thus it constitutes the opposite of the polyp in music, [Wagner's] "infinite melody"' (CW 1). Hence, Bizet's orchestration is *classical*. When taken together, Bizet's music (according to Nietzsche) achieves the most painful and tragic accents ever heard on stage 'without the *lie* of the great style' (CW 1).

All of this contrasts with Wagner, whose music is 'brutal, artificial, and "innocent"[4] at the same time' (CW 1). These orchestral

---

[4] The accusation of 'innocence' is an innuendo that specifically refers to the subject matter of *Parsifal*, Wagner's final music drama, which we will consider more fully in a subsequent section.

tendencies, which are at the same time the tendencies of the modern soul (according to Nietzsche), are what really makes Wagner's music 'timely' and consequently decadent. Here we have a music of tragic accents, but with grimaces, gesture, counterfeit. Consequently, Wagner's music is nothing but 'hot air' – the African *sirocco* – which makes Nietzsche break out into a disagreeable sweat when listening to it (CW 1).

As we can see, the nature of this contrast sets the stage for what follows, for Nietzsche then tells us that Bizet's music 'treats the listener as intelligent, as if himself a musician'; this is in all respects the opposite of Wagner, who in both his theoretical works and in the application of his 'infinite melody' – that is, as both a philosopher and a musician – drones on *ad infinitum*. 'Wagner treats us as if – he says something so often – till one despairs – till one believes it' (CW 1). Clearly there is something discordant, unmelodious and unmusical when one's philosophical and artistic drives are not in harmony.

But for one whose drives *are* in harmony, music and philosophy go hand-in-hand. 'Has it ever been noticed', Nietzsche continues, 'that one becomes more of a philosopher the more one becomes a musician? – The gray sky of abstraction rent as if by lightning . . . the great problems near enough to grasp; the world surveyed from a mountain – I have just defined the pathos of philosophy', and in one pregnant passage, the deeds of Zarathustra, whose inspirations culminate in unexpected answers to vital philosophical questions (CW 1).

Consequently we find at the beginning of section 2 that Bizet's work also 'redeems' and that 'Wagner is not the only "redeemer"'. The intersection of geography with culture, and the dichotomy between Nietzsche's art and that of Wagner, is for the first time verbalised as a means to continue advancing the proposition that 'better music' makes a 'better philosopher'. Once again we find Nietzsche appealing to Bizet's *Carmen* as the musical embodiment of *amor fati* and therefore the artistic depiction of the pessimism of strength:

> This music is cheerful, but not in a German or French way.
> Its cheerfulness is African; fate hangs over it; its happiness

is brief, sudden, without pardon. I envy Bizet for having had the courage for this sensibility which had hitherto no language in the cultivated music of Europe – for this more Southern, brown, burnt sensibility. (CW 2)

When we contrast this with the music of the 'north' – that is with Wagner's music – all we find is a counterfeit redemption. Love as compassion, depicted as virginal redemption, is just another iteration of the pessimism of degenerating instincts. The fatality of love, as depicted in the tragic climax to *Carmen*, is human passion, egoistic possession and, above all, the essence of what is vital. Nietzsche sums up this point when he tells us that such a conception of love 'is the only one worthy of a philosopher', in that it 'raises a work of art above thousands' (CW 2).

Section 3

The rhetorical analogy between geography and culture as if it were the logical ground from which the dichotomy between Nietzsche and Wagner should be judged as antipodes now resolves itself into the proposition that 'music should be Mediterraneanized' at the beginning of section 3, and with it, Nietzsche's stylistic contrast between Bizet and Wagner drops away. For lurking behind the mask of Bizet and the 'south' is the prophet of Zarathustra in the flesh, who now prepares us for the formal charges against Wagner.

Accordingly, it is here in section 3 that we find the first of four principal charges against Wagner, namely, that *Wagner's music dramas are decadent*. The charge itself is introduced through the cognate notion that decadence is the pathological magnification of one aspect of the whole at the expense of the whole.[5] Consequently 'the first thing that his art offers us is a magnifying glass' in which 'everything looks big, *even* Wagner' (CW 3). As Nietzsche goes on to state, Wagner's problem – the problem with which he was pathologically fascinated, and with which he

---

[5] The definition of decadence is formally given in section 7, but is clearly the basis of what follows here.

occupied both himself and his audience for the duration of his artistic career – was the problem of redemption. Indeed, the rich leitmotif of 'redemption' is a theme that prevails in every single one of Wagner's operas. But as Nietzsche declares, it is a counterfeit. 'What a clever rattlesnake! It has filled our whole life with its rattling about "devotion," about "loyalty," about "purity"; and with its praise of chastity it withdrew from the corrupted world. – And we believed it in all these things' (CW 3).

Using the neutral, sexless pronoun 'it' to androgynise Wagner as a snake, what follows next is a cursory survey of every single one of Wagner's canonical music dramas in which the theme of redemption is 'rattled off'. In this respect, the architecture of section 3 is designed in the main to pronounce the charge against Wagner which, as an organising idea, functions as a kind of axiom from which we must deduce the charge of decadence through Nietzsche's cursory survey of Wagner's music dramas.[6] Yet notwithstanding, Wagner's 'problem', Nietzsche admits, is seductive (CW 3).

In the midst of adducing the 'proof' of Wagner's decadence, Nietzsche pauses for a particularly mean-spirited refrain against Cosima Wagner, which, in context, is meant to flesh out the nature of Wagner's decadence. He does this by taking up the theme of the Wandering Jew from *The Flying Dutchman* who, in the character of the Dutchman himself, has been condemned to wander the seas eternally unless he can be redeemed from his fate through the love of a faithful woman. Nietzsche points out, and not very subtly either, that Wagner himself had been the prototypical Wandering Jew his entire life – restless, unstable and condemned to be misunderstood by his contemporaries. It was only through the love of a faithful woman, Cosima, who had taken upon herself to be that 'willing animal sacrifice' for Wagner's legendary ego, and who became in effect the 'willing conducting rod

---

[6] Officially, Wagner's canon begins with *The Flying Dutchman*, which is the earliest opera in point of time that Nietzsche maligns here in the text. But Nietzsche's acquaintance with Wagner's early canon is sporadic at best. Aside from the *Ring* cycle itself, Nietzsche was only perhaps really acquainted with *Tristan und Isolde* and *Die Meistersinger*, the music dramas that were most proximate to his relationship with Wagner, and the ones to which he remained the most sentimentally attached.

for lightning, storms, and rain near him', that he was redeemed (HAH1 430).

> Translated in reality: the danger of artists, for geniuses – and who else is the 'Wandering Jew'? – is woman: adoring women confront them with corruption. Hardly any of them have character enough not to be corrupted – or 'redeemed' – when they find themselves treated like gods: soon they condescend to the level of the women. – Man is a coward, confronted by the Eternal Feminine – and the females know it. (CW 3)

Thus, in being 'redeemed' Wagner ceased to be 'eternal', but for that very reason, so too did his art, for it too suffers from timeliness, corruption and decadence. Yet not only was Wagner corrupted, he became 'feminine' to boot. It was no secret, after all, that Wagner enjoyed wearing decidedly feminine attire about the house, including silk underwear, in order to minimise his discomfort. But it was probably just as well that Nietzsche neglected to mention, as the expense of acquiring this secret, just how frequently his services as Wagner's personal valet had been commissioned. Indeed, when he had last been approached with the humiliating request to send Wagner some silk underwear from the Basel firm of C. C. Rumpf shortly after the first *Ring* festival ended, Nietzsche had confessed his 'pleasure' at being able to do this 'small service', as it brought back fond memories 'of the times in Tribschen'.[7] Nevertheless, as Nietzsche endeavours to warn us here, the dangers arising from the cult of the genius have their origins in the vanity of the artist, and that vanity is magnified by the corruption of women who treat them as gods (see HAH1 162). Consequently the 'love' that Wagner lauds to the skies in his music dramas is really just a sublimated form of parasitism on the part of the female – namely Cosima – who seeks to find fame through her husband (see HAH1 399). Meanwhile of course, only truly 'free spirits' (such as Nietzsche–Zarathustra himself)

---

[7] SL (1969: 147 [KSB 5: 190]), letter to Richard Wagner, 27 September 1876.

have nothing to do with women, for they, 'like the prophetic birds of antiquity, as the true-thinking and truth-speaking men of the present, must prefer *to fly alone*' (HAH1 426). This was a low blow all the way around.

Nietzsche continues his analysis of Wagner's decadence with a somewhat tangential discussion of the trends in wider German culture, but the point is made very clear that Germans interpret what is genuinely an advance in art as culture as a symptom of decline. In this connection, one is reminded of Schopenhauer's criticisms of Kant's susceptibility to art, and how Kant, who is the representative of all that is 'north' and 'German' when it comes to art, would spawn a culture that saw it fit to wave the Mosaic Decalogue of German theology in the face of Goethe's immortal masterpieces.

> One knows Goethe's fate in moraline-sour, old-maidish Germany. He always seemed offensive to Germans; he had honest admirers only among Jewesses . . . Klopstock already felt called upon to deliver a moral sermon to him . . . Even *Wilhelm Meister* was considered merely a symptom of decline, 'going to the dogs' as far as morals go . . . all the petty courts, every kind of 'Wartburg' in Germany crossed themselves against Goethe, against the 'unclean spirit' of Goethe. (CW 3)[8]

'This is the story that Wagner put into music', Nietzsche goes on to note. Just like Goethe, Wagner had once been the original immoralist, but that was when he was a 'free spirit', when he himself had yet to be 'redeemed' by Cosima. Only then was he finally

---

[8] Kaufmann's translation footnotes the word 'Wartburg' as if Nietzsche is referring to the story of the ink spot that originated on the wall in Wartburg after Luther had allegedly thrown an inkwell at the devil who appeared to him; however, the context makes it clear that Nietzsche is actually referring to the song contest that takes place in the Minnesingers' Hall of Wartburg Castle during Act 2 of *Tannhäuser*, and of the character of Tannhäuser himself, that 'interesting sinner' who sings of profane love and is disgraced for it, only to be redeemed by the innocent virgin Elizabeth, who pleads at the throne of Heaven for his redemption in Act 3.

able to make Goethe palatable to the Germans. 'He *redeems* Goethe, that goes without saying; but in such a way that at the same time he himself sides shrewdly with the higher virgin' (CW 3).

So what happened after Wagner himself was 'redeemed'? Schopenhauer's effect on Germany – and *not* the effect that Nietzsche wanted – had transformed the art of Goethe into the handmaiden of Schopenhauer's ethical teaching, a subject matter to which Cosima was surely attuned.[9] The consequence: Wagner became corrupted when, following Cosima's entreaties and supplications, he tried to depict this as music drama. The proof: 'the moral and religious absurdities' of *Parsifal* (CW 3).

With these remarks, the diatribe against Cosima, and her corruption of Wagner (and by extension, Schopenhauer), more or less comes to a close, but what is once again worth pointing out here is that Nietzsche is accusing Wagner of accelerating the downfall of a culture that was already in decline in precisely the same way that (according to Nietzsche) the historical Socrates had done by capitalising on the conditions of his own milieu. Thus Wagner is, as we have pointed out, merely another disciple of the father of modernity, Socrates, that first pessimist of degenerating instincts, and as such, his entire approach to art as culture must be diagnosed as the sign of decline. We will see this very accusation come to the fore in section 5.

Sections 4–5

It is here at the beginning of section 4 that Nietzsche recounts the story of Wagner's *Ring* cycle from the standpoint of its philosophical genesis, and in so doing, continues to press the charge that *Wagner's music dramas are decadent*. From the standpoint of *The Ring*'s overall narrative, Nietzsche's intent here is to argue that there are two seemingly opposed and contradictory philosophies behind it – one that has its origin in Wagner's pre-Schopenhauerian days as a 'revolutionary free spirit' and

---

[9] For an especially illuminating note about how the 'Voltairean minded Schopenhauer' was 'shoved aside' at the hands of German theology, see UF 30[9], summer 1878.

'immoralist' and is derived from the philosophy of Feuerbach, and the other that has its origins in his post-Schopenhauerian conversion and is derived from the philosophy of Schopenhauer. And since it was fairly well known that Wagner had redirected his creative energies away from *Siegfried* in favour of conceiving *Tristan und Isolde* following his initial intoxication with and conversion to Schopenhauer in 1854, and only resumed work on the third act in 1869,[10] we might say that Siegfried, the hero of *The Ring*, becomes the hermeneutic focal point for Wagner's transformation from an 'immoralist' to a 'decadent' between Acts 2 and 3 of *Siegfried*, including the eponymous hero's downfall and 'redemption' through a woman, Brünnhilde, in the so-called 'Schopenhauerian ending' of *The Twilight of the Gods*. In any case, this is the picture Nietzsche wishes to paint for his readers in this section.

According to the philosophy of the 'revolutionary' Wagner (so Nietzsche tells us), all the ills of the world had come from 'customs, laws, moralities, institutions, from everything on which the old world, the old society rests' (CW 4). It was only natural therefore that the solution to those ills, in the eyes of his 'revolutionary' character Siegfried, was to abrogate the old order by declaring war on it. '*That is what Siegfried does*', Nietzsche tells us, for here we find, in Wagner's pre-Schopenhauerian conception of his hero, the original 'immoralist'. Indeed his very genesis, Nietzsche points out, was through adultery and incest, and it was Wagner, moreover, who had invented this radical contribution to the saga (CW 4). Hence,

> Siegfried continues as he has begun: he merely follows his first impulse, he overthrows everything traditional, all reverence, all *fear*. Whatever displeases him he stabs to death. Without the least respect he tackles old deities. But his main enterprise aims *to emancipate woman* – 'to redeem Brunhilde.' Siegfried and Brunhilde; the sacrament of free

---

[10] According to Cosima's diaries, Wagner completed the final full score for *Siegfried* on 5 February 1871. See CWD 1: 332.

love; the rise of the golden age; the twilight of the gods for the old morality – *all ill has been abolished*. (CW 4)

In fact, according to the original ending of *The Ring*, Brünnhilde was supposed to have sung a paean to love which followed the downfall of the old gods and their replacement with a new, human form of society that had 'returned to nature'. But all of this changed, according to Nietzsche, once Wagner became acquainted with Schopenhauer's ethical teaching and became, in Nietzsche's estimation, a decadent. Suddenly the original ending to *The Ring* was deemed far too naïve and optimistic, which meant that Wagner's characters would need to convert from free-spirited immorality into proselytes of the Wisdom religion following the cosmically attuned sage of Frankfurt. No longer would Wagner tolerate paeans glorifying the free-spirited and the emotionally indulgent panacea of love, but with a little exertion on our part, we could elevate our gaze to the grand drama of the periodic creation, preservation and absorption of the world throughout its countless kalpas, and then recognise that our own being, as the microcosm of this cycle, was tied to the endless wheel of becoming that had sprung from *tanhâ* or the thirst for sentient existence, from which our very salvation lay, as in the case of Brünnhilde herself, in studying the ascetic ideal of Schopenhauer's philosophy, or in the case of Siegfried, transforming into the 'pure fool' that would eventually become Parsifal. As far as a piece of rhetoric is concerned, this is the narrative that Nietzsche crafts for his readers here.[11]

---

[11] There is considerable willingness in the literature to take Nietzsche's explanation of *The Ring* at face value. Young (2010: 495–6), for instance, takes Nietzsche's characterisation of Wagner's shift from 'optimism' to 'pessimism' in section 4 to be a 'completely correct account' of Schopenhauer's influence on *The Ring*. But the issue here is far subtler than that. The relationship between one's artistic intuitions and the conceptual determinants that the artist uses to fix those intuitions raises an epistemological problem that deserves far more attention than it has at present received. Without broaching that problem *per se*, it is worth pointing out that Wagner himself touches on these very points when discussing the so-called 'Feuerbach ending' of *The Ring* in one of his letters to August Röckel. In particular, Wagner credits Schopenhauer's epistemological critique of the relationship between perception and conception which finally gave him the key to understanding why his prior conceptual constructs had failed to harmonise with his

There is, however, a more substantive criticism lurking behind the charge that *Wagner's music dramas are decadent*, and it is a criticism that should be understood with reference to our chief claim that Nietzsche's competition with Wagner is predicated on proving his psychological hegemony over his two great intellectual mentors.

Coinciding with his 'conversion' to Schopenhauer was, of course, Wagner's recognition of the extraordinary valuation that Schopenhauer had placed on music itself as the art form *par excellence*. For music did not, like the rest of the arts, merely depict the phenomenal world; rather, by speaking directly to the will itself as the ground of all phenomenality, music was able to represent the totality of the phenomenal world itself in its least derivative formulation. Of course, with this extraordinary rise in the value of music, Wagner became exalted, even by his standards, and at that point 'the musician himself all at once rose in price to an unheard

---

underlying artistic intuitions. In pertinent part, Wagner tells Röckel that 'While, as an artist, my intuitions were of such compelling certainty that all I created was influenced by them, as a philosopher, I was attempting to find a totally contrasting explanation of the world which, though forcibly upheld, was repeatedly – and much to my own amazement – undermined by my instinctive and purely objective artistic intuitions. My most striking experience in this respect came, finally, through my Nibelung poem; it had taken shape at a time when, relying upon my conceptions, I had constructed a Hellenistically optimistic world for myself which . . . in working out this plan, nay, basically in its very design, I was unconsciously following quite a different, and much more profound, intuition, and that, instead of a single phase in the world's evolution, what I had glimpsed was the essence of the world itself in all its conceivable phases, and that I had thereby recognized its nothingness, with the result, of course – since I remained faithful to my intuitions rather than to my conceptions –, what emerged was something totally different from what I had originally intended. But I also recall once having sought forcibly to assert my meaning – the only time I ever did so – in the tendentious closing words which Brünhilde addresses to those around her, a speech in which she turns their attention away from the reprehensibility of ownership to the love which alone brings happiness; and yet I had (unfortunately!) never really sorted out in my own mind what I meant by this "love" which, in the course of the myth, we saw appearing as something utterly and completely devastating. What blinded me in the case of this one particular passage was the interference of my conceptual meaning. Strange to relate, this passage continued to torment me, and it required a complete revolution in my rational outlook, such as was finally brought about by Schopenhauer, to reveal to me the cause of my difficulty and provide me with a truly fitting key-stone for my poem, which consists in an honest recognition of the true and profound nature of things, without the need to be in any way tendentious' (SLRW: 357–8, letter to August Röckel, 23 August 1856).

of degree: he now became an oracle, a priest, indeed more than a priest, a kind of mouthpiece of the "in itself" of things, a telephone of the beyond' (GM III 5). From that point forward, Wagner had found confidence to speak about ascetic ideals themselves as if he himself understood and embodied them.[12]

It was just this turn of events in Wagner's conversion that exasperated Nietzsche most, for the genuineness of an artist, Nietzsche thought, lay in his ability to deify the 'real world' by falsifying it. This is precisely what gives the artist, according to Nietzsche, a 'good conscience' (GM III 25). Nevertheless – and this was the pointed critique that Nietzsche made about Wagner's art in the *Genealogy* – there is a tendency for an artist like Wagner to actually get caught up in the fantasy world of his own creation, and all too easily fall into the error of believing that he himself is or can become 'what he is able to depict, think up, express'. But the reality, according to Nietzsche, is that '*if* [the artist] were precisely that, he would certainly not depict, think up, express it; a Homer would not have written an Achilles nor Goethe a Faust if Homer had been an Achilles of if Goethe had been a Faust' (GM III 4). As Nietzsche goes on to tells us, 'a perfect and whole artist is separated to all eternity from the "real," the actual'; and yet the fact that 'he makes an attempt to encroach for once upon what is most forbidden precisely to him' means, in point of fact, that what the artist qua artist is doing is abdicating or surrendering his artistry (Ridley 2002: 130; see also Ridley 1998: 79–82). This is what Nietzsche calls the 'typical velleity of the artist' (GM III 4).

Since the true artist, according to Nietzsche, is separated from the real 'to all eternity', the artist-as-velleist, rather than a beautifier of the world, becomes an actor in a fantasy of the real world. Like Socrates, he becomes 'the buffoon who *got himself taken seriously*' (TI 'The Problem of Socrates' 4). But what is perhaps the most interesting feature of the artist-as-velleist is that through

---

[12] No doubt what irked Nietzsche most was that Wagnerians had continued to pontificate on the marvels of Wagner's recent essay 'Religion and Art' (1880), all while making the consubstantiality of Wagner's person explicit. On at least one occasion, the Wagnerians proclaimed Wagner himself to be Christ – a comparison that Wagner, of course, merrily accepted (CWD 2: 571, 9 December 1880).

his velleity, he becomes the perfect expression of the 'bad conscience', of one who creates his art, not out of joy and the overfullness of life, but out of *ressentiment*.¹³

In other words, what Nietzsche is claiming here is that when it comes to the velleity of Wagner's art, the lines between what is 'real' and what merely 'beautifies the real' become increasingly confused and unclear; but it is also what makes Wagner's art all-the-more seductive – so much so that Wagner himself believed in his own worlds. At the same time, if he were really what he believed himself to be, he would have no need to depict it and then act as if the fantasy world he had created were the end-in-itself – in this case, being that 'telephone of the beyond'. So it is precisely this idle indeterminacy of the will to create and then act on one's creations that makes the artist-as-velleist a resentful dreamer who, as far as Nietzsche is concerned, is certainly no philosopher, and is definitely no metaphysician. Accordingly, when it comes to Wagner's espousal of the ascetic ideal in his music dramas (and most especially in *Parsifal*), it is nothing more than an empty-headed watchword, for the ascetic ideal means 'absolutely nothing' to Wagner (GM III 5).

It must be said, then, that Nietzsche's vindictiveness on this point is especially destructive. For what Nietzsche now argues in effect is that Wagner's new meal ticket, as it were, *is* the ascetic ideal; but it is not a meal ticket that Wagner had arrived at by his own reasoning, for artists who have been 'the all-too-pliant courtiers of their disciples and patrons, and flatterers with a good nose' for the trends and fashions of the day, are for that reason far too fragile to stand alone. They need, as Nietzsche tells us, 'a protective armor, a backing, a previously established authority' in order to disseminate their views (GM III 5). And since artists can only depict what they are not, they must rely on their 'protective armor' in order to depict it. So in precisely the same way that Wagner had once indulged in Feuerbach and the revolution to reinforce his artistic principles, and above all his 'revolutionary' character of Siegfried, he had now found his new meal ticket as the

---

¹³ See Ridley (2002) for an excellent discussion of these points.

high priest and hierophant of Schopenhauer and the ascetic ideal with his 'degenerate' character of Parsifal. 'Who could consider it even thinkable that [Wagner] would have had the courage for an ascetic ideal without the backing that Schopenhauer's philosophy offered him, without Schopenhauer's authority, which was gaining predominance in Europe in the seventies?' (GM III 5).

The answer, to put it bluntly, is that it never would have happened. Remember, only in declining cultures is it necessary for theoretical underpinnings to justify creative expressions in order to gain a widespread acceptance for them, and in this sense perhaps nothing is more seductive for 'the people' than the 'moralization of decadence' (Conway 1997: 105–9). So once again Wagner, just like Socrates, is 'the buffoon who *got himself taken seriously*' (TI 'The Problem of Socrates' 4). The conclusion that we should draw is that Wagner's final tone poem, *Parsifal*, should be regarded as a secret, malicious and derisive act which panders to the current degenerative tendencies of modernity with its weak, enfeebled and dissipated drives, mocking a society currently fascinated with material asceticism in secret cahoots with anthropomorphic theology. But perhaps what is most interesting of all is that now Wagner is accused of 'ruthlessly chang[ing]' his views once he 'converted to Schopenhauer', a phenomenon that led to 'a complete theoretical contradiction . . . between his earlier and later aesthetic beliefs' (GM III 5).[14] The trope here is obvious: whatever 'conversion' experience Wagner had as a result of Schopenhauer's treatment of 'genuine Christianity', his celebration of it in his final work is a pious fraud.[15]

It is no secret then that 'the *philosopher of decadence* gave to the artist of decadence – *himself*', as these are the very elements of a declining culture that Nietzsche has set himself to overcome. And so it is here in section 5 that Nietzsche once again reframes the text as the need to overcome the decadence of modernity, with Wagner in particular as the prototypical case. He does so, as he

---

[14] Compare PW 6: 74–5 where Wagner had accused Nietzsche of doing the exact same thing.
[15] On these points, see NCW 'Wagner as Apostle of Chastity' 1–3.

had done in the preface, by reminding us of the epistemic gap that exists between himself and all of modernity in understanding the effect of Wagner's music. Wagner's art 'has made music sick' Nietzsche tells us at the beginning of section 5. Just as unity is to multiplicity, so too is the archetype to its copies, the genus to its species: Wagner 'sums up modernity', and so is by definition its most illustrious representative. Once Wagner realised his affinity for all that was most timely, he simply accelerated its tempo. Wagner is, according to Nietzsche, 'A typical decadent who has a sense of necessity in his corrupted taste, who claims it as a higher taste, who knows how to get his corruption accepted as law, as progress, as fulfillment' (CW 5).

Wagner, as the most characteristic representative of decadence, merely hastened the downfall of a culture that was already going 'speedily downhill' (NCW 'A Music Without a Future'). This also explains, incidentally, why all of Europe failed to recognise Wagner as a decadent, for they were akin to him, but were simply poorer, pallid, more feeble imitations. Here we have a very good reason why Wagner 'is not resisted', and why the 'misunderstandings about him parade as "gospel"', to which Nietzsche adds spitefully, 'he hasn't by any means converted only the *poor in spirit*' (CW 5).[16]

Laying aside the rhetorical fireworks in this section, which in many ways obscure the principal point, when we examine Nietzsche's criticisms of Wagner as the prototype of decadence who, in his propinquity to 'the whole of European decadence', merely accelerated its sickness, one cannot help but be reminded

---

[16] Once again, Nietzsche's claim that he has been liberated from *ressentiment*, and with which he parades around with such carefree insouciance throughout his published works, runs in stark contrast with what he actually says in his notebooks and letters. In a letter to Malwida von Meyesenbug, shortly before he published *The Case of Wagner* in the autumn of 1888, Nietzsche admits that 'there is indeed a great *emptiness* around me. Literally, there is no one who could understand my situation. The worst thing is, without a doubt, not to have heard for ten years a single word that actually *got through* to me – *and* to be understanding about this, to understand it as something necessary! I have given humanity its profoundest book [*Zarathustra*]. How must one atone for that! . . . One could die of being "immortal"! . . . The old seducer Wagner, even after his death, is taking from me the few remaining people on whom I could have some influence' SL (1969: 302 [KSB 8: 377–8]), letter to Malwida von Meysenbug, end of July 1888).

once again of the 'decadent' Socrates who, even though he was able to capitalise on the conditions of his milieu, failed as a physician of *culture*, because he had succumbed to the pessimism of degenerating instincts, allowing reason and morality to dictate the organic logic of will and life (TI 'The Problem of Socrates' 9). And yet to have truly paved the way for a new culture that would have been, in a very real sense, 'post-Socratic', Wagner would have had to become strong enough to confront and overcome the timeliness of his existence. Unfortunately, and like Socrates himself, Wagner succumbed to the pessimism of degenerating instincts, leaving us in his wake with Wagnerians, Germans, the Reich – all negative and pejorative symptoms of a declining culture.

To pave the way for a new tragic age and a culture that is necessarily post-Wagnerian, one must be able to do what Wagner himself could *not* do, according to Nietzsche: one must be strong enough to confront the timeliness of one's existence through the purely self-creative act. Once again Nietzsche reminds us of the epistemic gap that he believes exists between himself and all of modernity in understanding the effect of Wagner's music. To overcome sickness, one cannot *be* sick. At bottom one's instincts must be 'healthy' (EH 'Why I Am So Wise' 2) and because Nietzsche had always (according to him) 'instinctively chosen the right means against wretched states' (EH 'Why I Am So Wise' 2), he could accept decadence as a speciality. In all other respects, he had instinctively inclined towards the *ascending* type of life, and this made him 'strong enough' to confront decadence and to overcome it. It is this stipulation that Nietzsche believes distinguishes him from 'the whole of European decadence', including Wagner, and it is this sentiment that lies at the foundation of his statement that 'Sickness itself can be a stimulant to life: only one has to be healthy enough for this stimulant' (CW 5).

Since it is a *given* for us to accept that only one who has recognised and confronted this declining life can overcome it, this leaves only Nietzsche–Zarathustra as the logical choice to usher in a new tragic age. From the standpoint of the second half of section 5, Nietzsche simply resumes his variations on a theme regarding Wagner as the résumé of modernity. There are, however, two important observations that Nietzsche makes here, but as they are psychological corollaries of what Nietzsche claims are the adverse physiological reactions to Wagner's music rooted in the very nature of his rhythms and tempi, we will explore what these observations mean more fully in the context of examining the charge that *Wagner's music is rhythmically, harmonically and formally flawed* in section 6. Nietzsche's two observations are the following:

1 As psychological types, Wagner's characters are all neurotics. Dramatically, they embody 'the convulsive nature of his affects'.
2 All the 'tones' of the modern world are found in Wagner's art: brutal, artificial and innocent. These are the tones of the exhausted (CW 5).

Section 6

With sections 6 and 7, we have arrived at the core of Nietzsche's polemic against Wagner. These two sections, when taken together, articulate every single one of the formal charges Nietzsche makes against Wagner, so it is important to examine how these two sections relate to all that follows. For instance, the principal charge of section 7 is that *Wagner is an actor above all in composing his music dramas*; yet this charge, which forms everything that follows from section 8 onwards, is built up from the three principal charges we encounter here in section 6.

Of course, the temptation is to read section 6 as if it were purely a burlesque – and to a certain extent it is.[17] But because the satirical nature of this section actually belies three very serious and consequential charges, we will need to look past the burlesque in order to examine its contents in some detail. In certain

---

[17] When one of the first reviewers of the text, Ferdinand Avenarius, criticised Nietzsche's style in *The Case of Wagner* as that of a *'feuilletonist* with a head full of ideas but still only that of a writer of popular literary articles without much serious intent', Nietzsche replied that 'when I have, literally, to carry the destiny of man, it is part of my trial of strength to be able to be a clown, satyr, or, if you prefer it, *feuilletonist* to the extent that I have been in *The Case of Wagner*. That the profoundest mind must also be the most frivolous one is almost a formula for my philosophy.' See SL (1969: 323 [KSB 8: 468–70]), critical note to letter to Franz Overbeck, 13 November 1888.

essential respects, two of the charges build upon the psychological observations Nietzsche had made about Wagner's music dramas in section 5, but in this section he endeavours to get at the charges through another tactic: by staging a theatrical piece of parody and sarcasm on the effect of Wagner's art.[18]

The first charge featured here is that *Wagner's art is nothing but theatricality and effects*. This is really more of a proto-charge, because it ultimately becomes the basis for the principal charge in section 7 that *Wagner was an actor above all in composing his music dramas*. But to understand the latter charge, we need to recognise how it is connected to the former.

The second charge featured here is that *Wagner's music is rhythmically, harmonically and formally flawed*. This charge is part and parcel of what Nietzsche judges to be the adverse physiological responses to listening to Wagner's music. At the same time, however, the psychological corollary to this charge is that this kind of formal flaw in the music is part and parcel with the degenerate psychology of modernity. The 'brutal, artificial, and innocent tones' of Wagner's art are the tones of the exhausted world which finds, on the one hand, its most ardent champion and defender of decadence in the person of Wagner, and, on the other, a public in perfect step with the degenerating instincts of his art.

So what is the significance of the charge that *Wagner's art is nothing but theatricality and effects*? Actually this charge is not as straightforward as it might at first seem, and the theatre piece that Nietzsche

---

[18] Indeed Conway (1997: 120–9) convincingly argues that the satyr play as a form emerges in Nietzsche's post-Zarathustran writings as a compelling figure for his criticisms of late modernity more broadly, and to that extent, the figure itself serves as a kind of ill-positioned *entr'acte* between late modernity and its successor epochs, and in particular, the political and artistic impotence of the forms that belong to the late period of declining cultures that Nietzsche purports to chronicle. At the same time, and because Nietzsche himself is an involuntary participant in the 'epilogue farce' that is late modernity, the figure of the satyr play, Conway argues, opens up an 'infra-tragic context' for heroism and with it the possibility of renewing the tragic cycle. There is no doubt that Nietzsche promises us the latter, and given the fact that he frames the 'open letter' of *The Case of Wagner* with the aphorism *ridendo dicere severum* ('through what is laughable, say what is sombre'), one might argue that Nietzsche is very much inhabiting the satyr play that comes after the Wagnerian tragedy in order to open up that 'infra-tragic context' for heroism, and with it, the possibility of renewing a new tragic cycle with his *Zarathustra*.

stages here at Wagner's expense does not make it any easier to parse. Fortunately, of the two charges, this is given more precedence in Nietzsche's philosophical development, while the second charge, especially in its more radical form, only appears comparatively late in his writings. There is no question, however, that Nietzsche fixated on the problem of Wagner's rhythms early in his philosophical development – his early notebooks and his draft notes for what eventually became his essay 'Richard Wagner in Bayreuth' testify to this fixation – but the charge of exaggerated and extravagant rhythms and their connection with physiological degeneration is one that more properly belongs to the final years of Nietzsche's productive life and *pari passu* his own deteriorating health. Even so, priority in time does not by itself help us to parse the charge of theatricality and effects, because the charge itself, or what we have called the proto-charge to the indictment that Wagner was an actor above all, is deeply interwoven with a number of key principles related to Nietzsche's own philosophical development. In this regard, there is perhaps no better early record of the origin of these two charges and their connection with Nietzsche's intense and lifelong preoccupation with the creative power of the artist than that found in 'Richard Wagner in Bayreuth'. As our analysis thus far has shown that Nietzsche's competition with Wagner is at the basis of our present text, this examination will no doubt help us evaluate how the specific charges we are considering in the present section play out, for here we get, in every sense of the word, an essay that struggles to come to terms with Wagner.

To begin, there are a number of passages in Nietzsche's early essay that meditate on the truly astonishing nature of Wagner's artistic drive, and in particular how all knowledge, all erudition and scholarship, indeed all culture, possessed for Wagner no more than an instrumental value for life and living, for which his task was to synthesise and subordinate it to his 'creative power'. Wagner's talent for learning, Nietzsche tells us, 'is wholly extraordinary even among Germans, the true nation of learners', and yet this was not achieved without some measure of danger.

> From all sides it grows on and in him, and the larger and heavier the edifice becomes, the greater becomes

the tension on the arch of his ordering and dominating thought . . . Wagner, the renewer of the simple drama, the discoverer of the place of the arts in a true human society, the poetic elucidator of past views of life, the philosopher, the historian, the aesthetician and critic; Wagner, the master of language, the mythologist and mythic poet who was the first to draw a ring around this marvellous, ancient, enormous structure and carve into it the runes of his mind — what an abundance of knowledge he had to gather together and encompass in order to be able to become all this! And yet the weight of all this did not crush his will to act, nor did the attractions of its individual aspects lead him astray . . . we others want to become all the more courageous by being able to see with our own eyes a hero who, even in regard to modern cultivation, 'has not learned to be afraid.' (WB 3)

Nietzsche's reference in the final clause to the one who has not 'learned to be afraid' is an allusion to Wagner's character Siegfried, which highlights once again the bold, intrepid and at times insolent daring that constitutes the principal characteristic of the hero's 'immoralism' that Nietzsche so admired.[19] So here we can see that what Nietzsche marvelled at and admired in Wagner were precisely those characteristics of a bold and intrepid nature in everything related to the creation and propagation of his art. At the same time, the effect of synthesising and subordinating everything to his 'creative power' means that Wagner's psychology as an artist is to simplify and unite. Wagner possesses 'an astringent power', Nietzsche goes on to note, 'and it is to this extent that he belongs to the great forces of culture'.

He has mastered the arts, the religions, and the histories of various nations, and yet he is the opposite of a polyhistorian, of a spirit that merely pulls things together and

---

[19] It should be noted, however, that these are the very same characteristics that lead, paradoxically enough, to Siegfried's own downfall.

organizes them, for he helps shape and breathe life into those things that he pulls together; he is a *simplifier of the world*. (WB 4)

Finally, and in a very beautiful passage that expresses the totalising nature of Wagner's art from the depths of his creative power, Nietzsche observes that

> in Wagner, everything visible in the world wants to deepen itself and intensify its inwardness by becoming audible, and it searches for its lost soul. At the same time, in Wagner everything audible wants to emerge and rise up into light as phenomenon for the eye, it wants, as it were, to assume bodily form. His art always leads him in two directions, out of the world as auditory drama into an enigmatically related world as visual drama and vice versa: he is constantly forced – and the viewer with him – to retranslate visible motion into soul and primal life and, on the other hand, to see the hidden fabric of the inner world as a visual phenomenon and to give it semblance of a body. All this is the essence of the *dithyrambic dramatist*, this term understood so broadly that it includes at once the actor, the poet, and the composer – and this term must necessarily be drawn from the single perfect manifestation of the dithyrambic dramatist prior to Wagner, from Aeschylus and his fellow Greek artists. (WB 7)

In these three excerpts, we have captured in a very succinct way all that Nietzsche revered about Wagner's creative power, and how he was able to transform it into a world of art in the most totalising way. In fact we know that the entire picture of what Nietzsche describes here as the culmination of Wagner's art is, from the standpoint of *Ecce Homo*, really just 'a picture of the pre-existent poet of *Zarathustra*, sketched with abysmal profundity and without touching for a moment the Wagnerian reality' (EH 'Why I Write Such Good Books' BT 4). We know therefore that at the root of Nietzsche's whole effort to select, assimilate and become the 'ideal Wagner' was his veneration of

Wagner's ability to subordinate everything to his artistic drive in a legislative way.[20]

But there is a dangerous tipping point to the nature of these powers, and in the unpublished notebooks and fragments that did not make the final cut, we get a better sense for what they are. Over the course of several notes in notebook 32, for instance, Nietzsche outlines a number of 'dangers' pertaining to Wagner's artistic drive.[21] Perhaps the most synthetic of these notes is note 10, which comments on the 'danger' of Wagner's legislative nature when it comes to the creation of his art. 'He seems to have considered immoderation and unbridledness to be natural', Nietzsche begins by telling us. Like Goethe, Wagner's taste and his ability ran in parallel, and this made Wagner, like Goethe, presumptuous in the creation of his art.

> Wagner wanted to create whatever had a powerful effect on him. He never understood anything about his models other than what he was also able to imitate. Character of the actor. Wagner has a legislative nature: he has an overview of many relationships and does not get caught up in trivialities; he organizes everything on a large scale and cannot be judged by the isolated detail – music, drama, poetry, state, art, etc. The music does not have much value, nor does the poetry, nor does the drama; the acting is often mere rhetoric – but everything forms a totality on a large scale and at the same level. Wagner the thinker ranks just as high as Wagner the composer and poet. (UF 32[10], beginning 1874–spring 1874)

---

[20] For Nietzsche's disillusionment with the 'real' Wagner, see, for instance, UF 27[44], spring–summer 1878; UF 34[3], April–June 1885.
[21] Notebook 32 reveals Nietzsche's attempt to sort out the strengths and weaknesses of Wagner and his art, and by extension, Nietzsche's individuation process in a much more striking way than do the notes from notebook 33. While many of the notes from notebook 33 are substantially similar to those found in notebook 32, they are far more conciliatory, especially as they are moving towards what ultimately becomes the basis of his essay on Wagner. It is for this reason that we prefer to mine the unalloyed contents of notebook 32 to help *us* sort out Nietzsche's criticisms of Wagner here.

Even though the nature of this note does not structure Nietzsche's criticisms of Wagner in a syntactical argument, the substance makes it clear what those concerns are: because all fields of study could be made subject to Wagner's legislative nature, in which his ability to synthesise them ran parallel to his ability to depict them, the real danger of Wagner and his art is that all scholarship is necessarily absorbed into his personality on the one hand, for the sole purpose of reproducing what has a cumulative, powerful effect on Wagner's personality on the other. In other words, because Wagner's personality possesses a synthesising function, he is able to reduce everything to the simplicity of a point, which, when reproduced in his art, has a *concentrated* effect. Meanwhile the object as it were is deemed to have no autonomy or character in its own right other than what Wagner is able to absorb into himself. It is precisely this feature, Nietzsche points out, that turns Wagner's legislative nature into an attribute that is characteristic of the actor. This is the gist of note 10.[22]

The dominating nature of Wagner's artistic drive meant that whatever he absorbed had to be transfigured into the realm of art.

---

[22] We should point out that the charge that Wagner is an actor is much more ambiguous, even equivocal, in these early notes than it is by the time we encounter it in *The Case of Wagner*, but it is especially equivocal when we compare it with the much more fully worked-out charge that Wagner's art relies on theatricality and effects, even at this early stage. As we have noted, however, this is primarily due to the fact that Nietzsche's charges against Wagner are deeply interwoven with a number of key principles related to his own philosophical development, for which Nietzsche's notebooks at this early stage become invaluable documents testifying to the fact that, even in the midst of drafting his essay about Wagner, Nietzsche was attempting to sort out what those principles were. There is no question that Nietzsche charges Wagner with being an actor in these early notes, but the charge is not nearly as pejorative as it is in *The Case of Wagner*. As we will discover, this suggests that the charge itself does not exclusively derive its pejorative thrust from the idea that Wagner's art is enmeshed in theatricality and effects, but is grounded rather in Nietzsche's assessment of how 'legitimate' Wagner's use of them are in his music dramas. It is the latter criterion which calls into question the 'sincerity' and 'authenticity' of Wagner's art, and this is what makes Wagner vulnerable to the charge that he is 'an actor above all'. This is why we maintain that Wagner's appeal to theatricality and effects is essentially a proto-charge, a stepping stone, to the charge that Wagner is an actor, for what changes is not the mere fact that Wagner uses theatricality and effects, but rather Nietzsche's assessment of the ends to which they are used.

And as all that he absorbed, collectively and as a totality, affected *him* (according to Nietzsche), it is only natural that Wagner would try to reproduce that effect in his art. This is what Nietzsche claims in the very next note:

> Wagner's first problem: 'Why isn't the expected effect realized, since *I* experience it?' This drives him to a critique of his public, of the state, of society. He posits between artist and his public the relationship of subject to object – totally naïve. Wagner's talent is a growing *forest*, not an individual tree. (UF 32[11], beginning 1874–spring 1874)

When we connect the content of this note with Wagner's ambition to create an artwork of the future – and especially one that would resurrect the tragic age of the Greeks – Nietzsche's observation, vindictive though it is, does seem to get to the nexus of his objections about Wagner's theatricality and effects. For even though Wagner was driven to create a collective and totalising effect out of all that he absorbed, his artistic drive still required him to present and display that effect to the greatest number of people possible in order to win them over to his art. What was his medium? In one word: theatre.

> Wagner attempts a renewal of art on the only basis that still exists, that of theater: here a *mass* is truly still aroused and makes no pretensions as in museums and concert halls. To be sure, it is an extremely crude mass, and to this very day it has proven impossible to regain control of the theatrocracy. Problem: should art forever go on living in a sectarian and isolated way? Is it possible to put it in control? This is where Wagner's significance lies: he attempts to establish a *tyrannis* with the aid of the mass of theater goers. There can be little doubt that if he had been born Italian, Wagner would have achieved his goal. The German has no respect for opera and always views it as something imported and un-German. Indeed, he refuses to take seriously the theater as a whole. (UF 32[61], beginning 1874–spring 1874)

In other words, Wagner's significance lay in his attempt to *popularise* the theatre. But as Nietzsche aptly observes, Wagner's public consisted of Germans who did not take the theatre seriously, and felt it to be un-German as a whole. Furthermore, as Wagner knew the Germans to be dull and boring, his only hope of winning them to his side, and thereby popularising the theatre and his art, was to present a spectacle of overwhelming effects to get even the 'dull, boring, unwieldy' German to take the theatre seriously. Wagner, in other words, 'sold out'.

> Wagner values simplicity of dramatic design because it has the most powerful *effect*. He gathers together all the *effective* elements in an age that, because of its insensitivity, requires extremely crude and powerful measures. The magnificent, intoxicating, confusing, the grandiose, the horrible, noisy, ugly, enraptured, nervous, everything is legitimate. Inordinate dimensions, inordinate measures. The irregularity, the overdose of splendor and ornament, give the impression of wealth and luxury. He is aware of what still has an effect on our human beings of today: yet at the same time he still idealized and had a very high opinion of 'our human beings of today.' (UF 32[57], beginning 1874–spring 1874)

In sum, Wagner was able to establish a tyranny over the mass of theatregoers by pandering to the lowest common denominator of German sensibility in order to vindicate his art[23] – and indeed, behind the smokescreen of Nietzsche's own vaudeville, this is precisely the substance of the charge regarding Wagner's theatricality and effects that we find in section 6. The burlesque begins with Nietzsche parodying Wagner as if the latter were conducting a forum on aesthetics to a group of his disciples and protégés about how to establish 'intimations' to the German public. Beauty is ruled out – naturally – for beauty belongs 'only to the few'.

> Why, then, have beauty? Why not rather that which is great, sublime, gigantic – that which moves *masses*? – Once

---

[23] Compare UF 32[22], beginning 1874–spring 1874.

more: it is easier to be gigantic than to be beautiful; we know that. We know the masses, we know the theater. The best among those who sit there – German youths, horned Siegfrieds, and other Wagnerians – require the sublime, the profound, the overwhelming. That much we are capable of. And the others who also sit there – the culture *crétins*, the petty snobs, the eternally feminine, those with a happy digestion, in sum, the *people* – also require the sublime, the profound, the overwhelming. They all have the same logic. 'Whoever throws us is strong; whoever elevates us is divine; whoever leads us to have intimations is profound.' – Let us make up our minds, honored musicians: we want to throw them, we want to elevate them, we want them to have intimations. That much we are capable of. (CW 6)[24]

Truly, the cynicism with which this parody was penned makes it seem as if Wagner himself engaged in nothing other than a shrewd, utilitarian calculus. And while there may be some level of reality to this claim, the main thrust of the present charge is that in a declining culture that has no real respect for art, and so 'requires extremely crude and powerful measures' in order to be moved, Wagner cobbled together all that was most effective in creating a large-scale pageant of the spectacular and overwhelming in order to win art for the masses. Yet as we know from 'Artwork of the Future', theatricality and effects merely affect the 'outer man' and do not get to the essence of the 'inner man'. For that we need music, and it is at this point that we are in a position to examine the second charge that *Wagner's music is rhythmically, harmonically and formally flawed*.

Like the previous charge, this one is hardly unambiguous, and while the origins of the charge can be traced to the very same notebooks and draft notes for what eventually became his essay about Wagner, Nietzsche's fixation with it only really seems to have acquired vehemence following a personal experience that he

---

[24] Compare NCW 'Where I Offer Objections'.

had at the hands of one of Wagner's own protégés in the summer of 1872.

To speak plainly, Nietzsche was to all intents and purposes a very amateurish musician. The style of some of his earliest compositions reveals a tendency to imitate the romanticism of Schumann, especially in his songs, but many of them suffer from what one might call 'tonal obstinacy' – a kind of sonority, especially in connection with his harmonic constructions, that seems to resist thematic development, preferring instead to subordinate the latter to a kind of revelry in the sounds themselves. As Liébert has aptly characterised it, 'the harmonic element that dominated his musical imagination threatened, under the effect of emotion, to degenerate into pure sonorous chaos, from which the melody emerged only rarely' (Liébert 2004: 23). Young echoes this sentiment, noting that Nietzsche's primary failing as a composer was that he 'lacked command of large-scale structure' and that he was 'never able to find an original voice' (Young 2010: 155). In this respect, Nietzsche's compositional instinct was the direct antithesis of what his German milieu esteemed as the essence of all 'classical' beauty in art: logic and order. Indeed the very fact that Nietzsche's compositional forms failed to appreciate the tonal architecture of large-scale structure at the expense of grandiose gestures that never get beneath the 'musical surface' reveals an instinctive aversion to mathematics in favour of pathos and affect.[25] But if we are to understand the significance of *The Birth of Tragedy* properly, Nietzsche's exposure to Wagner's music, as the aegis-bearing witness to the rebirth of Dionysus, reaffirmed for him that the 'knowledge-hungry Socratism' of modernity, whose innermost art expression was precisely this 'arithmetical abacus of the fugue and the contrapuntal dialectics' (BT 19), would finally be subjugated before the rebirth of tragedy out of the spirit of

---

[25] In his assessment of Nietzsche's musical incompetence, Scruton (1997: 380) notes that Nietzsche had 'mastered certain stock rhetorical gestures, but lacks the sense of musical structure that will enable him to develop and elaborate his sparse ideas'. Young (2010: 496) echoes this, noting that '[t]he person who was really a miniaturist was *Nietzsche himself*. As a composer of anything longer than five minutes he rambles, his music exhibiting neither the old logic nor a new one. . .'

music. But whether that music would be Wagner's or Nietzsche's remained, for the time being, undecided. That, however, did not stop Nietzsche from trying to settle the question of his abilities once he had become involved in Wagner's circle.

Indeed, shortly after the publication of *The Birth of Tragedy*, Nietzsche put the finishing touches to what was perhaps his most ambitious composition to date: a piece for two pianos called the *Manfred Meditation*.[26] Naturally, he was curious about its artistic merits and felt that he required a competent judgement regarding his musical abilities. Unfortunately, the individual whom he solicited to judge those abilities turned out to be a major miscalculation. On 20 July 1872, Nietzsche approached none other than Hans von Bülow, Wagner's erstwhile protégé and newly minted ex-husband of Cosima, and now a broken man desperately trying to distance himself from the Wagner cult.

Bülow had been married to Cosima at the time she had given birth to Wagner's two daughters – Isolde in April 1865 and Eva in February 1867 – and she had already become pregnant with Wagner's third child before Bülow realised the adulterous nature of their relationship. Needless to say, Bülow was devastated by Wagner's behaviour towards him, all the more so since he had been singularly devoted to Wagner and his works, and had been responsible for premiering both *Tristan und Isolde* and *Die Meistersinger* in Munich. It was at the height of this melodrama that Nietzsche first entered the picture, for when he first showed up at Tribschen on Whit Monday, 17 May 1869, he was greeted by Wagner's mistress, Cosima von Bülow, who was already in her third trimester and living in an adulterous relationship with Wagner. It was the scandal of Lucerne. Yet the eager professor, who 'even quotes from *Opera and Drama* in his lectures',[27] must have seemed to the Wagners like the perfect salve for their immediate troubles: as a classical philologist,

---

[26] Nietzsche's score for the *Manfred Meditation*, along with other selected works, can be found in Nicholas Hopkins's edition of his works for the piano.

[27] CWD 1: 96, 17 May 1869.

Nietzsche could toil on Wagner's behalf to gain wider academic acceptance for his ideas, thus creating a diversion from the public opprobrium attached to their relationship. Needless to say, Nietzsche accepted this commission, so these were, for better or for worse, the circumstances in which Nietzsche's relationship with the Wagners, and by extension his relationship with Bülow, began.

It appears baffling, then, to consider why Nietzsche would have troubled the distraught Bülow for a critique of one of his own musical compositions, unless we entertain conjectures about how their personal bond had been sufficiently strengthened. While it is true that Nietzsche had recently been in contact with Bülow, the contact had been expressly authorised at the Wagners' request and for the sole purpose of sending Bülow a copy of *The Birth of Tragedy*.[28] Prior to this, Nietzsche had no intimate dealings with Bülow, and he certainly could not have circumvented the Wagners, especially given his *own* knowledge of the extremely fragile circumstances surrounding their relationship with Bülow.[29] In any case, it appears that Nietzsche weighed up the unique position in which he found himself as the ambiguous ally and confidant of Bülow, and then indulged the completely selfish motive of trying to enlist a disaffected ex-Wagnerian into a critique of his own music, for which the opportunity had now fallen, as it were, directly into his lap.[30]

---

[28] DBCW 2: 16, 3 January 1872.
[29] It is certain that Bülow came to Basel in late March/early April 1872 to give a series of concerts, as Cosima's own diary records this communication from Nietzsche (CWD 1: 466, 11 March 1872). During his visit to Basel, Bülow spent time with Nietzsche and, according to Nietzsche's sister, it was during these face-to-face visits that Bülow gave vent to his personal feelings about Wagner. In particular, certain 'bitter remarks' were made about Cosima, and Nietzsche was made to feel just how deeply Bülow's devotion to the Wagners had been repaid with treachery. It was also during this time that Bülow first drew upon the mythological love triangle of Ariadne–Theseus–Dionysus as a simile for his personal sufferings with the Wagners, in which he equated Cosima with Ariadne, Theseus with himself and Wagner with Dionysus. According to Nietzsche's sister, Bülow's implication in using the simile was to suggest that after him (that is, Bülow), 'a god had come'. If this story is even remotely accurate, it would support the conclusion that whatever passed between Nietzsche and Bülow strengthened the personal bond between the two men, at least enough for Nietzsche to initiate a correspondence with Bülow independent of the Wagners. See Förster-Nietzsche (1912–15) 1: 257–8.
[30] SL (1985: 261–2 [KSB 4: 26–7]), letter to Hans von Bülow, 20 July 1872.

Whatever the circumstances, what came back to Nietzsche on 24 July 1872 was a remarkably candid but excoriating critique of his composition. What is especially noteworthy for our purposes are the passages in Bülow's letter which deal with his professional estimation of Nietzsche's music in trying to imitate that of Wagner. In weighing up the artistic merits of Nietzsche's composition, Bülow told him very plainly that

> Your *Manfred Meditation* is the most extreme example of fantastic extravagance and the most unedifying and most anti-musical composition I have met for some time. Again and again I had to ask myself whether the whole thing was not a joke and whether it had not perhaps been your intention to write a parody of the so-called Music of the Future. Was it not on purpose that without exception you put every rule of harmony to scorn from the higher syntax to the most ordinary conventions of correct composition? But for the psychological interest – for despite all their confusion, your feverish musical productions display an exceptionally distinguished spirit – your *Meditation*, from the musical standpoint can only be compared to a crime in the moral world. I was utterly unable to find the faintest trace of any Apollonian elements in its composition, and as for those of the Dionysian order, I must confess that your piece reminded me more of the morrow of a Bacchanalian festival than the festival itself. If you really feel a passionate call to express yourself in the language of music it is essential that you should master the first elements of that language. A reeling imagination reveling in the memory of Wagnerian chords is not a fit basis for creative work. The most outlandish Wagnerian audacities, apart from the fact that they spring quite naturally from the dramatic texture and are justified by the words . . . are always correct from the standpoint of language – indeed they are so down to the smallest detail of notation. If the insight of a thoroughly educated musical scholar like Dr. Hanslick is inadequate to this purpose, it follows that to form any proper estimate of Wagner as a musician, a man must be a musician

and a half ... Once again, no offense I hope – for you yourself called your music 'execrable' – you are right; it is even more execrable than you imagine ... you could not possibly employ any surplus leisure you may have more badly than by torturing Euterpe in the way you do ... Please discern in my uncompromising frankness (rudeness) the proof of my equally sincere respect. Really, after all I have said, I cannot make this lame excuse. I simply could not help giving full vent to my indignation at all such antimusical experiments in tone. Perhaps I ought to direct a portion of this indignation against myself, for, seeing that I am responsible to *Tristan*'s having been performed once more, I am indirectly to blame for having plunged so lofty and enlightened a mind as yours, my dear Professor, into such regrettable pianoforte convulsions.[31]

Bülow's critique was truly unforgiving, but it was neither insensitive nor unsympathetic, and in general, he is quite perceptive regarding Nietzsche's welfare as a whole and the unique and dynamic interaction he was sharing with the Wagners at the time. Nonetheless, the distress that Nietzsche must have felt at Bülow's critique is evident from the fact that it took him over three months to respond.[32] But Nietzsche's actual reply to Bülow is not nearly so revealing of his compositional instinct as is the draft letter that he never sent. In the draft, Nietzsche explains to Bülow that, even though his music is self-taught, and he knows how to compose in the 'pure style' and with 'a certain degree of purity', sometimes all the same

I have been overcome by such a barbarically excessive urge [to compose], compounded of defiance and irony, that I have as much difficulty as you in perceiving sharply what is serious, what is caricature, and what is decisive mockery in my latest music ... This has unfortunately made it quite

---

[31] SL (1985: 263–6), letter to Nietzsche, 24 July 1872.
[32] See SL (1985: 267–9 [KSB 4: 78–80]), letter to Hans von Bülow, 29 October 1872.

clear to me now that the whole piece, together with this mixture of pathos and malice, did correspond absolutely to a real mood, and that I experienced pleasure as never before in writing it. So it is a sad outlook for my music and even more for my moods. How does one characterize a state of mind in which delight, scorn, exuberance, and sublimity are all jumbled together? Here and there I end up in this dangerous, moonstruck region. At the same time, I am infinitely far – you will believe me – from judging or admiring Wagner's music from the viewpoint of this half-psychiatric musical excitement. Of my music, I know only one thing: that it enables me to master a mood which, if it is not gratified, is perhaps a more dangerous one. In honoring Wagner's music, I honor precisely this highest necessity – and where I do not grasp it, being an inadequate musician, I presuppose it by an act of faith . . . What I want is the truth; you know that it is more pleasant to hear it than to speak it. So I am doubly indebted to you. But I ask only one thing of you – do not make *Tristan* responsible for my sin. *After* hearing *Tristan* I would certainly never again have written any such music – *Tristan* will cure me of my music for a long time. If only I could hear it again! I shall try, then, to take a musical cure . . . The whole thing, as a matter of fact, has been a highly instructive experience for me; the educational problem, which occupies me in other areas, has now been posed for me in the domain of art, with particular cogency. To what frightful aberrations is the solitary individual nowadays exposed![33]

The confession that Nietzsche lays plain in this letter regarding the state of mind from which his own compositional instinct flowed is particularly noteworthy for our analysis here, as the psychological ground from which Nietzsche's own criticisms of Wagner's music would soon follow – indeed he plainly says so in the last sentences of the letter itself. In particular, Nietzsche tells

---

[33] SL (1969: 106–7 [KSB 4: 76–8]), draft letter to Hans von Bülow, 29 October 1872.

us that despite the insufficiency of his musical training, he is periodically overcome with a 'barbarically excessive urge' to express himself in music, as was the case with his *Manfred Meditation*, and that this prevents him from really perceiving what he is actually expressing. Because of his inadequate musicianship, Nietzsche is unable to translate these moods into a suitable musical form, yet two facts remain psychologically decisive: 1) there is a tremendous sense of pleasure in the expression of these moods – moods in which 'delight, scorn, exuberance, and sublimity are all jumbled together'; and 2) the musical expression of these moods helps Nietzsche gratify and master them, lest they lead to 'a more dangerous one'. Taken together, the nature of these moods which find expression in musical form, and for which the form of Wagner's music in particular had revealed them to Nietzsche in their most undiluted character, helped him honour this highest necessity within himself. From the standpoint of individual psychology, there is simply no other reason to imitate what Nietzsche understood to be Wagner's music as a means to access these moods.

On the other hand, if the musical by-product of a 'reeling imagination reveling in the memory of Wagnerian chords' is a 'half-psychiatric musical excitement' as Nietzsche himself also confesses here,[34] then he would have known first-hand just how 'harmful' it would be for the artistically inclined solitary individual to give himself up to the heights of passion, and how that might have translated into the wider educational problem 'now posed for me in the domain of art, with particular cogency' – the very issue before us, in fact, in Nietzsche's 'warning' about Wagner's music. For what does Nietzsche now tell us about passion here in section 6? *In sum*: it is the cheapest thing in the world. 'Let us reach an understanding about passion. Nothing is cheaper than passion. One can dispense with all the virtues of counterpoint, one need not have learned a thing – passion is one ability we always have' (CW 6). And the cheapness of passion, according

---

[34] In the German original, Nietzsche uses the word *psychiatrisch* to denote, according to Middleton, 'nervous and emotional states of overexcitement which can be discharged in music – hence, music as catharsis'. SL (1969: 106 [KSB 4: 76–8]), critical note to draft letter to Hans von Bülow, 29 October 1872.

to Nietzsche, is made plain by the fact that Wagner creates a pure sound world that dispenses with 'all the virtues of counterpoint' and ignores all the rules of harmony. 'And this is the definition of passion', Nietzsche goes on to tell us. 'Passion – or the gymnastics of what is ugly on the rope of enharmonics' (CW 6).

This latter statement, although ostensibly pinned to *Parsifal* in the text, more properly belongs to Nietzsche's assessment of *Tristan*, the only one of Wagner's music dramas that Nietzsche really studied in any musical depth, and of which his *Manfred Meditation* stood as the one abortive attempt to emulate its sounds, and consequently, its effects. The 'enharmonic' features of *Tristan* begin with the now famous 'Tristan chord' in the second full bar of the prelude and continue for the entirety of the music drama – thus the musical phenomenon of *Tristan* as a whole more aptly suggests the figure Nietzsche uses here in section 6 of 'exercising our ear muscles'. *Tristan* ostensibly opens in A minor (the first note is a lone A on the cello). In hearing this lone A, we as listeners would then expect to hear certain harmonic structures that are common in that key. Yet as soon as we hear the harmonic ambiguity of the 'Tristan chord' in the second bar, it becomes apparent that Wagner is not committing to a traditional key at all, as the dissonance introduced is not only harmonically undecipherable, but is not immediately resolved, and this in turn creates a sense of 'tonal groundlessness' for the listener in which there dawns an increased sense of freedom for the music to move in ways and to 'pivot' in directions that would otherwise be 'prohibited' by our harmonic expectations. Indeed, Scruton observes that the Tristan chord 'can be understood only in terms of the chromatic voice leading that leads towards and away from it, and which it strangely and poignantly arrests. It is ill at ease yet stationary, standing isolated in the music like an outsider in the gathering' (Scruton 2004: 96–7). And yet through each chord progression, the harmonic structures that *are* created resolve for us one series of harmonic expectations, while there yet lingers within the very same chord the beginning of another chromatic progression that does not belong to those just resolved. It is a musical tension like no other, and one that has been repeatedly imitated ever since Wagner composed it.

The sheer intoxication of *Tristan*'s harmonic waves, in which every potential harmonic expectation seems to dissolve in the very moment that another is born, must have seemed like the perfect musical reproduction of the philosophy of becoming. Yet despite all the passionate intoxication that Nietzsche surely felt from the harmonies of *Tristan*'s music, Wagner's composition is hardly reducible to a revelry of sounds. While Nietzsche's *Manfred Meditation* merely reels in the revelry of Wagnerian harmonies, Wagner's ability, according to Liébert, to use and manipulate with virtuosity 'the frameworks, rules, and techniques of classical syntax' seems to have entirely eluded Nietzsche's musical capacity, and so Nietzsche in all likelihood never really perceived the strict architecture of the work that undergirds those harmonies. It is here, Liébert goes on to conclude, that 'the composer in Nietzsche no longer corresponded with the listener' (2004: 25), a conclusion that resonates with Bülow's warning to Nietzsche that 'to form any proper estimate of Wagner as a musician, a man must be a musician and a half'. And yet this idea that Wagner's music is an exercise in 'enharmonic ugliness' that puts 'every rule of harmony to scorn' for the sake of passion forms the foundation of Nietzsche's charge here that *Wagner's music is rhythmically, harmonically and formally flawed*. It is, as Nietzsche claims, 'infinity, but without melody' (CW 6).

Yet as one might suspect, the principal problem here is not that a given composer – in this case Wagner – happens to create infinity without melody. The problem for Nietzsche, as we have just discovered, has to do with the psycho-physiological effects on the individual listener who is subjected to this 'infinity without melody'. And Nietzsche's draft letter to Bülow makes this point perfectly clear. Once Nietzsche perceived the catalytic capacity of Wagner's music to have so easily induced his own heightened states of passion, and especially when he found out that the expression of those states was hardly 'musical' (at least according to Bülow), he recoiled. It was shortly thereafter that Nietzsche really began to fixate on the psycho-physiological effect of Wagner's rhythms.[35] Yet the ultimate irony of Bülow's revelation was the manner in

---

[35] See, for instance, UF 32[42], beginning 1874–spring 1874.

which Nietzsche shifted those very same limitations regarding the nature of his *own* music on to that of Wagner, assuming almost without batting an eyelid that what Wagner was composing must likewise fail to be music. Some of the earliest notebooks of 1878, following his break with Wagner, bear this out with particular cogency:

> Wagner cannot *narrate* with his music, cannot *prove* anything with it, but instead assaults, overthrows, torments, causes tension, terrifies – what he lacks in training, he makes up for in his principle. *Mood* replaces composition: he goes about his business too directly. (UF 27[29], spring–summer 1878)[36]

Wagner's music is *dramatic music*. It speaks the language of both the eye and the ear, 'but for someone who does not see what is taking place on stage', Nietzsche notes in *The Wanderer and his Shadow*, 'dramatic music is nonsense', for it really requires 'that we also have ears where our eyes are located'; and this requirement, Nietzsche snidely observes as he passes the blow he had received from Bülow on to Wagner, 'would do violence to Euterpe' (HAH2 163, 'Dramatic Music'). But with this kind of demand on eye and ear, and especially when music is supposed to express the innermost essence of the phenomenon, dramatic music starts to function as the '*language of the explainer*, who speaks continually, however, and allows us no time' to catch our breath (UF 30[111], summer 1878). This is, in short, what Wagner's 'infinite melody' is trying to achieve: it is the language of the explainer who is incessantly commenting on the drama upon the stage. 'This is perhaps the most essential of all his innovations', Nietzsche tells us in his *Mixed Opinions and Maxims*:

> His celebrated artistic technique, arising from and adapted to this desire – the 'infinite melody' – strives to break and sometimes even to mock all mathematical symmetry of

---

[36] Compare UF 27[47], spring–summer 1878.

tempo and energy, and he is overly rich in inventing these effects, which sound to older ears like rhythmical paradoxes and blasphemies. He fears petrification, crystallization, the transition of music into something architectonic – and so he sets three-beat rhythm against the two-beat one, frequently introduces the five- and seven-beat, repeats the same phrase immediately, but extending it so that it lasts two or three times as long.[37]

The danger of this 'infinite melody', Nietzsche goes on to conclude, is that its goal is a sonorous movement without limit or measure, and when it is matched with the completely naturalistic art of acting and the language of gesture, they can hardly impart any measure to the 'infinite melody' with which they are paired. The result is a kind of totalising effect on our senses, for even though our attention is intermittent, where we attend sometimes '*only* to the music, sometimes to the drama, sometimes to the stage', there is nonetheless *always* a demand being made upon our sense faculties, and this eventually wears down one's nerves. Yet according to Nietzsche, this is precisely what Wagner understands about his art. The most ambitious combination of means will always guarantee the strongest effect principally because of this relentless demand upon our sense channels to receive them.

At the same time, if the psychological corollary to the charge that *Wagner's music is rhythmically, harmonically and formally flawed* is that the music itself reflects the decadent and degenerate psychology of modernity, and if it is true that the definition of decadence is the pathological magnification of one aspect of the whole at the expense of the whole, then what is most important to the modern theatregoing public is hardly the music, let alone a beautiful melody, but the very colour of the tones themselves which crystallise the agitation, overexcitement and exhaustion of their own physiological condition; hence, Nietzsche's mockery in section 6

---

[37] HAH2 134, 'How the Soul Should Be Moved According to Modern Music', and NCW 'Wagner as a Danger' 1; compare SL (1969: 162 [KSB 5: 261]), letter to Carl Fuchs, end of July 1877.

that what is truly important in throwing people 'belongs partly in physiology'. There is no need for a beautiful melody when we can pay especial attention to how the colour and tone of certain instruments will affect our physiological responses and then build up a series of sound effects from that. For nothing stirs up passion like the refinement of a tone that can 'persuade even the intestines' or 'bewitch the marrow of the spine'. It is this art, Nietzsche explains, that will throw people. 'People will give credit to our spirit if our tones seem to pose many riddles' (CW 6).

Thus, the stylistic contrast between Wagner and Bizet with which Nietzsche–Zarathustra first framed his gospel of self-overcoming is now given a complete exegesis from the standpoint of Nietzsche's psycho-physiological explanation of decadence.[38] The 'brutal, artificial, and innocent tones' of Wagner's art are at the same time the tones of the exhausted world – with perhaps the single exception of the poet of *Zarathustra* who has conquered them. Yet if we consider how Nietzsche's own music was first received, and especially how his 'anti-musical experiments in tone' had originated in, and so easily propagated, his *own* heightened states of passion, it seems virtually indisputable that Nietzsche simply assumed that Wagner's compositions must have arisen from the same psychological need as his own, and that therefore his technical competence as a musician must be every bit as suspect, for he soon shifted those very same criticisms on to Wagner's music in order to justify to himself that its effect on him was identical with the very same errors he was accused of committing by Bülow. This, however, is the definition of the psychologist's fallacy.

All the same, however, with this wearing down of our nerves, we are ready to assent to anything that Wagner says. This is the basis of the third charge in section 6 that *Wagner's music is 'idealistic' in the pejorative sense*. The basis of this charge is actually quite easy to understand, and the analysis that we have provided up to this point has done much of the work for us already. The notion that Wagner is repetitive to the point

---

[38] Compare UF 27[32], spring–summer 1878.

that one becomes either desensitised or hypnotised makes us all, either willing or unwilling, confederates in his ultimate design. When Nietzsche tells us, as we have already pointed out in section 1 in connection with Wagner's 'infinite melody', that 'Wagner treats us as if – he says something so often – till one despairs – till one believes it' (CW 1), we now have a bit more leverage to understand how this plays out in the charge that Wagner's music is 'idealistic'. For whether one has been enervated or hypnotised is immaterial: we are primed all the same for the 'meaning' that Wagner tells us belongs to the music. And in this connection, it is significant that Nietzsche cites Wagner's essay 'Religion and Art' in section 6 to indicate what he means by Wagner's idealism. Hence some acquaintance with Wagner's essay will help us better understand the charge of idealism and how it is connected with the previous charges.

The immediate object of Wagner's essay is to examine the affinities that music has with genuine religious feeling, and how music, which validates those feelings, might emancipate them from the thraldom of intellectual dogmatism under which the vast majority of humanity suffers an artificial and counterfeit religious life. Wagner frames the magnitude of this problem in the very first sentences of his essay by noting that

> One might say that where religion becomes artificial, it is reserved for art to save the spirit of religion by recognising the figurative value of the mythic symbols which the former would have us believe in their literal sense, and revealing their deep and hidden truth through an ideal presentation. (PW 6: 213)

In what follows, Wagner argues that dogmatic religion, under the auspices of scholastic philosophy and the Christian priesthood, has been directly responsible for the appalling degradation of religious symbolism by insisting that its highest symbols be accepted as literal truths. Once those symbols became stiffened into intellectual dogmas, religion became emotionally barren and intellectually sterile. But as dogmatic religion has always sensed this problem, it has always called upon art to save it, and it is here that Wagner appeals to the unique power of music to liberate our religious feelings from the tyranny of intellectual dogmatism, by arguing that music presents an ideal form which at the same time conveys affective values that are both immediate and certain to our inner experience. Indeed, the peculiar ability of music to convey 'what is' to the human spirit 'stops all strife between reason and feeling'; yet this concord is given through an art form that is 'completely removed from the world of appearances', and so seems to usurp our heart as if 'by act of Grace' (PW 6: 224). In this special sense, Wagner goes on to claim that music is 'the only art that fully corresponds to the Christian belief', and is therefore the only art 'to save the noblest heritage of the Christian idea in its purity from "over-worldly reformation"', especially from the throes of the decaying Church and the absurdity of religious dogma, the products of what he calls 'Jesuitic casuistry and rationalistic pettifogging' (PW 6: 224–5).

For Wagner, the essence of all religious feeling ultimately stems from our desire for oneness, and when stripped of all dogmatism, the preliminary step towards henosis centres on changing the polarisation of desire. As desire in the usual sense moves towards objects and objective achievements in some sense, the preference for, and the attachment to, the object, and the discrete sense of egoism that is affirmed by it, act as barriers to a consciousness that is continuous and impersonal. But to change the polarisation of desire so that, instead of moving towards objects and objective achievements as the terminus, there is a movement towards the unconditional and all-embracing in consciousness, seems, to the ego-bound valuation of things, to be equivalent to psychical death, since it entails the negation of personal will and thus a reversal of the egoistic clinging to life. Needless to say, Wagner was deeply impressed with the many examples afforded in the history of the world of those who were able to effect this total abrogation of their will, including Prince Siddhārtha and Jesus of Nazareth. Indeed, when stripped of all the dogmas pervading Church Council Christianity, the ultimate essence of Christ's ethics centres on a concern for otherness that consisted in both a self-giving to the God or transcendental principle, and a valuation of others that was at least equal to the valuation he had for his own person. In this respect, the ethic here is radically anti-egoistic, and it implies a practical negation of the personal will.

Yet notwithstanding, Wagner did not require the hypothesis of Christianity to express the nature of this principle, either for Wotan in *The Ring* or for the eponymous hero in *Parsifal*.[39] As he once remarked to Cosima, 'music and religion are directed at the will, but because compassion is aroused, the individual is raised above himself to the species level, and to this extent the world is equivalent to God'.[40] And it is here, of course, that Wagner had tried to establish, through the musical deed of his final music drama *Parsifal*, something of the sanctity and reverence of this total abrogation of the will with which the original Gospels leave us, without *Parsifal* itself being a 'Christian' work.[41]

But the problem, of course, for Nietzsche – and one that he knew perfectly well – is that if music does possess anything like the ability to tap into the 'innermost essence of the phenomenon', or can in any way access the volitional element of our consciousness directly, then Wagner's art, at least in Nietzsche's estimation, is spoon-feeding the rabble by beautifying the ascetic ideal which, as we already discovered, means 'absolutely nothing' for Wagner. Using 'infinity minus the melody' in order to either enervate or hypnotise us, Wagner's whole purpose, according to Nietzsche, is to 'ennoble' our will by teaching us the mystery of the ascetic ideal. Yet there is something about all of this which strikes one as being a piece of pure theatre, since the mysterious depths of the human soul are now put on display as a spectacle designed for the consumption of the masses.

---

[39] CWD 2: 59, 7 April 1878.
[40] CWD 2: 126, 31 July 1878.
[41] In a letter she wrote to Dr Eiser in February 1877 in response to his proposal to interpret the libretto to *Parsifal* by comparing it with Calderón's *autosacramentales*, Cosima insisted it was not a 'Christian' work. 'Calderón used his genius to dramatize Church dogmas for the people, but *Parsifal* has nothing in common with any Church, nor indeed with any dogma, for here the blood turns into bread and wine, whereas it is the other way around in the Eucharist. *Parsifal* picks up where the Gospels leave off; and its poet continued to structure and create his material, heedless of all that already existed.' See Borchmeyer (1991: 401–2 note 59).

'Let us choose the hour when it is decent to look black, to heave sighs publicly, to heave Christian sighs, to make an exhibition of great Christian piety', Nietzsche mockingly observes at the end of the section, for if all it takes 'to ape the high tide of the soul' is to create a religious spectacle designed for the masses, then we can avoid meditating on the profound nature of these philosophical problems altogether, for 'the "swelled bosom" shall be our argument, the beautiful sentiment our advocate' (CW 6). For just as long as the artist can cobble together the semblance of a religious spectacle that is designed to mimic the effects of what the undiscerning masses expect should be part and parcel of the religious experience, then surely Wagner's music will provide 'redemption'. Meanwhile, those who take the ascetic ideal seriously and approach the problem in earnest (in other words, Nietzsche himself) will most certainly be 'without song and singers' (D 548).[42] It is fairly easy therefore to understand the resentment that flows from this charge, although it hardly makes it any more excusable. Nevertheless, with the analysis we have provided in section 6, we are now in a position to analyse the charge that *Wagner is an actor* in the sections that follow.

Sections 7–8

To understand this charge, and how it is connected with the three central charges we examined in detail in section 6, it is worth emphasising once again that Nietzsche's entire challenge to Wagner revolves around proving who has the right to carry the mantle of the 'philosopher who practices music' for culture. In order to show this, Nietzsche has to demonstrate that Wagner's art had succumbed to the very features that Wagner himself had identified as those responsible for a declining culture, while at the same time showing that his art, and in particular his *Zarathustra*, had realised the features that Wagner

---

[42] On this point, Nietzsche's observation about the ascetic tendencies of his own life to his *de facto* mother and friend Malwida von Meysenbug is not only touching, but is particularly revealing in light of some of the resentment that we find in his criticisms of Wagner. See SL (1969: 171 [KSB 6: 4–5]), letter to Malwida von Meysenbug, 14 January 1880.

had identified with a culture on the ascendant – art as the immediate vital act of life. As we have already pointed out, Wagner, in his analysis of the decline of the arts, had identified luxury or decadence as the feature central to Socratic culture (PW 1: 76–7, 'Artwork of the Future'), while our own analysis has shown that Nietzsche's post-Wagnerian position did nothing if not try to prove that Wagner and his art had become yet another victim of Socratic culture. It follows, therefore, that in bringing this challenge to a head, Nietzsche's case of Wagner is necessarily predicated on proving Wagner's decadence. For if, in preaching his gospel of self-overcoming, Nietzsche can prove to us that Wagner's art had succumbed to decadence while convincing us that he, Nietzsche, had recognised and overcome it, then by Wagner's *own* definitions, his art would have to be acknowledged as the symptom of decline. Once this is accomplished, only Nietzsche would remain as the logical and legitimate successor to Wagner to carry the mantle of the 'philosopher who practices music' for culture. What Nietzsche must prove, therefore, is that Wagner as both philosopher and artist is nothing less than a counterfeit metaphysician running a redemption racket through the seductive nature of his music, which is nothing more than theatricality and effects.

In this regard, the charge that *Wagner is an actor* is the culmination of the previous charges, and is in some sense the climax of Nietzsche's challenge to Wagner. Once we string the previous charges together, we get a very interesting narrative about how exactly it is that Wagner is an actor, for the indictment itself (as one might expect) is implicitly designed to exonerate Nietzsche. Using the analysis we have provided so far, let us briefly examine the narrative that Nietzsche is attempting to craft for his readers that culminates in the charge that *Wagner is an actor*.

According to Nietzsche, Wagner understood that music could directly access and, to some extent, influence the volitional-based element of our consciousness. Human embodiment, following Schopenhauer, was nothing more than a species of the will in nature which, under the lens of the intellect, brought the will into the focus of a fine point, and was for that reason called the highest grade of its objectivation in nature. But to incorporate these philosophical presuppositions into the very fabric of one's musical compositions meant that, as an artistic device, music began to function as the 'language of the explainer' for the drama on the stage: in other words, because music was now believed to reveal the true significance of the motives and forces that pervade the dramatic action, it could speak without pause as a kind of running commentary on all the varied and nuanced distinctions of the will within the drama.

Unfortunately this artistic development brought the pairing of music with the drama into an unavoidable contradiction, for if we grant that music is supposed to convey the motive feeling of a particular character in sounds, then these sounds will provide us with a particular expression of feeling in music, but they do so more or less synchronically and holistically. On the other hand, the dramatic poem, which speaks to us conceptually and is paired with a sequence of movements and expressions on the stage, is subject to a different kind of temporal unfolding to our understanding. This means that the language of music and the language of concepts express their content according to totally different temporal laws and cannot be made to run parallel to one another: sometimes entire symphonies are required to express *one* dramatic sentiment, and when this *does* occur, what is the stage drama supposed to be doing? Wagner, however, desired synchronicity between the music and the concept, for if music is supposed to function as the 'language of the explainer', then Wagner had to bring the world of sound into the most precise alignment with the world of dramatic depiction, and this could only really be achieved under the assumption that music is a 'mere means of expression' whose ends do not lie in the music itself, but rather in the service of the dramatic action unfolding on stage.[43] As soon as Wagner regarded music as a 'mere means of expression', his tones were specifically conceived to evoke the drama. All the instruments of the orchestra, each of which has its own unique tone quality, could now be conceived as the sonorous analogue of an eternal and inscrutable will, and thus all the many tones, shades and hints at this undercurrent could now be depicted through the physical characteristics of sound. Melody was no longer necessary – indeed it could be completely dispensed with – since what mattered most was this pleasure in nuance, this

---

[43] For an excellent discussion on these points, see UF 32[52], beginning 1874–spring 1874.

pleasure at appreciating all the subtle touches of affect in enhancing the drama. Thus by utilising music as a mere means for what really matters – the drama – Wagner was composing, not as a musician, but as a dramatist, by appealing to the power of music for the sole purpose of achieving and enhancing dramatic effect as an end in itself. Truly, as Nietzsche would observe in one of his final notebooks, Wagner 'uses music for something other than music, he intensifies poses, he is a poet'. Wagner 'can paint' with his tones, and it is this peculiar talent for music in the service of the drama that has enabled him to paint poses, façades, gestures and, above all, a spectacle of his own philosophical and religious idealism which has 'appealed to "beautiful feelings" and "heaving bosoms" ... with the help of music Wagner does all sorts of things which are not music: he suggests swellings, virtues, passions. For him music is a means' (UF 16[29], spring–summer 1888). But for Nietzsche, any musician who actually advocates for 'music as a mere means' (which he repeatedly accuses Wagner of doing) betrays the actor.[44]

With this brief narrative, then, we finally have a coherent account of how all the other charges work together to culminate in the charge that *Wagner is an actor.* But what exactly does 'being an actor' mean? For even though the charge is unquestionably pejorative, it is also fairly technical, so if we are to understand its significance, and why Nietzsche makes such a monumental fuss over it in the sections that follow, then we really need to understand it in the wider context of Nietzsche's challenge to Wagner.

On the surface, the charge that Wagner is an actor whose art is engaged in theatricality and effects would hardly constitute any kind of nineteenth-century art scandal, since this was the rule and not the exception in late eighteenth- and early nineteenth-century operatic productions. So the charge that Wagner (or anyone else for that matter) is an actor is not, in and of itself, a categorical condemnation. The real problem, as we have previously pointed out, has to do with whether or not theatricality and effects play a legitimate role in Wagner's music dramas, for if it is true that his whole approach to composition is to bring the world of sound

---

[44] Compare NCW 'Where I Offer Objections'.

into the most precise alignment with the world of drama, then believing music to be a 'mere means of expression' for the drama would more or less imply that the composer was composing almost entirely from the standpoint of calculating a dramatic effect. Consequently, if Wagner is, according to Nietzsche, the most characteristic representative of decadence, then the charge that Wagner is an actor acquires its pejorative thrust from the idea that he ushered in the degeneration of *all art* into *acting for effect*, and thereby accelerated the downfall of a culture that was already in decline. These are the points that Nietzsche sets out to establish in the sections that follow, and by doing so he sets the stage for his final, categorical condemnations of Wagner and modernity in the postscripts and epilogue that follow, and how he was uniquely positioned to overcome them.

In order to initiate the discussion that ensues, Nietzsche opens section 7 by framing the problem of culture as the decline of all art into that of acting, and to support the argument that follows, he returns once again to his definition of decadence to do much of the analytical work. We have already touched on how Nietzsche's definition is connected with the charge that *Wagner's music is rhythmically, formally and harmonically flawed*, but to really get a sense for how this definition of decadence is responsible for the deterioration of style and what Nietzsche calls here the 'overall change of art into histrionics', it is well worth citing a letter that Nietzsche sent to his musical friend Carl Fuchs shortly before the publication of *The Case of Wagner*, as it very neatly explains how the degeneration of large-scale rhythmic structures into rhythmic perturbations at the cellular level leaves only the dramatic gesture or 'music as effect' as the uniting principle of the work.

In his letter to Fuchs, Nietzsche begins by arguing that the recent trend in musical practice to include phrase markings as part of a published musical score is 'wicked pedantry', because the very idea that a composer should provide detailed performance markings on how a musician is supposed to shape a series of notes from one bar to the next is built upon the entirely false premise that 'there *is* a correct, that is, *one* correct exposition' of the performance – an assumption that Nietzsche goes on to note seems 'psychologically and experimentally *wrong*'. In the moment of creation, Nietzsche continues, the composer perceives all of the subtle shadings of sound and intonation and holds them in a 'precarious equilibrium', but once the composer tries to formalise them, the musical composition as a whole tends to break up into increasingly smaller units precisely because the realisation and interpretation of the music is now tied to the performance system associated with the phrase markings at the cellular level.[45] Then, having observed these wider trends in trying to tie the musical composition to its realisation as a performance, Nietzsche homes in on Wagner:

> we considered this animation and enlivening of the smallest articulations, as it enters Wagner's *practice* in music and has spread from there to become almost a dominant performance system (even for actors and singers), with counterparts in other arts – it is a *typical symptom of deterioration*, a proof that life has withdrawn from the whole and is now luxuriating in the infinitesimal. 'Phrase marking' would, accordingly, be the symptom of a decline of the organizing power, or, to put it differently, a symptom of the incapacity to bridge *big* areas of relations rhythmically – it would be a decadent form of *rhythm* . . . The more the eye is focused on the single *rhythmic* form ('phrase'), the more myopic it becomes with regard to the broad, long, big forms . . . An alternation in the optics of the composer – this is happening everywhere, not only in the surfeit of rhythmical life in the infinitesimal – also in our capacity for enjoyment is restricting itself more and more to the tender, small, sublime things . . . as a result of which one only creates such things.[46]

---

[45] As Nietzsche opines here, '*there is no sole saving interpretation*, either for poets or musicians'. In other words, the fact that composers write a piece of music by no means implies that they know best how to perform it – and how true this is can be gauged by the fact that very few people prefer to listen to Stravinsky conducting his own music or Rachmaninoff playing his own piano pieces.

[46] SL (1969: 306–7 [KSB 8: 400–1]), letter to Carl Fuchs, 26 August 1888; compare NCW 'Wagner as a Danger' 1.

From the content of this letter, Nietzsche makes it quite clear that the overall architecture of a composition, or what he calls the 'broad, long, big forms' of its realisation, depends upon, and to some extent presupposes, some kind of uniform time metric that organises the composition as a whole. But Wagner's practice in music had introduced phrase markings at the cellular level for the express purpose of formalising the music *as a performance*. Thus the very idea of a uniform time metric had been increasingly displaced in favour of highlighting these rhythmic and dynamic accentuations of the music, which were completely bound up with the performance on the stage. In addition, the duration of these rhythmic accentuations, which are often very brief, as well as the composer's increased focus on animating them from one bar to the next, meant that what truly mattered was the performative nature of the music. Consequently, the overall architecture of a composition as governed by the 'broad, long, big forms' of its rhythms had degenerated into what Nietzsche calls a rhythm of affect or emotion which luxuriates in the infinitesimals of sound performance. In other words, Wagner's music *is* the performance, the dramatic gesture, which unites the work as a whole.

With this explanation, we finally have the key to Nietzsche's charge that *Wagner is an actor* in both its technical and pejorative senses, and with it the interpretative framework for the remaining sections of our text, which are almost entirely predicated on this charge. Given what we understand so far about Nietzsche's wider challenge to Wagner, one might expect that accusing Wagner of being an actor does not have any real consequences for broader culture unless Nietzsche can convince his readers of his central thesis about decadence, and then connect it with the fact that Wagner's approach to art typifies the degenerating instincts of the modern world.[47] In this respect there is an interesting but short-lived discussion about literary decadence at the beginning of section 7, where Nietzsche tries to explain how this 'over-all change

---

[47] See, for instance, the very pregnant passage here, where Nietzsche tells us that Wagner's decadence was no 'whim' or 'accident', but rather that he was 'something *perfect*, a typical decadent in whom ... every feature is necessary' (CW 7).

of art into histrionics' has corrupted style in art more generally. In fact the observations here that 'life, *equal* vitality, the vibration and exuberance of life pushed back into its smallest forms' echo Nietzsche's letter to Fuchs about the 'typical symptoms of deterioration' more broadly, where 'life has withdrawn from the whole and is now luxuriating in the infinitesimal'.[48] The discussion, however, is premature, for Nietzsche soon drops it in favour of amplifying the central charge that Wagner is an actor by examining the very ground from which Wagner creates his art. This is the real thrust of section 7 as well as the sections that follow.

Nietzsche begins by telling us that Wagner composes, not by sounds, but by the 'hallucination of gestures', for which he then 'seeks the sign language of sounds' (CW 7). Given what we have expounded so far, the amplification here is fairly straightforward: if music is the means and drama is the end, then Wagner is more concerned with accentuating the dramatic potential of each sound. In fact, the realisation of the sounds themselves becomes tied to their performative value from one bar of music to the next, and this means that what unites the music itself, considered as an organic whole, is *not* the music, but rather the drama. Thus what makes Wagner an actor in the technical sense is the fact that the drama comes first in terms of its temporal creation, while the music is essentially derived from the drama as a 'mere means' for calculating its performative effect.[49]

Yet Nietzsche's attack on the ground from which Wagner creates his art has a far more radical object, and for anyone familiar with the effusive praise that Nietzsche showers upon himself and how *he* creates in *Ecce Homo*, telling his readers that Wagner composes from the 'hallucination of gestures' is tantamount to declaring that Wagner does not compose from the inspiration of genius. In other words, what we find here when it comes to examining the ground from which Wagner creates his art is an implicit contrast between the composite, artificial and inorganic

---

[48] SL (1969: 307 [KSB 8: 401]), letter to Carl Fuchs, 26 August 1888.
[49] It was no secret, in fact, that Wagner wrote his own libretti and that it took him years to set their dramatic potential to music.

means with which Wagner laboriously cobbles together his tiny, cellular sound animations, and the genuine and effortless inspirations from which the poet of *Zarathustra* creates.

To bring this contrast into clear relief, we need only consider what Nietzsche tells us about his own genius in *Ecce Homo*, and how his *Zarathustra* in particular had come to him as a *bona fide* inspiration. In a section entirely devoted to the fulsome description of his afflatus, Nietzsche declares that he had merely been the 'mouthpiece, merely the medium of overpowering forces' in which the inspiration for his *Zarathustra* dawned upon him. 'Like lightning, a thought flashes up, with necessity, without hesitation regarding its form', Nietzsche reports, for

> everything happens involuntarily in the highest degree but as in a gale of a feeling of freedom, of absoluteness, of power, of divinity . . . everything offers itself as the nearest, most obvious, simplest expression . . . here the words and word shrines of all being open up before you; here all being wishes to become word, all becoming wishes to learn from you how to speak.

Nietzsche then concludes his testimony with a posture of his own: 'This is *my* experience of inspiration; I do not doubt that one has to go back thousands of years in order to find anyone who could say to me, "it is mine as well"' (EH 'Why I Write Such Good Books' TSZ 3). Evidently then, the effect of having 'to go back thousands of years' to find creative inspirations on the order that Nietzsche reports here seems to preclude whatever form of inspiration might be claimed for Wagner's art; and indeed, when we compare Nietzsche's description of the joy, the freedom and the power found in having his *Zarathustra* 'revealed' to him, Wagner's approach to composition sounds downright devitalising.[50]

---

[50] All in all, this is a very interesting turn of events, for in *Human, All Too Human*, Nietzsche specifically denies the notion of inspiration which he seeks to exalt in *Ecce Homo*. In section 155, Nietzsche tells us that 'the imagination of a good artist or thinker continually produces good, mediocre and bad things', and that it is his *'power of judgement'* that 'rejects, selects, [and] ties together', using Beethoven's notebooks – and Wagner's

It is in these connections that we finally find an explanation for one of the most curious accusations with which Nietzsche confronts Wagner in section 7; namely, that he is 'the *greatest* miniaturist in music' (CW 7). In the more obvious sense, Nietzsche means that Wagner was never able to compose music from the standpoint of music, but rather intensified poses by making musical patchwork, motifs and sound formulas, all of which were derived from the dramatic gesture. But the deeper cut is that Wagner never composed from inspiration, but rather from the gesture, and therefore from what is counterfeit and false. It is no wonder then that Wagner's approach in cobbling together his patchwork of motifs and formulas at the cellular level 'exhausts his strength' (CW 7), for he is simply faking it; whereas by contrast, Nietzsche's vigour and patience were perfect in the days following the composition of his *Zarathustra*: 'Often one could have seen me dance; in those days I could walk in the mountains for seven or eight hours without a trace of weariness' (EH 'Why I Write Such Good Books' TSZ 4). Taken together, what we find in section 7 is that Nietzsche's art is effortlessly and authentically inspired, while Wagner's is at best laboriously cobbled together from the pretence of authenticity, but which in reality is an artistic fraud.

With this conclusion, we return once again to the same fundamental series of complaints with which Nietzsche attacked Wagner in section 87 of *The Gay Science*; namely, that no musician is better at the infinitely small, and hence the microcosmic, than Wagner.

> But quite apart from the *magnétiseur* and fresco-painter Wagner, there is another Wagner who lays aside small

favourite composer – to illustrate 'how he gradually gathered together the finest melodies and selected them, as it were, out of multiple beginnings' (HAH1 155). In the very next section, Nietzsche tries to provide a physiological explanation for what artists call 'inspiration', telling us that it is simply a matter of the 'productive power' having been 'dammed up for a long time' which gives the artist the illusion that it has come forth as 'something miraculous' (HAH1 156). Needless to say, Wagner was not slow to react to Nietzsche's slighting of the artistic genius, as Cosima records in one of her diary entries: 'R. talks in disgust about Nietzsche's denial of inspiration as shown by the Beethoven sketchbooks; it would be better, he says, if such sketches were not published – as if the search for a form for a particular inspiration were a denial of its existence!' (CWD 2: 123, 27 July 1878).

gems: our greatest melancholiac in music, full of glances, tenderness, and comforting words in which no one has anticipated him, the master in tones of a heavy-hearted and drowsy happiness. (CW 7).

These comments, which echo the conciliatory remarks Nietzsche makes about Wagner's music in *Nietzsche Contra Wagner*, are intended almost as a foil. For like section 87 of *The Gay Science*, the conclusion Nietzsche wants us to reach remains the same. Even though Wagner excels at the infinitely small, he does not know it, which means that his art is at its best precisely when he is least aware of it.[51] While the true artist will always be his own work of art, which is the very condition that forces him to create from some kind of artist's conscience, what we continue to find in Wagner's case is a widening chasm between the artist and his works of art. But the reason for this, as we now know from the conclusion of section 7, is precisely because Wagner subordinates his entire art to that of the grand gesture, and therefore to what is essentially untrue.

From this point forward, the idea that Wagner is a fake or a fraud so completely dominates the remaining sections of *The Case of Wagner* that it becomes, as it were, the standard around which Nietzsche rallies himself for his final assault. Because Nietzsche has, at this point, judged Wagner's use of the theatre to be in the service of dubious ends, we now know that what makes Wagner especially vulnerable to the charge that he is an actor is that his art specialises in what is deceptive and untrue. It is in this connection that we find perhaps the most serious amplifications of this charge, including what we find here in section 8 with the claim that Wagner's dominant instinct was to act.

In the more immediate sense, the effect of this claim is to undermine what is perhaps one of the central theses of Wagner's 'Artwork of the Future' regarding the so-called 'rebirth of culture', and in this respect, Nietzsche's chief concern is to continue prosecuting the assault on how Wagner's art, according to his own

---

[51] GS 87, and NCW 'Where I Admire'.

definitions, must be acknowledged as the symptom of decline. By claiming that Wagner's dominant instinct is to act, Nietzsche is in some sense highlighting to his contemporary readers precisely how Wagner himself believed that he would bring about the renewal of art as culture.

To be clear, when it came to creating the artwork of the future, and in particular Wagner's monumental *Gesamtkunstwerk*, Wagner had insisted above all that the artwork of the future be grounded in the immediate conditions of life. And as it turned out, the only two art forms which, in Wagner's estimation, *were* grounded in the immediate conditions of life were poetry and drama – the very arts that just happened to be Wagner's own specialities. The artwork of the future, therefore, was made to rest on the shoulders of the 'artist of the future', the very artist who specialised in depicting and synthesising art forms that are grounded in the immediate conditions of life. Hence the implications of this assertion were not too difficult to draw out, then or now, for who did Wagner nominate to be the 'artist of the future' in his original analysis? 'Without a doubt, the poet. But *who* will be the poet? Indisputably the *performer*' (PW 1: 195-6, 'Artwork of the Future'). In other words, the artwork of the future was made to rest of the shoulders of the performer, and Wagner, as we very well know, principally nominated himself in that role. So if what Wagner says is true, then according to his own admission, the synthetic unity of all the arts rested on, and was made subordinate to, the performance of the actor. The true agglutinating agent of Wagner's *Gesamtkunstwerk*, and what enabled Wagner to lord it over the other arts, was his tyrannical instinct for acting. This is precisely what we find Nietzsche attacking in section 8.

Through his actor's genius, Nietzsche tells us, all the other art forms in existence became a 'mere means' for his art of calculating effects, while at the same time, the 'extremely crude mass' of the theatregoing public, which makes no pretensions to 'real art', allowed Wagner to establish his tyranny of acting and to become master over the mass of theatregoers. 'Wagner's art has the pressure of a hundred atmospheres', Nietzsche tells us in section 8. Yet one should not be fooled. Wagner was no more of a musician than he was a poet or a dramatist. Rather, 'he *became* a musician, he *became* a poet because the tyrant within him, his actor's genius, compelled him. One cannot begin to figure out Wagner until one figures out his dominant instinct' (CW 8). Thus, to understand his 'dominant instinct' is to recognise that at the basis of his 'artwork of the future' is something completely fake. Only his tyrannical instinct for acting held it all together, and the fact that this is so, according to Nietzsche, is made more apparent by the observation that Wagner abandoned 'all lawfulness' in music in order to turn it into the 'theatrical rhetoric' of underscoring gestures and of expressing 'the psychologically picturesque' (CW 8). Once again, the idea that Wagner uses music as a mere means for acting and that his art is more interested in creating false pathos and effect puts him on a par with the French masters, for whom Wagner never had any love, and means in effect that his art is no better than those very same 'French "sensational pieces"' that he had railed against in his critique of modern opera in 'The Destiny of Opera' (PW 5: 133).[52] Wagner 'is the Victor Hugo of music as language', where music is not really music, but language, and language moreover as the handmaiden of drama (CW 8). The conclusion that Nietzsche wishes us to draw, of course, is that when one's dominant instinct is to act, then one's art is concerned with 'effect, nothing but effect'.

But with this conclusion, there is a much deeper censure at the basis of the claim about Wagner's dominant instinct, for if it is true that his art is concerned with 'effect, nothing but effect', then the real problem, according to Nietzsche, is that Wagner's creative instincts are guided more by a concern for what *appears* to be true than what actually *is* true. In the first place, Nietzsche thinks, Wagner's instinct for what is fake was applied so consistently and tyrannically over every aspect of his life that eventually he understood better than anyone else alive that insisting on the simulation of truth can be every bit as effective – perhaps even more so – than what actually is the truth. And when the former can rally such seductive allies as pathos and effect to its cause, the naked truth can hardly compete.

---

[52] On this point, compare NCW 'Where Wagner Belongs'.

Unfortunately, this approach to truth, which works it over into a veil of illusions so that it becomes more palatable for the mob, certainly runs afoul of the teachings of Schopenhauer, the very philosopher whom Wagner professed to follow. Yet given the nature of Nietzsche's overall challenge to Wagner as both an artist and philosopher, it should go without saying that appeals to Schopenhauer were frequently made in order to settle final points of dogma. This is no exception, for when we survey Schopenhauer's teachings on the nature of truth from his essay 'On Religion', we find him telling us, through the dialogue of his two interlocutors Demopheles and Philalethes, that the 'naked truth does not belong before the eyes of the profane mob', which prefers on the contrary a 'thick veil' of illusions before she can appear before them. 'This is why it is entirely unfair and unreasonable to demand of a religion', Demopheles goes on to note, 'that it should be true in the literal sense'; and it is also incidentally why both rationalists and supernaturalists end up looking absurd in the process, 'since they both proceed from the assumption that it should be, under which the former then prove that it is not, and the latter stubbornly assert that it is'. In reality however, allegory and myth are the actual elements of religion for the masses, since they 'very nicely [satisfy] the ineradicable metaphysical need of mankind and [take] the place of pure philosophical truth, which is infinitely difficult and perhaps never attainable' (PP 2, 'On Religion', 174).

If, therefore, religion *en masse* is a fraud, at least it has the merit of being a pious fraud; but all this stands beneath the dignity of the genuine philosopher in any case. For if simplicity is the seal of truth, 'then the naked truth must be so simple and comprehensible that we must be able to teach it in its true form to everyone without mixing it with myths and fables (a pack of lies) – that is, disguising it as *religion*' (PP 2, 'On Religion', 174).

To say it more politely then – as Nietzsche surely had at the close of section 3 – 'philosophy is not suited for the masses. What they need is holiness.'[53] And yet when we weigh the evidence of

---

[53] Nietzsche's original is in French: *'la philosophie ne suffit pas au grand nombre. Il lui faut la sainteté'* (CW 3).

'the moral and religious absurdities' that constitute Wagner's final music drama *Parsifal*, we can see that Schopenhauer's approach to the truth is clearly not Wagner's intention. Instead Wagner's instincts find their prerogative in creating 'a pack of lies', and then acting as if they were true by appealing to the musical and theatrical effects that he appends to them, as if they somehow analytically revealed that truth. So once again, the very condition that might force an artist to create from some kind of artistic conscience is totally lacking in the case of Wagner.

The very fact that Wagner cannot create, let alone discriminate, what is true, nor seems much interested in pursuing what is true outside of the theatrical effects he creates, means that he is neither a philosopher, whose ostensible pursuit is the truth, nor an artist who falsifies what is true with a good conscience. Wagner is simply a pretender. In fact, he is the pretender *par excellence*, and it is in this connection that Nietzsche identifies his entire *raison d'être* with the psychology and morality of the actor.

> One is an actor by virtue of being ahead of the rest of mankind in one insight: what is meant to have the effect of truth must not be true. This proposition . . . contains the whole psychology of the actor; it also contains – we need not doubt it – his morality. Wagner's music is never true. But *it is taken for true*; and thus it is in order. (CW 8)

Wagner is in the vanguard of modernity only to the extent that he understood better than anyone else alive that fakery is more seductive than truth. This is the reason why he has been able to defraud everyone else, for the mass of theatregoers are all 'art idiots' anyway, at least in Nietzsche's eyes. This is the real reason why Wagner is a fraud.

Thus in tracing the charge that Wagner is an actor above all, which began in section 5 by describing Wagner, the modern artist *par excellence*, as 'the Cagliostro of modernity', we now have the full effect of what Nietzsche means by Wagner's talent for acting. To say that Wagner is committed on a priori grounds to feigning what he is not means that what comes first for Wagner is pretence, play-acting and make believe. And when one's creative instincts are preoccupied with what is fake, then the artist by definition cannot create what is true. It need hardly be said that the whole gravitas of Nietzsche's argument is to undermine and discredit Wagner as a thinker and a musician, or as anything other than a showman along the lines of P. T. Barnum who gives the people *panem et circenses* through elaborately staged hoaxes.

With this conclusion, we can see once again that Nietzsche continues to press his narrative about Wagner as a means not only to condemn him and the decadence of modernity that he personifies, but also to indicate at the same time how he, Nietzsche, has overcome them both. We get a sense of this through some of the closing lines of section 8, in which Nietzsche appeals to one of his recurring analogies – art as a material substance that is consumed by one's physiological functions – to establish the point that Wagner's art is impoverished and void of nutrition:

> The Wagnerian, with his believer's stomach, actually feels sated by the fare his master's magic evokes for him. The rest of us, demanding *substance* above all else, in books as well as in music, are scarcely taken care of by merely 'represented' tables and are hence much worse off. To say it plainly: Wagner does not give us enough to chew on. (CW 8)

But because the Cagliostro of modernity, Wagner, and his pathos for acting toppled every taste and conquered every resistance to maintaining a separation of the arts, there was an overall change and decline of all the other arts into histrionics after Wagner had finished with them.

Sections 9–10

At this point in the essay, Nietzsche has formally made his case against Wagner, and in the sections that follow, he more or less attempts to draw out the implications that follow from his definition of acting as it applies to Wagner. Section 9 is primarily concerned with Wagner's dramatic plots, while section 10 is taken up with an examination of Wagner's prose works. Both, however, are intended to scrutinise Wagner's productions under the definition of acting in order to demonstrate the conclusion that in both music and philosophy, the secret artistry of his instinct was to act. The prosecution on these points is very important, for as we have repeatedly pointed out, only by discrediting Wagner in both domains will Nietzsche prove that *he* has won his duel with Wagner over who has the right to carry the mantle of the 'philosopher who practices music' for culture.

The first feature Nietzsche attacks in section 9 is Wagner's plots, and in particular, how Wagner conceives them. In this connection, two recurring claims about Wagner's art are especially prominent: first, that every aspect of his art is executed with an eye to the ultimate effect it creates, and second, that the 'extremely crude mass' of the theatregoing public allowed Wagner to establish his tyranny for acting and to become master over them.

In creating his plots, Nietzsche begins by telling us that Wagner's only real concern is for the ultimate effect they will have on the audience. Thus Wagner begins by conceiving, as it were, the dénouement: here he can safely create scenes of great pathos that he is certain will have the effect of completely knocking over his audience. From there everything else is derived, including the plot itself, which is essentially a series of strong scenes in succession tied together in some kind of artificial syntax to give us, the audience, the impression of dramatic necessity.

> What he envisages first is a scene whose effectiveness is absolutely safe, a genuine *actio* with an *hautrelief* of gestures, a scene that *throws* people – this he thinks through in depth, and from this he then derives the characters. All the rest follows from this, in accordance with a technical economy that has no reasons for being subtle . . . To begin with, he tries to guarantee the effectiveness of his work to himself; he starts with the third act; he *proves* his work to himself by means of its ultimate effect. With such a sense of the theater for one's guide, one is in no danger of unexpectedly creating a drama. Drama requires *rigorous* logic: but what did Wagner ever care about logic? To say it once more: it is *not* the public of Corneille of whom Wagner had to be considerate – but mere Germans. (CW 9)

The sense of this excerpt seems straightforward enough, but there is a more subtle point worth exploring here, and one that Nietzsche himself makes in a footnote regarding the origin of the word 'drama' and the nature of its unfortunate translation as 'action'. The relevance of this footnote to Wagner and his music dramas will soon become clear.

According to Nietzsche, the ancient drama, strictly speaking, had no 'action' at all. Instead, Nietzsche claims, dramas were 'events' – that is, δρώμενα (*dromena*) – in the hieratic sense. The most ancient drama represented 'the legend of the place [or] the "holy story" on which the foundation of the cult rested'. In addition, from what little we know of the ancient playwright Aeschylus and his relationship to the Eleusinian Mysteries, Aeschylus was familiar enough with them to have been charged with 'profanation' of the mysteries by allegedly imitating their rites on the stage.[54] Hence, the reason why the ancient playwright would have 'aimed at scenes of great pathos' is precisely because the dramas themselves were ritual performances of a religious or holy nature which, in their staging, would have exercised an overpowering effect upon contemporary audiences, who knew the legends of the place, the holy story, and the associated rituals all too well (CW 9, critical note). Therefore when we compare our understanding of these 'ritual performances' with the kind of drama that Wagner, the 'modern-day Aeschylus', conceives, the result according to Nietzsche is a complete misunderstanding on Wagner's part about the nature of the ancient music drama and the so-called return to its origins as part of his 'artwork of the future'. When understood in their proper light, Nietzsche's criticisms in this footnote are devastating, because they strike at the very heart not only of Wagner's vision of bringing about the rebirth of tragedy, but even more so at who Wagner thought himself to be in trying to bring this about.

In the first place, by telling us that Wagner's chief concern was to calculate his final effect under the misunderstanding that 'drama' meant 'action', Nietzsche is trying to indicate that Wagner's motives

---

[54] Aristotle, *Nicomachean Ethics*, 1111a8–10.

differ from those of the ancient playwrights on whom he modelled his so-called 'dramas'. For in 'aiming at scenes of great pathos', the latter could count on the spirit of the folk to participate in the holy scenes and the rituals that were recreated on the stage in order to bring about a genuine communion of dramatic pathos. But if all Wagner is doing is creating a series of strong scenes in succession that are tied together by the most fatuous plot points of 'dramatic action', then Wagner *qua* dramatist is plainly exposed for the actor that he is. Wagner may have rightly observed that the ancient tragedy was the kind of art form that was inspired by, and flourished through, the spirit of the folk (PW 1: 136, 'Artwork of the Future'), but his dramas are simply scenes of great pathos that are calculated from the gesture of pathos itself. On this latter point, Nietzsche cannot help but give full vent to his fury, ridiculing the dramatic 'knots' he finds in *Tristan und Isolde* and *Die Meistersinger* in order to illustrate just how little their scenes of great pathos depend on the 'action', and therefore how 'unnecessary' these scenes are in the classical sense.

In the second place, and perhaps less obviously, by exposing Wagner's dramas as shrewd calculations that are derived from the gesture of pathos itself, Nietzsche is also telling us that Wagner is no 'high priest' in the sense that Aeschylus might have been, no matter what the throng of his sycophantic admirers might say. For even with the veneer of myth, which parrots the 'holy story' or the 'legend of the place' from the Attic stage, Wagner presides over no true folk, but only that 'extremely crude mass' of the theatregoing public – 'mere Germans' – who are just as steeped in decadence as Wagner, that ardent champion and defender of decadence himself. Indeed, when we strip away the mythic content from Wagner's music dramas, so Nietzsche tells us, we get the decadent problems of bourgeois modernity.

> 'But the *content* of the Wagnerian texts! their mythic content! their eternal content!' – Question: how can we test this content, this eternal content? – The chemist replies: translate Wagner into reality, into the modern – let us even be crueler – into the bourgeois! What becomes of Wagner then? – Among ourselves, I have tried it. Nothing is more entertaining, nothing to be recommended more highly for

walks, then retelling Wagner in *more youthful* proportions: for example, Parsifal as a candidate for a theological degree, with secondary school education (the latter being indispensable for *pure foolishness*) . . . Indeed, transposed into hugeness, Wagner does not seem to have been interested in any problems except those which now preoccupy the little decadents of Paris. Always five steps from the hospital. All of them entirely modern, entirely *metropolitan* problems. Don't doubt it. (CW 9)

Ultimately, however, it is the final paragraph of section 9 that puts the finishing touches on Nietzsche's assault on Wagner's characters and plots. And while the rhetoric itself retains the spirit of the essay itself as a satyr-like play which comes after the modern tragedy that *is* Wagner,[55] Nietzsche's rhetoric is deceptively substantive. In particular, his claims here amount to the following: Wagner, that champion of vitalism, who supposedly gives life and the necessity of its cycles priority over the category of the intellect, actually creates characters who are life-negating. The proof: none of his characters can affirm their own activity without succumbing to 'modern ideas', nor can they will the direction of future life in the form of progeny. 'Have you ever noticed . . . that Wagner's heroines never have children? – They *can't*. – The despair with which Wagner tackled the problem of having Siegfried born at all shows *how* modern his feelings were at this point' (CW 9). Instead, Nietzsche suggests, Siegfried must 'emancipate' Brünnhilde, Parsifal must become a saint, and most of the rest of them need some form of redemption that lies outside their vital being, found either in the transformation of consciousness at death (Tristan and Isolde) or through the grace of another (the Dutchman, Tannhäuser, or Kundry and the Knights of the Grail). The inescapable conclusion, of course, is that if Wagner is a 'high priest' of anything, it is decadence. Truly he is in the vanguard of modernity, but he is no 'modern-day Aeschylus'.

---

[55] For Nietzsche's claim that Wagner should have seen his *Parsifal* as the satyr-like play of his own Wagnerism, see NCW 'Wagner as Apostle of Chastity' 2.

With these remarks, Nietzsche turns his attention to Wagner's prose works in section 10. Considering that Wagner's writings are ostensibly the foundation of his philosophical musings on art, as well as the theoretical basis for how philosophy and art would be merged, this section is the final piece of evidence Nietzsche adduces to prove that in matters of philosophy as well as art, Wagner is a fraud.

Nietzsche begins his line of attack by ridiculing Wagner's deification at the hands of the Germans, and then moves on to point out just how odd and unusual it is for a musician to write about the meaning of his own music.

> Not every music so far has required a literature: one ought to look for a sufficient reason here. Is it that Wagner's music is too difficult to understand? Or is he afraid of the opposite, that it might be understood too easily – that one will *not* find it *difficult enough* to understand? As a matter of fact, he repeated a single proposition all his life long: that his music did not mean mere music. But more. But infinitely more. – '*Not mere* music' – no musician would say that. (CW 10)

As this passage clearly suggests, there is something dubious about a musician who writes about the meaning of his own music. But it is especially dubious for a musician who professed to follow Schopenhauer's teachings about music as the art form *par excellence*. For if it is true that music accesses the ground of all appearance most directly; if the power of music really does possess the ability to convey meaning in an immediate and irrefutable way, and is for this reason why 'the other arts speak only of shadows while music speaks of the essence' (WWR 1, 52), then why in the world is Wagner writing prose works about his own compositions, as if the writings themselves will tell us *more* about the nature of his music than what the music, in principle, should tell us on its own?

With the allusion here to Schopenhauer's doctrine of the principle of sufficient reason, namely that we should inquire into the ground or reason for why something is and not otherwise, Nietzsche once again parries Wagner using Schopenhauer in order to expose just how philosophically unacquainted Wagner was with the philosopher whom he revered. Instead, Nietzsche accuses Wagner of being an unconscious disciple of Hegel, not only in the sense that his prose works were, like Hegel's philosophical writings, turgid, long-winded and obscure, but also in the sense that Wagner's music is, like the dialectical process of the Idea itself, forever 'becoming' and 'developing'. Wagner required a literature, Nietzsche tells us, not because he embodied Schopenhauer's teachings in music, but because he was in actuality a lifelong commentator on the 'Idea', and it is here that Nietzsche cites a particularly obscure section from an essay by Wagner called 'A Communication to my Friends' (1851) in order to support his argument.

In accusing Wagner of being a disciple of Hegel, there are two lines of criticism here worth noting. First, by calling attention to this early essay, Nietzsche's intention is to expose the stylistic parallels that exist between Wagner and Hegel. The passage from 'A Communication' is as tortuous as Wagner's passages get, and not only does it sound conspicuously Hegelian in terms of its ideology, it is also written in the typically bad style that is characteristic of Hegel.[56] But the essay is also relevant in the sense that it predates Wagner's acquaintance with Schopenhauer. This fact is likewise noteworthy because despite that acquaintance, Wagner's style never really changed. Indeed, unlike Nietzsche, who recognised the beauty and clarity of Schopenhauer's writings, and who had done everything in his power to outshine him, Wagner continued to write in the same 'Hegelian' way as he always had. In fact, Wagner's post-Schopenhauerian prose works continued to be every bit as turgid, long-winded and obscure as before. The unstated conclusion, which echoes those found in section 4, is that Wagner hardly underwent any real 'conversion' experience, either religiously or artistically, after he became acquainted with Schopenhauer. Wagner simply misunderstood the philosophy that was implicit in his most characteristic works of art.[57]

---

[56] Compare the section in question in PW 1: 346–8, 'A Communication to my Friends'.
[57] Compare GS 99.

Unfortunately Wagner was not simply a disciple of Hegel in the stylistic sense. By accusing Wagner of being a lifelong commentator on the 'Idea', Nietzsche is also telling us that his art is more deeply interwoven with the essence of Hegel's philosophy in the pejorative sense. In the first place the 'Idea', when philosophically considered, is hardly clear and distinct. But just as clear concepts and honest investigations in philosophy had been replaced by the 'hollowest word-mongering' and a host of theatrical gestures, such as speaking of the 'Idea' with raised eyebrows and a sombre voice, so too do we find Wagner's grand musical offerings to be nothing more than musical patchwork and motifs whose efficacy was realised, as the Hegelian philosophy's had been, by 'impressing, flabbergasting, mystifying, and throwing sand in the reader's eyes through all manner of tricks' to achieve its ends (FW 'Predecessors' 4). Once again, then, we find Nietzsche advancing the same criticism about Wagner's art that we found in section 7; namely, Wagner never really composed from inspiration or genius, but rather laboriously cobbled together his tiny, cellular sound animations by uniting them with an actor's gesture and a host of theatrical tricks. Hence Schopenhauer's most famous follower, Richard Wagner, was not Schopenhauerian at all. Wagner's music was the artistic likeness of the wordsmithing, ink-slinging, mindless scribbling of German philosophy at which Schopenhauer had once thrown his most furious thunderbolts.[58]

When we consider, however, that Nietzsche's intention as a whole is to discredit Wagner as being anything other than a philosophical and artistic fraud, there is another thread that we need to trace out to the arguments that Nietzsche makes here, as it follows upon the idea that Wagner simply misunderstood the philosophy that was implicit in his most characteristic works of art. After all, the misunderstanding could be innocent enough, in which case it would matter very little that Wagner's art, and the philosophy that he introjected into it, had anything to do with one another. In that case, the fact that Wagner happened upon Hegel as a means

---

[58] See PP 1, 'On University Philosophy', for an especially delicious polemic on German philosophy as the handmaiden of theology.

to gain credibility for his early artistic views only shows that artists in general, and Wagner in particular, need that 'protective armor', that 'previously established authority' in order to disseminate their views (GM III 5). But if Wagner is a fraud in the most essential sense, then it is perfectly consistent for him to have pandered to the lowest common denominator of German sensibility as a means to vindicate his art. After all, the same Germans who 'raved about Hegel' are that 'extremely crude mass' of the theatregoing public. Wagner understood this. He realised that if he could seduce men's spirits after the same manner as Hegel, he might win over that 'extremely crude mass' of German sensibility, which 'makes no pretensions to real art', and thereby establish his tyranny for acting over that same mass of theatregoers.

> Let us remember that Wagner was young at the time Hegel and Schelling seduced men's spirits; that he guessed, that he grasped with his very hands the only thing the Germans take seriously – 'the idea,' which is to say, something that is obscure, uncertain, full of intimations; that among Germans clarity is an objection, logic a refutation . . . Let us keep morals out of this: Hegel is a *taste*. – And not merely a German but a European taste. – A taste Wagner comprehended – to which he felt equal – which he immortalized. – He merely applied it to music – he invented a style for himself charged with 'infinite meaning' – he became the *heir of Hegel*. – Music as 'idea.' – And how Wagner was understood! The same human type that raved about Hegel, today raves about Wagner; in his school they even *write* Hegelian. (CW 10)

In this passage, then, we finally have the full effect of what Nietzsche means by claiming that Wagner's art is the aesthetic consequence of Hegel's system, not Schopenhauer's – a claim that is no compliment to either Hegel or Wagner.[59] At the same time, by pitching Schopenhauer's challenge to Hegel alongside Nietzsche's own challenge to Wagner into the generally convoluted mess regarding

---

[59] Compare BGE 244.

'European' versus 'German' events in history (and therefore who is succeeding whom), there is one final line of attack that Nietzsche brings to bear in maintaining that Wagner was the unconscious disciple of Hegel. In particular, Wagner's propinquity to Hegel and not to Schopenhauer meant that Wagner had succumbed to the German *Geist* in becoming one with 'the great delayers of history', a criticism that not only echoes those found in section 357 of *The Gay Science*, but also anticipates those we will find in Nietzsche's first postscript. In GS 357, for instance, Nietzsche tells us that by obstinately clinging to God and divinity, the German contemporaries of Schopenhauer had delayed the latter's triumph of atheism, and so failed to align themselves with part of the great chain of being that would become 'heirs of Europe's longest and most courageous self-overcoming'. In this *genuine* movement of European history, 'Hegel in particular was its great delayer par excellence, with his grandiose attempt to persuade us of the divinity of existence, appealing as a last resort to our sixth sense, "the historical sense"' (GS 357). Before long, however, the very idea that history should be seen as the self-expansion of the world spirit captivated – and 'Germanised' – all of Europe, even France. And now of course, with his *Parsifal* on offer, Wagner had finally shown his true colours by aligning himself with the great philosophical delayer of the Germans as well. In other words, the final criticism that we find here in section 10 is that Wagner became every bit as 'idealistic' as Hegel, and therefore in matters of culture, he became every bit as 'German'. Wagner became the heir to Hegel in matters of style, in matters of substance, and above all in matters of culture. Here was Nietzsche's answer to the question that had persistently badgered Wagner during his entire artistic career: what is German?[60]

> It was not with his music that Wagner conquered them, it was with the 'idea' – it is the enigmatic character of his art, its playing hide-and-seek being a hundred symbols, its polychromy of the ideal that leads and lures these youths to

---

[60] Compare PW 4: 151–69, 'What is German?'

Wagner; it is Wagner's genius for shaping clouds, his whirling, hurling, and twirling through the air, his everywhere and nowhere – the very same means by which Hegel formerly seduced and lured them! In the midst of Wagner's multiplicity, abundance, and arbitrariness they feel as if justified in their own eyes – 'redeemed.' ... After all, they are, without exception, like Wagner himself, *related* to such bad weather, German weather! (CW 10)

With these final comments, Nietzsche concludes the section by reaffirming the rhetorical analogy he had introduced in sections 1–3 between geography and culture, the intersection of which effectively symbolises the stylistic contrast, and through that the 'spiritual' dichotomy that exists between himself and Wagner. The grey, gruesome and foggy music of Wagner belongs with the geography of the 'north', while the 'dance of the stars', the music of the spheres, and the 'exuberant spirituality' of both belongs to the geography of the 'south', something that the great 'idealistic delayer of history' and of German culture, Wagner, knows nothing about.

Sections 11–12

The final two sections of the text are concerned with summing up Nietzsche's criticisms of Wagner and, as far as Nietzsche is concerned, with deducing the adverse consequences that follow for culture from an uncritical acceptance of Wagnerism. In weighing up these criticisms, including those we found in section 10, the real question is why they should matter for Nietzsche's case against Wagner. After all, accusing an artist of deception is scarcely news in the broader sense, so one can hardly expect to be taken seriously when the object of one's polemic is to blame an artist for engaging in their métier. Still less can one blame an artist for reflecting on and writing about it. In fact, there is so little here that is ostensibly threatening once we step back to consider it that the fact that Nietzsche dedicated an entire pamphlet to Wagner clearly indicates that he did feel threatened. This in itself should tell us a great deal about how the charges that we find within it, including the consequences Nietzsche deduces for culture, are intimately bound up with Nietzsche's attempt to 'overcome' Wagner.

A word of warning here: to think of Wagner as some kind of static obstacle that Nietzsche overcomes in the same way that an athlete might leap over a hurdle on their way to the finishing line is to fatally misunderstand Nietzsche's relationship to Wagner. As our analysis has shown time and again, Nietzsche's case against Wagner is completely driven by his competition with him. Wagner is *the* central philosophical and artistic problem of Nietzsche's project as a whole, for in Nietzsche's estimation, Wagner either united, or came the closest to uniting, the philosophical and artistic drives for the purposes of culture. Rightly or wrongly, Wagner had become the *de facto* 'philosopher who speaks music'. This is precisely where the battle is for Nietzsche, and it is what makes his confrontation with Wagner so necessary. By laying out his indictment, and by labouring to prove that Wagner does not measure up to the bar that Nietzsche judges he had set for himself in both his music and philosophy, Nietzsche is at the same time trying to establish the proposition that he has achieved what Wagner had not. We must never forget or lose sight of the fact that Nietzsche's project as a whole was *Wagner's problem first*. This is not about overcoming a hurdle. This is precisely what Nietzsche says it is: 'a declaration of war, in aesthetics'.[61] This is about victory, hegemony and taking pleasure in the spoils of war. What Nietzsche is trying to establish for his readers (and for posterity) is that he is more Wagnerian than Wagner. By diverting the great stream of Wagner's thought into run-off, Nietzsche would assume the philosophical and artistic current for himself.

To be sure, nothing demonstrates the factuality of this motive, and the true origin of the animus against Wagner on this point, than a letter Nietzsche wrote to his disreputable musician-friend and confederate Heinrich Köselitz (Peter Gast) six days after Wagner's death, just as the first part of his masterpiece *Zarathustra* – in other words, the 'proof' of his achievement over Wagner – had been 'finished

---

[61] SL (1969: 240 [KSB 8: 446–7]), letter to Malwida von Meysenbug, 4 October 1888.

exactly in that sacred hour in which Richard Wagner died in Venice' (EH 'Why I Write Such Good Books' TSZ 1).

It was hard to be for six years the opponent of a man whom one has admired above all others, and I am not built coarsely enough for *that*. Eventually, it was the old Wagner against whom I had to defend myself; as for the real Wagner, I shall be in good measure his heir . . . Last summer I felt that he had taken away from me all the people in Germany worth influencing, and that he was beginning to draw them into the confused and desolate malignancy of his old age.[62]

And not six months later, amid draft notes for his *Zarathustra*, we find Nietzsche rather candidly admitting his methodology, which details the 'artistic nature' of his 'breaking away' as a means to create,[63] as well as the following note that confesses the very motive on which his methodology is based: 'To become artist (one who creates), saint (one who loves), and philosopher (one who knows) *in one person:* – *my practical goal*!' (UF 16[11], autumn 1883).

Thus, as we can so clearly see, the real problem that Wagner posed for Nietzsche was that, at every step of the way, he threatened to overshadow and eclipse Nietzsche's own project of becoming, as his 'Schopenhauer as Educator' essay had long ago foretold, the artist, the philosopher and the saint for culture (SE 5). This is precisely what Nietzsche is telling us in his letter to Gast: Wagner had 'taken away' the few people in Germany worth influencing, who could not discriminate between the truly Wagnerian project in the hands of Nietzsche, and the two-bit carnival at Bayreuth where redemption was being handed out 'to the people' by Wagner, the counterfeit

---

[62] SL (1969: 208 [KSB 6: 333–4]), letter to Peter Gast, 19 February 1883.

[63] Compare 'To seize *for myself* the total *immorality* of the artist in regard to my material (humankind): this was the work of my last few years. To seize for myself *intellectual freedom* and *joy*, in order to be able to create and not to be tyrannized by alien ideals. Basically, it matters little *what* I had to break away *from*: yet my favorite mode of *breaking away* was artistic in nature: i.e., I constructed an *image* of what had captivated me up until then: like Schopenhauer, Wagner, the Greeks (genius, saints, metaphysics, all previous ideals, the highest morality) – simultaneously a *tribute out of gratitude*' (UF 16[10], autumn 1883).

metaphysician and the high priest of theatricality and effects. So here again, when we examine the criticisms we find in section 10 about Wagner's music and its relationship to his prose works, it is important to recognise that these criticisms presuppose Nietzsche's *own* project about the musicality of language and his role in becoming the authentic 'philosopher who speaks music' for culture *contra* Wagner.

We need only briefly recall a couple of noteworthy sections in *The Gay Science* and *Beyond Good and Evil* that help to ground Nietzsche's challenge here about the relationship between language and music and its role in judging Wagner's whole art as 'unmusical'. First, given the importance that Nietzsche attaches to the power of music to convey meaning in an immediate and irrefutable way, we now know that section 106 of *The Gay Science* ('Music as an Advocate') is extremely valuable for the insight it gives into the world of Wagnerian propaedeutics and Nietzsche's application of those teachings for his own project; namely, that one must be capable of 'making music' even out of one's ideas or philosophy of life with the intent of communicating their value in an immediate and irrefutable way. To 'make music' through the medium of language is, in effect, to connect the abstract ideas of reason with their affective significances by appealing to the common denominators that both spoken language and music in the more restricted sense share – that is tone, stress, intonation and rhythm – and then uniting them through the fixable signs of the language in order to go beyond the 'dictionary definition' of the word. Done properly, of course, this is to convey meaning or content in an immediate and irrefutable way, for like music in the more restricted sense, it is not possible to *refute* a tone. At the same time, however, we know that Nietzsche went further than this in thinking that he *had* done it properly, for when it came to judging the deed of his *Zarathustra*, Nietzsche bragged often enough that he had given humanity its profoundest book and also the most perfect in its language.[64] And in *Ecce Homo*, Nietzsche tells us that *Zarathustra* actually is music itself for which no less than a spiritual

---

[64] See, for instance, SL (1969: 299 [KSB 8: 340]), letter to Karl Knortz, 21 June 1888, and SL (1969: 302 [KSB 8: 377]), letter to Malwida von Meysenbug, end of July 1888.

rebirth in the art of hearing would be necessary before one found ears to hear (EH 'Why I Write Such Good Books' TSZ 1). When paired with his criticisms of style in language in *Beyond Good and Evil*, and how little German style seemed to depend on the sounds of the language themselves – so much so that even its good musicians (read Wagner) wrote poorly – the point was only too easily proved for Nietzsche that, compared with him, even Germany's best musician is no 'real musician'.[65] By contrast with Nietzsche's *Zarathustra*, which is both philosophically profound *and* musical in nature, and is, incidentally, truer to Schopenhauer's doctrine about music, here we find Wagner, the alleged disciple of Schopenhauer, devoting a whole literature to the 'meaning' of his music. From the standpoint of philosophy, the work should be musical. From the standpoint of music, the work should be its own value and meaning, and should not require a theoretical or philosophical exegesis in order to become *more* meaningful. Here was the proof that Wagner did not unite the philosophical and artistic drives for the purposes of culture, and certainly could not wear the crown of the 'philosopher who speaks music' for culture.

If, then, Wagner's art no longer signified the rebirth of art as culture, then Wagner and his art could only be seen as one more symptom of a declining culture that had begun with Socrates. As far as Nietzsche was concerned, philosophy and art had always been for the very few, and yet Wagner had managed to win over that 'extremely crude mass' of German sensibility in both philosophy and art in order to establish his tyranny over them. What does this signify as a feature of artistic cultures on the decline? As Nietzsche tells us in section 11, it signifies the emergence of acting, fakery and pretence in art. Wagner became the great rabble-rouser for art's sake. Wagner *popularised* art in the same way that Socrates had *popularised* philosophy, and so he possessed, like the despised Socrates, 'the strongest democratic-demagogic tendency' (UF 23[14], winter 1872–73). This is the great warning of Nietzsche's penultimate section. 'In declining cultures, wherever the decision comes to rest with the masses, authenticity

---

[65] Compare BGE 246–7.

becomes superfluous, disadvantageous, a liability. Only the actor still arouses *great* enthusiasm' (CW 11).

In declining cultures, Nietzsche continues, 'the *golden age* dawns for the actor', for if the judgement of what constitutes a 'great success' in art rests with that 'extremely crude mass' of the theatregoing public – the same public that 'makes no pretensions to real art' – then the very notion of expertise, and of those who work tirelessly to hone their skills down more specialised paths, can simply be overthrown by the egoistic self-promoter whose real talent lay in rousing the rabble. This is the function of the actor in declining cultures, and the sense of the warning here associated with them. With his philosophical and artistic presumption, the *poseur* Wagner gave 'meaning' to his 'total work of art', and in doing so, he rallied all those who laboriously toiled away under the many branches and tributaries of learning in music and philosophy, infusing them with a newly found 'meaning' and pretence for themselves.

> The conductors, machinists, and stage singers were the first he convinced. Not to forget the orchestra musicians – these he 'redeemed' from boredom. The movement Wagner created even reaches over into the field of knowledge: gradually, relevant sciences emerge from centuries of scholasticism . . . All of these are, as I own gratefully, the best among Wagner's admirers, those most deserving of our respect – they are simply right to admire Wagner. They share the same instinct, they recognize in him the highest representative of their type, they feel changed into a power, even a greater power, ever since he kindled them with his own ardor. For here, if anywhere, Wagner's influence has been *beneficial*. Never yet has so much been thought, desired, and worked in this area. Wagner has given all of these artists a new conscience. What they now demand of themselves, *get* from themselves, they never demanded of themselves before Wagner came along – formerly, they were too modest. (CW 11)

As we read through the content of this excerpt, which occupies a considerable portion of section 11, it should be apparent that

Nietzsche's 'warning' here about the emergence of the actor in music is hardly a categorical condemnation. But given what we now know about Nietzsche's case of Wagner, it is much easier to understand why Nietzsche's rhetoric on these points is equivocal. For if Nietzsche is to have any hope of laying a legitimate claim to the Wagnerian succession, then his principal task, as we have illustrated in depth and repeatedly emphasised, is to prove that he has become 'more Wagnerian than Wagner' (and likewise 'more Schopenhauerian than Schopenhauer'). This takes a very simple propositional form: whatever Wagner did, Nietzsche did better. What this means, in effect, is that what seems to be a warning from one side is really gratitude and praise on the other.[66]

As the tenor of this excerpt makes clear, Wagner's influence on all these varied experts in music and scholarship really *was* beneficial because it raised them out of the depths of the excessively narrow and restrictive concerns of scholasticism that inevitably follow as a result of pursuing increasingly minute forms of inquiry and analysis. Like a true physician of culture, Wagner restrained this fragmentation of our drive for knowledge by putting it into the service of a comprehensive world-view, an artistic vision, thereby consolidating and unifying it. Thus Wagner, like Schopenhauer, demolished secularisation in learning and scholarship, and with it, the barbarising power of the sciences, by arousing meaning at the deepest level of being.[67] Hence the debt of gratitude on these points should be evident, for considering that 'blind science' and 'knowledge at any price' were the essential causes of our degenerating instincts for life and the fundamental failure of the Socratic culture, the significance of both Schopenhauer

---

[66] In this connection, see also Thomas Mann, who notes that he had always taken Nietzsche's 'immortal critique of Wagner' as simply 'a panegyric in reverse, another form of eulogy' (1985: 100).

[67] As noted previously, these virtues had long dominated Nietzsche's thinking about where the 'supreme dignity of the philosopher' is revealed as a 'physician of culture'. One need only consult his 'philosophers book' to see just how psychologically invested he was in this conception. See, for instance, UF 19[27] and 19[41], summer 1872–early 1873, for a couple of excellent representative examples.

and Wagner lay precisely in their attempt to restore the relationship between art and life for the purposes of culture.[68] All of this means, however, that Nietzsche clearly recognised the advantages that would accrue to himself in stirring up a more 'democratic' enthusiasm for philosophy and art, and thus of 'rousing the rabble' in precisely the same way he accuses Wagner of doing with his own art. And judging by the laundry list of 'influential people' Nietzsche did try to persuade at Wagner's expense during the final years of his productive life, including those who might otherwise have been condemned to the category of 'art idiots' in his more private moments, we can be fairly certain that the few people in Germany still worth influencing constituted a coveted prize for one who was bold enough to have declared a war on Wagner in aesthetics as a means to succeed him.

To be clear then, Nietzsche's praise of Wagner is intimately bound up with his criticisms of him, and that means that the one side cannot really be understood without the other. Once we appreciate that both sides work together to promote the single unified objective that Nietzsche is 'more Wagnerian than Wagner', his warning about the emergence of acting into music makes much more sense, since Nietzsche's indictments of Wagner are designed to exonerate himself by implication. So while there is definitely gratitude and praise for Wagner's achievements in restraining the omnidirectional nature of our drives, demolishing the thraldom of excessive learning, and arousing meaning at the deepest level of our being, if by the same token that 'extremely crude mass' can be just as easily aroused by the idea of 'music as performance' and 'expression at any cost', and cannot discriminate between the truly Wagnerian project in the hands of Nietzsche and the *panem et circenses* of Bayreuth, then Wagner has simply ushered in the degeneration of all art into acting for effect; and those who have followed him, including 'the few people in Germany still worth influencing', have mistakenly found in

---

[68] Compare UF 35[11], spring–summer 1874.

him the highest representative of their type – decadence. This is the flipside and final warning with which Nietzsche leaves us in section 11:

> A new spirit prevails in the theater since Wagner's spirit prevails there: one demands what is most difficult, one censures severely, one praises rarely – what is good, even excellent, is considered the rule. Taste is no longer required; not even a voice. Wagner is sung only with a ruined voice: the effect is 'dramatic.' Even talent is precluded. *Espressivo* at any cost, as demanded by the Wagnerian ideal, the ideal of decadence, does not get along well with talent . . . Neither taste, nor voice, nor talent: Wagner's stage requires one thing only – *Teutons!* – Definition of the Teuton: obedience and long legs. (CW 11)

It is noteworthy that Nietzsche closes section 11 by likening the 'democratic understanding' (or misunderstanding) of Wagner and his art with Bismarck and the founding of the Reich. Both, Nietzsche thinks, are hollow forms of giganticism that have replaced authenticity in thought and deed. 'To judge by the Wagnerites I have known till now', Nietzsche confided to his surrogate mother and spiritual friend Malwida von Meysenbug shortly after he first published *Beyond Good and Evil*, 'the whole Wagner business seems to be an unconscious approach to Rome, which is doing the same thing inwardly as Bismarck is doing outwardly.'[69] But, as he tells us in *Beyond Good and Evil*, 'this is the age of the masses. They lie on their bellies before everything that's massive.' It matters not that Wagner has become the high priest of theatricality and effects and that his art is counterfeit and untrue. The same is true for politics. 'To them the statesman is "great" if he builds them a new Tower of Babel or some monstrosity of empire and power' (BGE 241). In the meantime, the true artistic genius (read Nietzsche) goes unnoticed; his '*victory over energy* remains without eyes to see it and consequently

---

[69] SL (1969: 256–7 [KSB 7: 257]), letter to Malwida von Meysenbug, 24 September 1886; compare NCW 'Wagner as Apostle of Chastity' 1.

without song and singers', for the 'great thought alone that gives greatness to a deed and a cause' in the microcosmic sense is constantly overshadowed by the desire for giganticism (BGE 241).

It is in this connection that we arrive, almost by logical deduction, at the three 'demands' that Nietzsche exacts from art in section 12, which closes the formal portion of *The Case of Wagner*.

1 That the theatre should not lord it over the arts
2 That the actor should not seduce those who are authentic
3 That music should not become an art of lying

As we can see, these three demands target the very core of Nietzsche's competition with Wagner. But for reasons that will become readily apparent as we seek to close the circle in the two postscripts and the epilogue, we will defer deducing the full implications of these demands, principally because of what we might already surmise about the Wagner case; namely, that Nietzsche's competition with Wagner necessarily entailed reaching into Wagner's own 'bag of tricks' in order to overcome him.

5
The Case of Nietzsche; or, How to Become More Wagnerian than Wagner

First postscript

At this point, we are ready to deal with the two postscripts and the epilogue. These final sections as a whole tend to be rather didactic, principally because if Nietzsche is to have any hope of 'overcoming' Wagner, it is in his interest to demonstrate how Wagner has fallen short of 'becoming Wagner' by summing up the adverse consequences of Wagnerism for culture. In this respect, the first postscript is concerned with executing a summary judgement on Wagnerism. This is 'The Price we are Paying for Wagner' which, as a catechism for Nietzsche's self-overcoming as well as the object of his victory, would finally attempt to sort out the truly Wagnerian project in his own hands from the actuality of Wagnerism, which has all the marks of a declining culture.

Given our analysis of Wagner's arguments about culture, and the fact that Nietzsche wholeheartedly endorses them as a means to test his art against his own theories about what governs the decline and rebirth of culture, it should come as no real surprise that Nietzsche opens his discussion by highlighting the small but robust German resistance to Wagner that is set against the backdrop of a declining culture with Wagner at its head. The reason for highlighting this resistance is, of course, that Nietzsche is leading it, but as soon becomes clear, the form and expression that it takes is every bit as important, for it shows that there is still a vestige of 'youth' or 'vitality' left within German culture in resisting Wagner at all.

Nietzsche begins by telling us rather notably that this German resistance to Wagner, which dogged him for three-quarters of his life, was *instinctual*, not ratiocinative. This point is significant when it comes to testing Wagner's art against his own theories, for we know that, according to Wagner, life and not intellect is the ultimate ontological category, and that means that the strength, vitality and flourishing of a given culture is bound up with the emphasis that that culture places on the categories of life and instinct over the categories of intellect and reason. Here we see this idea play out in the context of the German resistance to Wagner: 'He was resisted like a sickness – not with reasons – one does not refute a sickness – but with inhibition, mistrust, vexation, and disgust, with a gloomy seriousness, as if he represented some great creeping danger' (CW First Postscript). Nietzsche continues by noting that only when Germany's 'honored aestheticians' began waging an 'absurd war against Wagner's principles with "if" and "for"' did they finally succumb to the enervation of their instincts by trying to refute Wagner with reasons, and warns us immediately of that fact, stating that 'an instinct is weakened when it rationalizes itself'. This too is significant, for we also know that, according to Wagner, the more a given culture emphasises the categories of intellect or reason over those of will and life, the more anaemic, enervated and decadent that culture has become. Hence what Nietzsche says next about the German resistance to Wagner in the context of ascending and declining cultures should be thoroughly unsurprising.

> If there are any signs that, in spite of the total character of European decadence, the German character still possesses some degree of health, some instinctive sense for what is harmful and dangerous, this *dim* resistance to Wagner is the sign I should like least to see underestimated. (CW First Postscript)

In this connection, Nietzsche then points out the potential advantages to being part of this German resistance. The Germans may be the great delayers of history, but this only means that they are comparatively younger than other civilisations in Europe. As we have just pointed out, the youthfulness of a culture has its advantages, for like all young cultures, the categories of life and instinct are stronger than those of mind and intellect, and so those Germans who have shown an *instinctual* aversion to Wagner (Nietzsche obviously means himself) have proven at the same time that there is still 'health' and 'well-being' in the promise of a European culture – one that has not yet succumbed to the degenerating instincts of the Socratic culture. Once again, then, the real answer to the question 'What is German?' cannot be found in Wagner's solution, which was to succumb to the final, struggling, moribund state of Socratic culture with its degenerating instincts for life. Wagner's solution had simply *delayed* what is genuinely German in matters of culture by clinging to the death throes of another. Yet the proof that German culture is still young and on the ascent, if only in the hands of Nietzsche himself, is that the aversion to Wagner is *instinctive*.

With this turn, Nietzsche's assault on Wagnerism with what is 'truly German' in matters of culture is now intended to call into question Wagner's own identity, and by extension his ability as a German to resolve the problem of German culture. Nietzsche's attack here in the context of 'true Germans' itching to be rid of Wagner occurs in perhaps the most famous footnote of his entire oeuvre, where he begins by asking,

> Was Wagner a German at all? There are some reasons for this question. It is difficult to find any German trait in him. Being a great learner, he learned to imitate much that was German – that's all. His own nature contradicts that which has hitherto been felt to be German – not to speak of a German musician. – His father was an actor by the name of Geyer. A Geyer [vulture] is practically an Adler [eagle]. – What has hitherto circulated as 'Wagner's Life' is *fable convenue* [a myth that has gained acceptance], if not worse. I confess my mistrust of every point attested to only by Wagner himself. He did not have pride enough for any truth about himself; nobody was less proud. Entirely like Victor Hugo, he remained faithful to himself in biographical questions, too – he remained an actor. (CW First Postscript)

Given Wagner's talent for acting, and especially his aptitude for feigning what he is not, the obvious thrust of Nietzsche's attack here is that Wagner's 'German identity' must be counterfeit too. Regrettably, the evidence Nietzsche marshals for this conclusion is as dirty as it gets, but the ire that must have surely stirred in Nietzsche's breast while dispensing it was no doubt the product of comparing his more recently refurbished sense of self against the knowledge of his one-time commission as Wagner's obsequious errand boy. Such errands, among others more or less humiliating to the pretence of philosophical dignity, included tracking down 'tulle with gold stars and polka dots' for the 1869 Christmas Nativity scene that the Wagners had constructed of Christ in the manger,[1] and hassling over the thankless duties Wagner had handed to him in the production of his autobiography *Mein Leben*. As early as January 1870, for instance, Nietzsche had been enlisted to help Wagner revise and edit the opening chapters of his autobiography – that 'myth' that had since 'gained acceptance'. Nietzsche's job had been to manage the content, polish the prose and proofread the manuscript for chronological errors,[2] but in the process he soon became acquainted with how one weighs up the messy material of one's own history for the purposes of artistic presentation[3] – the very skill, indeed, he would later claim as so important for us to learn from artists, and one that he found 'needful' in giving style to his *own* character.[4] Yet here in the midst of correcting galley proofs, as well as hassling over printing costs for small selections of the autobiography to be published as Wagner's Christmas gift to Cosima,[5] Nietzsche was also tracking down the right coat-of-arms for the frontispiece. Wagner's letter to Nietzsche, dated 16 January 1870, reveals that the central problem connected with this little errand, and the extent to which Nietzsche was roped into addressing it, stemmed from the fact that while the bird of prey on Wagner's

---

[1] DBCW 1: 18, 15 December 1869.
[2] SLRW: 768–9, letter to Friedrich Nietzsche, 14 January 1870.
[3] Compare SL (1969: 56 [KSB 3: 37–8]), letter to Gustav Krug, 4 August 1869, where he alludes to precisely this point.
[4] See, for instance, GS 290 and 299.
[5] DBCW 1: 13n, 30 November 1869.

crest closely resembled an eagle, it was actually supposed to be a cinereous vulture. Since there was the distinct possibility that one might be mistaken for the other, Wagner prevailed upon Nietzsche to doctor the engraving so that a 'vulture' would clearly be recognised, complete with its characteristic ruffle.[6]

Now what makes Nietzsche's attack especially dirty is that one's coat-of-arms is supposed to represent one's family's genealogy across time. Hence the fact that Wagner's crest depicted a visually ambiguous form of vulture, and that the vulture in turn was intended to pay homage to his stepfather, Ludwig Geyer, who was himself an actor, clearly implies that Wagner himself came from a line of dissemblers, and that Geyer was Wagner's real father. However, there is an even more destructive aspect to Nietzsche's rhetoric here. The common Semitic noun for both 'vulture' and 'eagle' is the same (רשנ *nšr*), and both Geyer and Adler were common Jewish surnames in Germany at the time. So when we stop to consider that Wagner himself had once accused the Jews of being not much more than expert imitators of other cultures without having a genuine culture of their own, there is no question that Nietzsche is accusing Wagner of being 'Jewish' and therefore of counterfeiting his 'German identity'. Once again, and true to form, Nietzsche had turned Wagner's theoretical arguments against Wagner himself. The attack here could not be more personal or relevant to Nietzsche's 'self-overcoming', nor perhaps more detrimental to the mythology of Wagner in the hands of the Völkisch, anti-Semitic movement of his mindless partisans.

In the context of this exegesis, what we find Nietzsche arguing is that since Wagner is not 'truly German', this means that his swan song, *Parsifal*, cannot possibly be an authentic contribution to German culture. Wagner was simply the expert appropriator of a 'foreign culture' and the imitator of its symptomology, while all that was 'young' and 'healthy' and 'authentically German' robustly resisted him. And what is the proof Nietzsche adduces for

---

[6] SLRW: 769–70, letter to Friedrich Nietzsche, 16 January 1870; see also Fischer-Dieskau (1978: 41).

this claim? When the inscription on Wagner's grave was changed from 'Redemption for the Redeemer'[7] to 'Redemption *from* the Redeemer' (CW First Postscript), the few healthy and authentic spirits still left in Germany made it known that they refused to accept the final, struggling, moribund state of Socratic culture as being one with their own, and so spurned the decaying and despairing decadent himself, who 'sank down helpless and shattered before the Christian cross' embracing it with his final music drama *Parsifal* (NCW 'How I Broke Away from Wagner' 1).

Once again, the arguments that we find here demonstrate only too clearly that the form of Nietzsche's victory over Wagner is completely embedded within, and depends upon, the theoretical consequences that follow from Wagner's own conception of culture. To openly proclaim that Wagner was not truly German, or German enough, and hence could not fill the void in the way that he himself had declared was so necessary to bring about the rebirth of a new European culture is simply another way of telling us that Wagner was not the self-appointed prophet and 'artist of the future' that he claimed himself to be. But because Nietzsche must, at the same time, convince his readers that *he* is the true heir to the Wagnerian project, it follows that the form of Nietzsche's victory over Wagner depends every bit as much on whether *he* has remained true to the theoretical consequences that follow from Wagner's own conception of culture. This is the only way that he can divert the great stream of Wagner's thought into the philosophical and artistic current he is claiming for himself, and supplant Wagner as the true prophet of a new European culture.

Up to this point, Nietzsche has done everything in his power to indicate that Wagner has not lived up to his own hype. The nature of the charges, which culminate in the judgement that Wagner is an actor, are clearly intended to discredit Wagner before his own theories. But now that Nietzsche is faced with executing the final sentence on Wagnerism, and of trying to wrap up *The Case of Wagner*, he is at long last confronted with

---

[7] The closing words of Wagner's final music drama *Parsifal* after the eponymous hero heals the wound of Amfortas with the holy spear.

the problem of 'overcoming' Wagner, and of proving that he is Wagner's legitimate successor. This is precisely what we find in the balance to the first postscript, where the battle lines that Nietzsche first drew in the preface finally come full circle. In particular, we now know that the meaning of Nietzsche's duel with Wagner is rooted in the dispute over who has unified the philosophical and artistic drives for the purposes of culture, and that means that there must in turn be a final resolution to the problem of whether art and the purely self-creative act are sufficient to confront the burden and weight of existence. As we noted in our analysis of the preface, *The Case of Wagner* is *a dispute over the nature of music itself.* Since we also know that music conveys meaning or content in an immediate and irrefutable way, the battle for Nietzsche was always going to be over the nature of that meaning, and how it is used to confront the facts of existence. Throughout our analysis, we have seen how Nietzsche believed that Wagner used and abused this power for purely theatrical purposes, and how Wagner's tyrannical instinct for the theatre, with its populist manner of speaking, was able to 'cement together the chaos of the people' (UF 32[22], beginning 1874–spring 1874) by pandering to the lowest common denominator of a culture that was already 'going speedily downhill'.[8] We can see with perfect clarity why Nietzsche had claimed in *Human, All Too Human* (reissuing it as a 'greatest hit' in his *Nietzsche Contra Wagner*) that music is the 'late fruit of every culture', and why Wagner's music in particular is the most illustrious representative of decadence and a declining culture. But for those who can recognise the symptoms of declining cultures and overcome them (Nietzsche, of course, means himself), it follows that such figures belong to a youthful culture still on the ascending curve of life, and so create art out of the 'overfulness of life', not out of its impoverishment.

At the same time, the fact that Wagner had 'taken away' the few people in Germany still worth influencing gives us some indication of the task Nietzsche had set for himself in 'overcoming'

---

[8] HAH2 171, 'Music as the Late Fruit of Every Culture'; NCW 'A Music Without a Future'.

Wagner. For how much more dangerous was it for Nietzsche that virtually all of Germany believed that the 'truly Wagnerian' project was in the hands of 'Wagner the actor', that expert appropriator of a 'foreign culture' and the imitator of its symptomology, who had finally won over the masses by spoon-feeding them, not the substance, but merely the *effects* of a religious experience? This is precisely what Nietzsche now proposes to take up in the remainder of the postscript by reminding his readers of the adverse consequences that follow from Wagner's 'contribution' to culture.

The complaints that Nietzsche issues here largely echo those found in section 11 where he laments the democratic-demagogic tendency that was introduced into art by Wagner's tyrannical instinct for acting. As with section 11, the principal concern Nietzsche raises is that once decisions about art come to rest with the masses, all 'authenticity' in art becomes superfluous. With the alarming rise in the number of art idiots, and the presumption of the layman over 'all severe, noble, conscientious training in the service of art' (CW First Postscript), Nietzsche is once again warning us of the descent into theatrocracy in the eerily Platonic sense.[9]

> The theater is a form of demolatry in matters of taste; the theater is a revolt of the masses, a plebiscite *against* good taste. – *This is precisely what is proved by the case of Wagner:* he won the crowd, he corrupted taste, he spoiled even our taste for opera! (CW First Postscript)

Nowhere is this descent into theatrocracy more terrible for Nietzsche than when it comes to the musical depiction of religious sentiment. After all, if Wagner is the philosopher that he pretends himself to be, then he should have heeded the words of his great teacher, Schopenhauer, who repeatedly proclaimed that the theme of philosophy must restrict itself to the realm of experience, and that the science of metaphysics, if there is to be one

---

[9] Compare a rather pregnant passage on these points in Plato, *Laws*, 700D–701A.

at all, must remain immanent, since any metaphysical conception one deduces about what is 'behind' or 'beyond' experience can only be valid in relation to that experience.[10] 'For this reason', Schopenhauer had explained, philosophy 'must remain cosmology, and cannot become theology. Its theme must restrict itself to the world; to express from every aspect *what* this world *is*, what it *may be* in its innermost nature, is all that it can honestly achieve' (WWR 2, ch. 48).

No doubt it is true that the mystic kernel of early Christianity produced a message of affective delight, but it did so at the expense of a doctrine of negative knowledge. Yet by confronting the actuality of mysticism, Schopenhauer had managed to address the problem of negative knowledge in terms of setting bounds for what is possible for philosophy (and, by extension, what is possible for art).[11]

> Now it is in keeping with this [limitation] that, when my teaching reaches its highest point, it assumes a *negative* character, and so ends with a negation. Thus it can speak here only of what is denied or given up; but what is gained in place of this, what is laid hold of, it is forced (at the conclusion of the fourth book) to describe as nothing; and it can add only the consolation that it may be merely a relative, not an absolute, nothing. For, if something is not one of all the things that we know, then certainly it is for us, in general, nothing. Yet it still does not follow from this that it is nothing absolutely, namely that it must be nothing from every possible point of view and in every possible sense, *but only that we are restricted to a wholly negative knowledge of it; and this may very well lie in the limitation of our own point of view.* Now it is precisely here that the mystic proceeds positively, and therefore, from this point, nothing is left but mysticism. (WWR 2, ch. 48, our emphasis)

---

[10] See, for instance, WWR 1, 15, and WWR 2, ch. 17.
[11] In fact, Schopenhauer sets this out so clearly that it is difficult to comprehend how scholars who comment on him could conclude that his final position advocates a kind of nihilism.

Once we heed Schopenhauer's analysis, which so clearly defines the proper objects of philosophy from those of mysticism, we can see that the vocation of the philosopher is to understand and interpret the universality of experience correctly, in which one's metaphysical conception merely provides the kernel or the key to the meaning and content of experience. And since metaphysics, on Schopenhauer's *own* account, is immanent, not transcendent, that likewise means that the effect of music must be immanent, inasmuch as music, and the metaphysical will that it embodies (in Schopenhauer's system at least), *ceases* to be a valid interpretation for the affections of experience once we regard it as an *ens extramundanum*. Thus while Christianity might have produced a message of ecstasy and affective delight, the mystical element of fusion in identity with the transcendent did not produce anything that we can reasonably *depict* in music. Yet here Wagner was, the high priest and hierophant of Schopenhauer's philosophy, claiming as late as 1880 that 'music reveals the inmost essence of the Christian religion', and that 'as pure form of a divine content freed from all abstractions, we may regard it as a world-redeeming incarnation of the divine dogma of the nullity of the phenomenal world itself' (PW 6: 223, 'Religion and Art'). So rather than heed the philosophy of Schopenhauer, who specifically argued that metaphysics remains immanent, not transcendent, Wagner went right along his merry way talking about music and the metaphysical will that it embodies precisely as if it were this *ens extramundanum*, and in increasingly wondrous and miraculous terms, thus either misunderstanding, ignoring or discarding the philosopher whom he professed to follow and revere. Hence in what follows, Nietzsche cannot help but give full vent to his indignation when he asks, quite sardonically, whether Wagner liberates the spirit.

> There is nothing weary, nothing decrepit, nothing fatal and hostile to life in matters of the spirit that his art does not secretly safeguard: it is the blackest obscurantism that he conceals in the ideal's shrouds of light. He flatters every nihilistic (Buddhistic) instinct and disguises it in music; he flatters everything Christian, every religious expression of decadence. Open your ears: everything that ever grew on

the soil of *impoverished* life, all of the counterfeiting of transcendence and beyond, has found its most sublime advocate in Wagner's art... (CW First Postscript)

Of all of the furious thunderbolts that Nietzsche hurled in Wagner's general direction, this passage is arguably the most celebrated. But once again, we need to understand that the reason for Nietzsche's animus is that *The Case of Wagner* is a dispute over the nature of music itself and how it is used to confront the facts of existence. And since the spoils from Nietzsche's duel with Wagner grant nothing less than the right to inherit the mantle of the 'philosopher who practices music' for culture, Nietzsche must show that Wagner's art got the *how* wrong when compared with his own.

In the first place, rather than using music to affirm the image of 'everything terrible, evil, cryptic, destructive and deadly underlying existence' (AT 4) without resorting to 'the *moral* interpretation and significance of existence' (AT 5), Wagner's final tone poem, *Parsifal*, does precisely this. And with this unfortunate descent into theatrocracy, 'mere Germans' no longer know the difference between good and bad music, and so really believe that 'Wagner the actor', that expert appropriator of the decidedly 'un-German' Socratic culture, is capable of handing out musical redemption with his final tone poem. In reality, however, Wagner's final act had merely pandered to the current degenerative tendencies of a culture that was already on the decline.

How do we know that Wagner's art got the *how* wrong when compared with that of Nietzsche? The provisional answer, of course, is that Nietzsche wants his *Zarathustra* to be seen as the legitimate counter-offer to the effects of Wagnerism, and that must mean that Nietzsche's *Zarathustra* (at least in his own estimation) got both the *what* and the *how* right. In order to advance this claim, let us take a couple of robust and highly instructive points regarding the conception and deed of *Zarathustra* in order to contrast them with the charges Nietzsche has brought against Wagner.

First, in terms of the profundity of its spirit and the authenticity of its achievement, *Zarathustra* is, in Nietzsche's estimation, far deeper, higher and more comprehensive than all the 'moral and religious absurdities' and 'all the counterfeiting of transcendence and beyond' (CW First Postscript) that we find in Wagner's music. Redemption may have been Wagner's problem, but he was above all 'a first-rate actor' (CW 8), and that means that his celebration of the spirit in *Parsifal* is a pious fraud. On the other hand, when it comes to his *own* 'redemption', we find Nietzsche telling his readers in *Ecce Homo* that he was no less than 'reborn' through the inspiration of his *Zarathustra* (EH 'Why I Write Such Good Books' TSZ 1), a claim that culminates in the sanctimonious admonition that 'one pays dearly for immortality: one has to die several times while still alive' (EH 'Why I Write Such Good Books' TSZ 5). And when it comes to the deed of *Zarathustra* itself, the lyrical hyperbole practically overflows with the 'proof' of just how authentic and original Nietzsche is, not only as the poet who says Yes to life, but as the very embodiment of one who can *make music out of it*. In this regard, the claims Nietzsche makes for himself are so extravagant that they are worth excerpting at some length. In particular, Nietzsche assures us that

> This work stands altogether apart. Leaving aside the poets: perhaps nothing has ever been done from an excess of strength. My concept of the 'Dionysian' here became a *supreme deed*; measured against that, all the rest of human activity seems poor and relative. That a Goethe, a Shakespeare, would be unable to breathe even for a moment in this tremendous passion and height, that Dante is, compared with Zarathustra, merely a believer and not one who first *creates* truth, a *world-governing spirit*, a destiny – that the poets of the Veda are priests and not even worthy of tying the shoelaces of a Zarathustra – that is the least thing and gives no idea of the distance, of the *azure* solitude in which this work lives. Zarathustra possess an eternal right to say: 'I draw circles around me and sacred boundaries; fewer and fewer men climb with me on ever higher mountains: I am building a mountain range out of ever more sacred mountains.'

Let anyone add up the spirit and good nature of all great souls: all of them together would not be capable of producing even one of Zarathustra's discourses. The ladder on which he ascends and descends is tremendous; he has seen further, willed further, been *capable* further than any other human being. In every word he contradicts, this most Yes-saying of all spirits; in him all opposites are blended into a new unity. The highest and the lowest energies of human nature, what is sweetest, most frivolous, and most terrible wells forth from one fount with immortal assurance. Till then one does not know what is height, what depth; one knows even less what truth is. There is no moment in this revelation of truth that has been anticipated or guessed by even *one* of the greatest. There is no wisdom, no investigation of the soul, no art of speech before Zarathustra; what is nearest and most everyday, here speaks of unheard-of things. Epigrams trembling with passion, eloquence become music, lightning bolts hurled forward into hitherto unfathomed futures. The most powerful capacity for metaphors that has existed so far is poor and mere child's play compared with this return of language to the nature of imagery.

And how Zarathustra descends and says to everyone what is most good-natured! How gently he handles even his antagonists, the priests, and suffers of them *with* them! – Here man has been overcome at every moment; the concept of the 'overman' has here become the greatest reality – whatever was so far considered great in man lies beneath him at an infinite distance . . . The psychological problem in the type of Zarathustra is how he that says No and *does* No to an unheard-of degree, to everything to which one has so far said Yes, can nevertheless be the opposite of a No-saying spirit; how the spirit who bears the heaviest fate, a fatality of a task, can nevertheless be the lightest and most transcendent – Zarathustra is a dancer – how he that has the hardest, most terrible insight into reality, that has thought the 'most abysmal idea,' nevertheless does not consider it an objection to existence, not even to its eternal recurrence – but rather one reason more for being himself the eternal Yes to all things, 'the tremendous, unbounded saying Yes and Amen.' – 'Into all abysses I still carry the blessings of my saying Yes.' – *But this is the concept of Dionysus once again.* (EH 'Why I Write Such Good Books' TSZ 6)

Here we have Nietzsche telling us, in all seriousness, that his genius for 'making music' out of his affirmative instinct for life has been raised to the rank of a supreme deed against which 'all the rest of human activity seems poor and relative'. Indeed, all the great souls of humanity put together 'would not be capable of producing even one of Zarathustra's discourses', for all along the great ladder of being on which he ascends and descends so freely and easily, Nietzsche–Zarathustra 'has seen further, willed further, been *capable* further than any other human being'. And since no spirit has penetrated the heights and depths of truth so profoundly, it follows that there had been 'no wisdom, no investigation of the soul, no art of speech before Zarathustra'. Obviously, then, the nature of his afflatus could only sound the depths of what is nearest and everyday in the most matchless way, taking the form of 'epigrams trembling with passion, eloquence become music, lightning bolts hurled forward into hitherto unfathomed futures'.

And how fortunate for us that there is no *ressentiment*, Christian or otherwise, to be found in Zarathustra either. We see this in how Zarathustra freely descends down the great ladder of being to meet others where they are and to say what is most good-natured to everyone. Indeed, the gentle manner in which he handles even his antagonists, the priests, and suffers with them and from them proves the degree to which Zarathustra's freely willed justice, pure lovingkindness and real noble-mindedness are rooted in *genuine* compassion – that wholly immediate, disinterested and instinctual sympathy for the sufferings of others that was the crown jewel of Schopenhauer's ethics, and the sole source of action that, according to him, has any genuine moral worth (BM 18). Here, humanity *qua* humanity is perpetually overcome, for when we compare Christian morality with Zarathustra's instinctual goodness, all that was once considered great in humanity lies beneath him at an infinite distance.

Finally, we must recall that in him all oppositions are blended into unities and well forth from a single fount with immortal assurance. Hence it is this ability to accept oppositions and, in effect, to transcend them that makes the psychological type of Zarathustra possible, and the highest type of everything that exists. We see this in how Zarathustra, the spirit who bears 'the heaviest fate' and the 'fatality of a task', can be at the same time the 'lightest and most transcendent' spirit, for truly the attributes of heaviness, severity and the forces of gravity necessarily entail those of lightness, joy and the forces of levity, and are, like all other oppositions, blended in him into ever higher unities. But unlike the Germans, who get lost in their opposites (EH 'Why I Write Such Good Books' CW 1), Zarathustra can take decisive action for the purposes of life; and so, even as the psychological type of Zarathustra 'says No and *does* No to an unheard-of degree', he is nevertheless 'the opposite of a No-saying spirit'. The spirit who thus has 'the hardest, most terrible insight into reality' can still say Yes to all things. This makes Zarathustra a dancer, one who can 'make music' out of the suffering of life.

Nietzsche then tells us at the beginning of section 7 that it was *he* who invented the dithyramb, not Wagner (EH 'Why I Write Such Good Books' TSZ 7). For the artist whose art 'always leads in two directions, out of the world as auditory drama into an enigmatically related world as visual drama and vice versa', the dithyrambic dramatist is forced to 'retranslate visible motion into soul and primal life and, on the other hand, to see the hidden fabric of the inner world as a visual phenomenon and to give it the semblance of a body' (WB 7). So even though the essence of the dithyrambic dramatist is at once the synthesis of 'the actor, the poet, and the composer' on Nietzsche's *own* admission (WB 7), we are meant to understand that only Wagner is the actor in the pejorative sense, while the poet, composer and mask of *Zarathustra* is the *bona fide* genius of culture. Consequently, the entire vision of the dithyrambic dramatist as we find it in Nietzsche's essay 'Richard Wagner in Bayreuth' really refers to 'the pre-existent poet of *Zarathustra*' – he plainly tells us this (EH 'Why I Write Such Good Books' BT 4), for after all, Nietzsche's 'psychological distillation' of Wagner is at stake, in which the Dionysian future of music would triumph over Wagner's ruin 'before the Christian cross'.[12]

Then, after devoting the remaining part of the section to excerpting Zarathustra's 'Night-Song', Nietzsche begins section 8 by warning his readers that 'nothing like this has ever been written, felt, or *suffered*'; indeed, that only a god such as Dionysus suffers after this manner. Yet, to complement his suffering, Dionysus needs Ariadne, for Dionysus is the formless light, while Ariadne is the current that opposes and embodies the light. Without embodiment, light cannot conceive its own content. Hence, as Nietzsche confesses here regarding Dionysus, the god who suffers, 'the answer to this sort of dithyramb of solar solitude in the light [namely, the 'Night Song'] would be Ariadne. – Who besides me knows what Ariadne is!' (EH 'Why I Write Such Good Books' TSZ 8). For the god who recognises the pain of time and becoming as the precondition for the creative act, the joy in creating is itself the great salvation from suffering.[13]

Now again, if any of this sounds familiar, it should, for as we have resolutely maintained, nothing less is at stake than the right to inherit the mantle of the 'philosopher who practices music' for culture. And since we now know that *The Case of Wagner* is a dispute over the nature of music itself and how it is used to confront the suffering of existence, we know that Wagner's music in particular is the ideological battleground through which the *what* of existence (its suffering) is confronted. Therefore, by setting up his *Zarathustra* in direct competition with Wagner and the effects of Wagnerism, Nietzsche, in his 'psychological distillation' of Schopenhauer and Wagner, is doing everything he can to show that *he* is the logical choice over his two great intellectual mentors in getting both the *what* (the suffering of existence) and the *how* right (by making music out of it) – so much so that

---

[12] See especially TSZ IV 'The Wizard' 2, where the Wizard is converted into the Intellectual Penitent, and thus the disciple of Nietzsche–Zarathustra, after the latter wrests the confession from the Wizard that his art merely 'dissembles' and that he is, in reality, 'not a great man'.

[13] See, for instance, TSZ II 'In the Happy Isles'.

this now includes winning the charms of Ariadne as the universal symbol of embodied suffering, as well as the actual woman who, akin to Nietzsche, suffered most from Wagner the Minotaur and the temptations of his labyrinth (in other words, Cosima herself). The conclusion that we are meant to draw is that only *Zarathustra* promises the truly Dionysian world-view, and with it, the coming of a new tragic age (EH 'Why I Write Such Good Books' BT 4). By contrast, Wagner's *Parsifal*, the so-called 'artwork of the future', had in reality succumbed to the degenerating instincts of the older, declining and entirely 'un-German' Socratic culture, with Christianity as its crown jewel, and so had fallen victim to his own theories about what governs the decline and rebirth of culture.

Of course, the question that we now need to address in the context of Nietzsche's case is whether this is actually true. Because Nietzsche has framed *The Case of Wagner* as a dispute over the nature of music itself in which he 'overcomes' the decadence of a declining culture through the hardest acts of self-creation, the implication is that Nietzsche really does believe that he had created an epistemic gap between himself and modernity when it came to the business of criticising Wagner's art. And since, in addition, Nietzsche believed that his 'microcosmic' approach to the problem of culture (which culminates in his *Zarathustra*) is what has fostered this epistemic gap, and therefore makes his criticism of Wagner possible, the issue we must finally resolve is what relationship Nietzsche's charges against Wagner have to his 'overcoming' him. For even as he seeks to sum up his case against Wagner in this postscript, it will become clear that Nietzsche, in the very act of challenging Wagner, resorts to many of the same 'devices' and 'tricks' that he openly accuses Wagner of using. As a matter of fact, nothing can more easily be proven. In this sense, how can we be sure *what* the charges against Wagner actually are? Once we realise that Nietzsche's case against Wagner is completely bound up with the case he is trying to make for himself, it becomes apparent that Nietzsche is playing a dangerous game in trying to become 'more Wagnerian than Wagner'.

For instance, who would possibly baulk at the suggestion that Nietzsche's forceful and insistent showcasing of his *Zarathustra* is itself one grand theatrical gesture, complete with all the 'moral and religious absurdities' and 'all the counterfeiting of transcendence and beyond' that we supposedly find in Wagner's music? Again, who would seriously dispute that Nietzsche leaves himself open to the charge that he, and not Wagner, has subordinated the problem of suffering to the theatrics of gesture in challenging him to a duel over who has suffered more profoundly in creating their respective works?

Nietzsche openly ridicules Wagner for the seductiveness of his art: Wagner is an 'old magician' and a 'clever rattlesnake' (CW 3). He is also 'the master of hypnotic tricks' (CW 5); and yet Nietzsche is fully aware of the power of 'music as an advocate', especially when it comes to the art of prose, to 'seduce' men's ears and hearts to both error and truth alike. Indeed, the primary lesson we derived from GS 106 is that rhythm is an unconscious exercise in hypnotics in which the mind does not know that it is being mesmerised. But perhaps more to the point is that *Zarathustra* is just such a seducer (EH 'Preface' 4), and more than a few times in *Ecce Homo* Nietzsche makes it clear that the great art of musical prose had been discovered by him and him alone.[14] Thus with 'my pen in hand and my notebook before me', ready to jot down 'something of which I have never thought, something that I wish to impress upon my mind' in Wagner's company,[15] Nietzsche must have learned very quickly indeed that it is not possible to refute a tone. Here is a dogma that he clearly coveted for himself, especially once we recognise that *Zarathustra* is intended to be the great musico-philosophical deed against Wagner.

The philosophy of Zarathustra, Nietzsche tells us, 'overflows' with life, and so naturally the great art of musical prose that conveys these 'glad tidings' must be 'healthy', for music, like 'health' and 'sickness', conveys irrefutable values. Once we accept the claim that Wagner 'has made music sick' (CW 5) and that a sickness cannot be refuted (CW First Postscript), we are more likely to accept the claim that the tones of *Zarathustra* may be healthy,

---

[14] Compare EH 'Why I Write Such Good Books' 4.
[15] SL (1969: 118 [KSB 4: 144–5]), letter to Richard Wagner, 18 April 1873.

irrespective of whether we actually resolve the further problem of whether tones themselves can be 'healthy' or 'sick'. So as far as 'theatricality' and 'effects' are concerned, Nietzsche is every bit as aware of how to use music to captivate and polarise his audience, even though he lays the blame for this exclusively at Wagner's feet. Perhaps for this very reason we can easily discount what Nietzsche–Zarathustra says about Bizet in the pamphlet – after all, Nietzsche did. 'What I say about Bizet', Nietzsche wrote to his friend Carl Fuchs in one of his final letters, 'you should not take seriously; the way I am, Bizet does not matter at all. But as an ironic antithesis to Wagner', Nietzsche conceded, 'it has a strong effect.'[16] Of course, the rhetorical or 'musical effect' Nietzsche has in mind is simply to polarise those who read him in favour of what *he* defines as 'healthy'. Music as Circe indeed.

Yet by far the most convincing test on these points comes from comparing the gesture of slander that we find with regard to Wagner's *Parsifal* in this postscript with Nietzsche's very 'untheatrical' reaction upon hearing the prelude in Monte Carlo the year before. After telling us that Wagner's art wears out our spirit through sensuous persuasion, Nietzsche concludes his thoughts on *Parsifal* by noting that

> In the art of seduction, *Parsifal* will always retain its rank – as *the stroke of genius* in seduction. I admire this work; I wish I had written it myself; failing that, *I understand it*. – Wagner never had better inspirations than in the end. Here the cunning in his alliance of beauty and sickness goes so far that, as it were, it casts a shadow over Wagner's earlier art – which now seems too bright, too healthy. Do you understand this? Health, brightness having the effect of shadow? almost of an *objection*? – To such an extent have we become *pure fools*.[17] – Never was there a greater master in dim hieratic aromas – never was there a man equally expert in all small infinities, all that trembles and is effusive, all the feminisms

---

[16] SL (1969: 340 [KSB 8: 554]), letter to Carl Fuchs, 27 December 1888.
[17] That is, like Parsifal himself, the pure fool, enlightened by compassion.

from the *idioticon* of happiness! – Drink, O my friends, the philters of this art! Nowhere will you find a more agreeable way of enervating your spirit, of forgetting your manhood under a rosebush. – Ah, this old magician! This Klingsor of all Klingsors![18] How he thus wages war against *us*! us, the free spirits! How he indulges every cowardice of the modern soul with the tones of magic maidens! – Never before has there been such a *deadly hatred* of knowledge! – One has to be a cynic in order not to be seduced here; one has to be able to bite in order not to worship here. Well then, you old seducer, the cynic warns you, *cave canem*. (CW First Postscript)

Perhaps what is most remarkable about this excerpt is just how typical it is of Nietzsche's approach to philosophy as a whole. If he is not depreciating and devaluing in order to annex and incorporate, he is ceremoniously ejecting through the front door what eventually creeps in through the back in the name of his 'self-overcoming'. In this respect, *The Case of Wagner* is no different, only more conspicuous, because the war for him is deadly serious. This excerpt in particular is a perfect example of what one might call 'rhythmic perturbations' at the 'cellular level', in which Nietzsche's tiny, spasmodic sound ejaculations are laboriously held together by the dramatic gesture of slander, and where once again his favourite theatrical prop, *ressentiment*, enters in with flourish and fanfare. Yet by all accounts, this is 'sick' music, Wagner's music, right down to the wearisome monotony of his rhetoric. At the same time, if Nietzsche is to have any hope of reclaiming 'all the people in Germany worth influencing',[19] then surely he must try to become 'Wagnerian' in the most recognisable sense.

Yet when we compare *this* Wagner, the Wagner of theatricality and effects, with Nietzsche's actual reaction to the prelude, it is apparent that Wagner had already achieved the very object Nietzsche coveted for himself, confirming in one stroke not only

---

[18] The 'black magician' in *Parsifal*, who seduces away the knights of the Grail.
[19] SL (1969: 208 [KSB 6: 333–4]), letter to Peter Gast, 19 February 1883.

the ideological battleground at the core of *The Case of Wagner*, but which image of Wagner it was actually necessary for him to 'overcome'. In a letter sent to his musician-friend and confederate Heinrich Köselitz (Peter Gast) dated 21 January 1887, and 'in purely esthetic [*sic*] terms', Nietzsche admits

> Did Wagner ever compose anything better? The finest psychological intelligence and definition of what must be said here, expressed, *communicated*, the briefest and most direct form for it, every nuance of feeling pared down to an epigram; a clarity in the music as descriptive art, bringing to mind a shield with a design in relief on it; and, finally, a sublime and extraordinary feeling, experience, happening of the soul at the basis of music, which does Wagner the highest credit, a synthesis of states which will seem incompatible to many people, even 'loftier' people, with a severity that judges, an 'altitude' in the terrifying sense of the word, with an intimate cognizance and perspicuity that cuts through the soul like a knife – and with a compassion for what is being *watched* and *judged*. Something of that sort occurs in Dante – nowhere else. Has any painter ever painted such a melancholy gaze of love as Wagner did with the last accents of his prelude?[20]

---

[20] SL (1969: 260 [KSB 8: 12–13]), letter to Peter Gast, 21 January 1887; compare 'Overture to *Parsifal*, greatest gift I've been granted for a long time. The power and severity of feeling, indescribable, I know nothing else that grasps Christianity so deeply and presents it so distinctly for our sympathy. Entirely exalted and moved – no painter has painted such an indescribably melancholy and tender *gaze* as Wagner . . . the greatest masterpiece of the sublime I know, the power and severity in capturing a terrifying certainty *in* the very compassion for it; no painter has painted such a dark, melancholy gaze as Wagner does in the last part of the overture. Nor has Dante, nor has Leonardo. It's as if for the first time in many years someone were speaking to me about the problems that trouble me; not, of course, with the answers I hold ready but with Christian answers – which ultimately have been the answers of stronger souls than those brought forth by our past two centuries. Admittedly, when listening to this music one sets one's Protestantism aside like a misunderstanding: just as, I won't deny, Wagner's music in Monte Carlo made me set aside even the *very good* other music (Haydn, Berlioz, Brahms, Reyer's Sigurd overture) that could be heard there like a misunderstanding of music. Strange! As a lad I intended for myself the mission of bringing the Eucharist to the stage; –' (UF 5[41], summer 1886–autumn 1887).

Given what Nietzsche says here about his initial reaction to the *Parsifal* prelude, is it in any way surprising that in the context of his *Ecce Homo*, composed one year later, *Zarathustra* now manages to 'outdo' *Parsifal*? Absolutely not. In *Parsifal* we find the finest psychological intelligence and definition of what must be expressed and communicated. Every nuance of feeling is 'pared down to an epigram', and above all, there is 'clarity in the music as descriptive art'. In *Zarathustra*, however, we find our protagonist sounding the depths of wisdom in what is nearest and most everyday through 'epigrams trembling with passion, eloquence become music, [and] lightning bolts hurled forward into hitherto unfathomed futures'.

Again in *Parsifal*, we find that there is a sublime and extraordinary happening of the soul at the basis of its music that enables it to synthesise seemingly incompatible states with an '"altitude" in the terrifying sense of the word'. But this achievement does not compare to the 'azure solitude' in which Zarathustra lives, for he has 'seen further, willed further, and been more capable than any other human being in history'. In Zarathustra, all opposites are blended into a new unity in which 'the highest and lowest energies of human nature, what is sweetest, most frivolous, and most terrible wells forth from one fount with immortal assurance'. And while the music of *Parsifal* exhibits compassion 'for what is being *watched* and *judged*' — a feature that is found perhaps nowhere other than in Dante — we must remember that 'Dante is, compared with *Zarathustra*, merely a believer and not one who first *creates* truth, a *world-governing spirit*, a destiny' (EH 'Why I Write Such Good Books' TSZ 6). After all, to recognise the cyclical necessity that governs nature is to recognise the great truth that creation and destruction entail one another. The creation of newer forms always arises from the conflict between older, existing forms.

> This is because the *one* will objectifies itself in all Ideas; and in striving for the highest possible objectivation, it now abandons the lower levels of its appearance after a conflict between them, in order to appear on a higher and thus more powerful level. No victory without a struggle. . .
> (WWR 1, 27)

Indeed, 'since the higher Idea or objectivation of the will can come forward only by overpowering the lower Ideas' (WWR 1, 27), it follows that resistance and pain mark the nature of all manifested forms. But in striving to overcome these older forms, resistance and pain become at the same time the necessary precondition for all subsequent creation. Knowing this great truth, a world-governing spirit such as Zarathustra can affirm the pain of time and becoming that is fundamental to the great circle of life itself, for he knows that the pain of manifestation is the precondition for all creative acts, and that the joy in creating is itself the great salvation from suffering.[21] Clearly, then, whatever Wagner does, Nietzsche does better.

As we are therefore presented with a choice between Nietzsche's 'psychological distillation' of Schopenhauer and Wagner on the one hand, and Wagner's 'companion piece and supplement to Schopenhauer's philosophy' on the other (GS 99), it is clear that the 'logical choice' should be Nietzsche's *Zarathustra*. Only the latter had managed to get both the *what* and the *how* right by fusing the philosophy of vitalism to 'the *most vital* **art form**' (UF 7[7], spring–summer 1883), and so had assimilated his two great intellectual mentors into a living paradigm of philosophical and artistic unity that would promise us a return to the Dionysian world-view (EH 'Why I Write Such Good Books' BT 4).

Only in this sense can we understand that what comes next in the postscript *really is* the psychological consequence of *Zarathustra* and the Dionysian world-view winning out over *Parsifal* and the Socratic world-view. Since it is Nietzsche's art and not Wagner's that promises to return us to the Dionysian world-view, it follows that Nietzsche's battle for the 'soul of Ariadne' must now take place in earnest. To inaugurate the battle, Nietzsche takes aim at the effects of Wagnerism on what he calls the 'female Wagnerian'.

---

[21] As we have already noted, Schopenhauer's ethics by no means imply his metaphysics, but with his 'will to power' and 'Dionysian world-view', Nietzsche essentially derived an ethical principle that is far more fundamentally consistent with Schopenhauer's own metaphysical conception. In Nietzsche's frame of reference here, this is part and parcel with getting the *what* and the *how* right.

Nietzsche begins his discussion by speaking of the 'female Wagnerian' as if she were some kind of determinate sub-species of female who had especially suffered at the hands of Wagner's degenerate artistic instincts. But it need hardly be said that Nietzsche's only real concern was with one 'female Wagnerian' in particular: Cosima Wagner. This becomes abundantly clear once we recognise that in challenging Wagner to a duel over the meaning of the philosopher who practises music for culture, Nietzsche is presenting his readers with a choice between one or the other of two competing alternatives for culture. Yet it is obvious that these two alternatives are intended to be mutually exclusive, since to choose Nietzsche over Wagner, the self-proclaimed 'antipode' of Wagner, implies that Wagner would have to be discarded. Since the suffering soul cannot serve two masters, even though by all accounts – namely his own – Nietzsche had won his duel with Wagner, the choice to elope with Dionysus over the pure fool that is Parsifal is not as easy and straightforward as it might seem to be at first. This is precisely how Nietzsche characterises the medical and psychiatric calamity that confronts the 'female Wagnerian'.

> What is a female Wagnerian, medically speaking? – It seems to me, a doctor can't confront young women too seriously with this alternative for the conscience: one or the other. – But they have already made their choice. One cannot serve two masters when the name of one is Wagner. (CW First Postscript)

The nature of this dilemma is compounded by the fact that Wagner's problem in particular – the 'problem of redemption' – so thoroughly and completely resonates with the degenerating instincts of the Socratic culture that it continues to seduce otherwise promising youth into the labyrinth. Remember, a sickness cannot be refuted: Wagner had already shown signs of his characteristic 'problem' before he ever met Cosima. But through her Catholic upbringing, which had militantly ingrained in her all manner of superstitious credulity, Cosima was naturally primed for Wagner's music, likewise also a 'sickness'. So when it came to augmenting 'Schopenhauer's effect' – once again *not* the effect Nietzsche wanted[22] – Schopenhauer's most famous follower, Wagner, managed alongside Cosima to transmogrify it into 'the moral and religious absurdities' that eventually became *Parsifal*.[23] As Köhler notes, 'when Nietzsche spoke contemptuously of Wagner's "prostration before the Cross," he was also thinking of his prostration before the woman who prayed at the Cross every day' (Köhler 2004: 513). In any event, the 'sickness' was complete.

> Wagner has redeemed woman; in return, woman has built Bayreuth for him. All sacrifice, all devotion: one has nothing that one would not give to him. Woman impoverishes herself for the benefit of the master, she becomes touching, she stands naked before him. – The female Wagnerian – the most charming ambiguity that exists today; she *embodies* the cause of Wagner – in her sign his cause triumphs! (CW First Postscript)

Yet after having devoted her entire life to Wagner's cause, Cosima would now find herself lost among the Wagnerians. Ariadne's golden thread, which had once rescued Wagner from his own labyrinth, which had once redeemed *him*, had now deserted her. After all, it had been five years since Wagner had died in Venice. Truly the 'old god was dead', and now the soul of Ariadne was every bit as lost as her erstwhile hero had once been in the labyrinths of his own creation. Fortunately Zarathustra, teacher of the 'overman', remained to instruct the soul of Ariadne that 'man is a thing to be surmounted' (TSZ I 'Introductory Discourse' 3); but before this critical step could even be acknowledged, Cosima would first need to come to terms with

---

[22] Compare UF 30[9], summer 1878 and GS 99 on these points.
[23] In one of his final draft letters to Cosima, Nietzsche notes his contempt for the nature of her influence on Wagner, telling her that 'You know very well how well I know the influence you exerted on Wagner – you know even better how much I despise this influence' (KSB 8: 604, draft letter to Cosima Wagner, early September 1888).

what is man and what is overman.[24] Wagner, after all, was just a man, not the second coming of Christ, as the soul of Ariadne had once believed. Thus here we assuredly find the final spearhead that Nietzsche–Zarathustra uses to wound Wagner–Parsifal on the cross. If only Zarathustra could convey his message to Ariadne to help her understand, perhaps she might in the end find herself confessing (and to Zarathustra's delight) that, after being 'abandoned by the hero, I dream about the superhero' (UF 13[1], summer 1883). Until that time, however, Nietzsche can only warn us here that

> He robs our youths, he even robs women and drags them into his den. – Ah, this old Minotaur! The price we have had to pay for him! Every year trains of the most beautiful maidens and youths are led into his labyrinth, so that he may devour them – every year all of Europe intones the words, 'off to Crete! off to Crete!' (CW First Postscript)

Perhaps, then, there is no more pregnant meaning behind the sense of Dionysus versus the Crucified (EH 'Why I Am a Destiny' 9), for no less than two competing alternatives for culture were at stake with philosophers practising music at their

---

[24] On these points especially, it did not take long for Nietzsche to reach out to Cosima following Wagner's death. Just six days after Wagner died in Venice, and in the very same letter in which he acknowledged that he would eventually become Wagner's 'heir', Nietzsche tells Gast that he had *already* sent a letter of condolence to Cosima. This is notable, for Nietzsche had cut off all relations with the Wagners since the episode with Dr Eiser in October 1877, when Wagner and Eiser had together conjectured that Nietzsche's poor health was the result of excessive masturbation. This is sometimes considered the 'cause' of the break between them. See, for instance, Magee (2000: 333–5), and more recently, Gilman's excellent article (2007). And indeed, Nietzsche's letter to Gast acknowledges that the estrangement had been for *six years*, thus dating the 'final blow' to 1877, precisely when these events occurred. See SL (1969: 209 [KSB 6: 337]), letter to Franz Overbeck, 22 February 1883, in which Nietzsche discusses the 'deadly offense' that came between them. But surely what had intensified Nietzsche's suffering during this time was that the woman of his affections would have known the entire story in all its embarrassing minutiae, and this latter fact might very well have pushed him over the edge. But with Wagner now out of the picture, it was presumably time for Nietzsche and his *Zarathustra* to move in.

head, and with his final collapse, Nietzsche certainly tried to convince the mistress of Bayreuth, and the official propagandist of Wagnerian dogma, that this was so. Now, why Nietzsche would bother trying to convince her remains a very valuable question; but if anything, the strained and complicated relationship Nietzsche had with Cosima, and the role she played as the high priestess of the Wagner cult, certainly reveals the extent to which she had successfully stage-managed Nietzsche's relationship with Wagner, one that primed him above all to assume the role of prostrate devotee who would willingly sacrifice himself in order to become finally 'worthy of tying the shoelaces' of such a god.[25] Remember that Cosima's sole concern was to deify Wagner's every word and deed. Just at a superficial level, Cosima's *daily* diary entries, which she began in 1869 after she permanently settled down with Wagner, and continued right up until the last day of his life on 13 February 1883, are perhaps the most definitive proof of this claim. But in addition, there are a handful of diary entries themselves that effectively proclaim the nature of this deification, and in doing so, resolve her conviction that the second coming was actually being fulfilled in the person of Wagner.[26] So those who, like Nietzsche, were lucky enough to be permitted entry to the hallowed halls of Tribschen, and then granted access to the adytum where the living god resided, were at the same time made to understand just how mundane their being was when compared with the Messiah figure of philosophy and music. Yet ironically, the dogma that taught Nietzsche the role of prostrate devotee who willingly makes sacrifices for one's god also taught him in the same stroke about the kind of woman who is enticed and magnetised by precisely this. This is what makes Nietzsche's battle for the 'soul of

---

[25] It is unfortunate that Cosima's letters to Nietzsche *still* have not been translated into English, even though the Nietzsche archive in Weimar published them in 1938. In this respect, English-speaking scholars are still comparatively in the dark about the extent to which Cosima controlled Nietzsche's earliest relationship with Wagner, and then shaped and determined what the influence would be, always of course for the benefit of Wagner. The facts, however, are plain. As Wagner's German biographer Joachim Köhler rightly notes, 'For Nietzsche as so many others, the way to Wagner led through Cosima's antechamber' (Köhler 2004: 507).

[26] See, for instance, CWD 2: 603, 20 January 1881.

Ariadne' so fascinating,[27] for the more Nietzsche tries to overcome Wagner by overcoming Cosima's *image* of Wagner, the more he seems willing to fall into the lap of the very woman who had deified Wagner in the first place, something that seems all the more fitting now that the 'old god is dead' and the new god, Dionysus, is there to supplant him.[28]

Second postscript and epilogue

With these closing remarks to the first postscript, Nietzsche's extensive, byzantine and psychologically invested challenge to Wagner has reached its apex. What remains in the second postscript and the epilogue simply underscores the principal conclusions, and in this regard what follows is a kind of summary indictment that is central both to how and in what sense Nietzsche has 'overcome' Wagner.

In this context, it is notable that Nietzsche begins the second postscript by formally underscoring the principal conclusion that

---

[27] One of Nietzsche's final letters is addressed to Cosima as 'Princess Ariadne' with the following note: 'Ariadne, I love you. Dionysus' (SL 1969: 346 [KSB 8: 572], letter to Cosima Wagner, beginning January 1889). And in his final letter to Jakob Burckhardt, Nietzsche notes that 'the rest is for Frau Cosima . . . Ariadne . . . from time to time we practice magic. . .' (SL 1969: 348, letter to Jakob Burkhardt, 5 January 1889).

[28] It should not go without mentioning that in the years following Nietzsche's final collapse, his sister Elisabeth, who, like Cosima, never had any real grasp of the intellectual life or spiritual depth of either Nietzsche or Wagner, nonetheless felt compelled to transform what life was left in him into the focus of a cult after she became clued in to her brother's cultural importance as the 'antipode' to Wagner. Succumbing to rather shameless and utilitarian motives, Elisabeth selected a home in Weimar, the seat of the great German muses Goethe and Schiller, and then put the ill philosopher 'on display', complete with flowing white robes, as the tangible god and living prophet of *Zarathustra*. Thus like Tribschen and Bayreuth, the Weimar home became a shrine of pilgrimage for the ardently devoted wishing to visit the living god within. And with her tendentious three-volume hagiography *Das Leben Friedrich Nietzsche*, the beginning of legend and mythmaking was born, an act that ran parallel to Wagner's own tendentious and artificial autobiography, *Mein Leben*. In this critical respect, both Cosima and Elisabeth pledged themselves as the first disciples of a cult that they were in large part responsible for founding. In many ways, the myth surrounding each figure is still very much in evidence and therefore at issue, yet for anyone who can surrender their prepossessions in order to see clearly into this period of Nietzsche's life, it is utterly heartbreaking in its effect. See Gilman (ed.) 1987: 237–62 for the full force of this less 'theatrical' final period.

frames *The Case of Wagner* as a whole; namely, that the essay is a declaration of war in aesthetics upon Wagner and all German taste in Wagnerism (CW Second Postscript). And since the nature of this war is rooted in a dispute over the nature of music itself, it would be reason enough, as Nietzsche laments here, for 'mere Germans' not to hear or understand the 'music' he had thus far made: 'I have given the Germans the most profound books they have – reason enough for the Germans not to understand a single word' (CW Second Postscript). Yet as he had begun the first postscript by highlighting the small but robust German resistance to Wagner and his role in leading it, Nietzsche tells us here that even though there has been a widespread misunderstanding of his declaration of war against Wagner, nonetheless 'on certain faces the lines of gratitude appear', and in certain cases, 'I even hear a modest exultation' (CW Second Postscript).

But to be 'understood in this matter', as Nietzsche claims he would prefer, would require him to admit the one thing that would give his hand away, namely, that the whole business of 'overcoming' Wagner really means becoming 'more Wagnerian than Wagner'. Because Nietzsche's personal challenge to Wagner is embedded within the theoretical implications of Wagner's own arguments about culture, his charges against Wagner necessarily depend upon successfully proving that Wagner's art embodies the very symptoms of declining cultures that Wagner himself had once identified in his own theories, in effect turning his own arguments against him. At the same time, Nietzsche is tasked with making a positive case for himself, for if he does in fact convince his readers that Wagner's art typifies a declining culture and not an ascending one – certainly no 'rebirth of tragedy' – he might, with all his grandstanding about *Zarathustra*, effectively lay claim to the Wagnerian succession for himself. It is only natural, then, that Nietzsche would recount his case against Wagner by first summarising the main features of Wagner's overall arguments about culture, which, in fact, he does here.

Thus, in declaring his war on Wagner and all German taste, Nietzsche begins by telling us something critical, namely, that he is not interested in celebrating 'other musicians' at Wagner's expense, for 'German culture' more generally was already on the decline. 'The decay was universal', Nietzsche observes (CW Second Postscript). Yet Wagner did not cause the decline of culture, for we know that this began long ago with 'Athenian self-dissection' (PW 1: 136, 'Artwork of the Future'), most notably in the figure of Socrates. Nevertheless Wagner ended up catalysing its sickness, because he was the most inwardly prepared to do so. Wagner, Nietzsche goes on to tell us, 'merely accelerated its tempo – to be sure, in such a manner that one stands horrified before this almost sudden, downward motion, abyss-ward' (CW Second Postscript). Instead of affirming the vitality of the instincts as he had once advocated, Wagner, like Socrates before him, had interpreted them as a decline, and so had allowed abstract intellect to displace the organic logic of will and life.[29] In the end, Wagner succumbed to the Socratic culture and so became, in effect, the leading disciple of Socrates, not Dionysus. As Nietzsche goes on to conclude,

> [Wagner] had the naïveté of decadence: this was his superiority. He believed in it. He did not stop before any of the logical implications of decadence. The others *hesitate* – that is what differentiates them. Nothing else. (CW Second Postscript)

What is especially notable here about dragging the corruption of 'other musicians' into the fray is that it fleshes out Nietzsche's argument about the universal signs of decay which he says he finds in all of German music, while at the same time it provides a reference point for Wagner's 'sudden, downward motion' into the abyss by comparison. This becomes quite evident when we connect it to the very next passage.

> What Wagner has in common with 'the others' – I'll enumerate it: the decline in the power to organize; the misuse of traditional means with the capacity to furnish

---

[29] As we know from Nietzsche's diatribe on Socrates, this is the formula for decadence. Battling the instincts goes *against* life, and is therefore associated with a *descending* or *declining* type of life. Compare TI 'The Problem of Socrates' 11.

any *justification*, any for-the-sake-of; the counterfeiting in the imitation of big forms for which nobody today is strong, proud, self-assured, *healthy* enough; excessive liveliness in the smallest parts; excitement at any price; cunning as the expression of *impoverished* life; more and more nerves in place of flesh. (CW Second Postscript)

So in terms of those 'universal signs of decay', Wagner was not the only musician who misused traditional means, imitated the big forms without self-assurance, or willed excessive liveliness and excitement at any price. Other musicians did the same, but they did so with less conviction. Remember, while other musicians hesitated before this universal decay, Wagner wholeheartedly embraced it. That means that the critical difference between Wagner and other musicians, in terms of their 'corruption', is simply one of degree. Obviously this has aesthetic implications for the case of Wagner: because other musicians, in terms of their corruption, present 'merely half' of Wagner's 'whole', they never captured the essence of decadence as completely as did Wagner. This is what makes him *incomparable* to other musicians.

> Those famous today do not write 'better' music than Wagner but merely less decisive music, more indifferent music – more indifferent because what is merely half is dated by *the presence of what is whole*. But Wagner was whole; but Wagner was the whole corruption; but Wagner was courage, the will, *conviction* in corruption – what does Johannes Brahms matter now? – His good fortune was a German misunderstanding: he was taken for Wagner's antagonist – an antagonist was *needed*. – That does not make for *necessary* music, that makes, above all, for too much music. – If one is not rich one should have pride enough for poverty. (CW Second Postscript)

As we can see, the trajectory of this argument, when we take it as a whole, could not more perfectly encapsulate the idea of an overall movement or tendency towards cultural decline as the background against which Wagner's 'sudden, downward motion' hastened to the abyss. Thus after fleshing out those common universal signs of decay and then telling us that Wagner had far surpassed them in terms of the absoluteness of his corruption, it is fateful that Nietzsche should mention Brahms as a specific example from among the pool of those other musicians. Yet the reason he does so makes perfect sense once we admit that Nietzsche is endeavouring to make a positive case for himself as a consequence.

In the first place, what is noteworthy about Brahms is that among the Germans, he really was taken to be Wagner's legitimate rival. But for a rivalry to actually exist – for one party to be the legitimate antagonist of the other – one must be above all the other's equal. As Nietzsche's remarks make clear, Brahms was just one from among a handful of those 'other musicians' who hesitated before this universal decay, so while his music displayed some of the same symptoms as Wagner's, it had yet to approach 'the whole corruption'. In this sense, Brahms could hardly be Wagner's equal and therefore his rival. This is what Nietzsche claims here when he says that the nature of this rivalry 'was a German misunderstanding'.

The *only* person who could be Wagner's legitimate rival, and therefore his equal, is one who was every bit as decadent, but who had found strength enough in himself to 'overcome' him.[30] There is no doubt that Nietzsche means himself, for this is what makes '*necessary*' music', not just 'too much music' languishing in decadence. Hence the upshot to having brought this 'sudden, downward motion' of the Socratic culture to its nadir is that Wagner had inadvertently paved the way for Nietzsche, Wagner's 'true heir', to usher in the upward swing towards a new tragic age. And as we know from *Ecce Homo*, this is precisely what Nietzsche actually claims. In fulfilling his vision of the 'philosopher who practices music', Nietzsche flatly tells us that he is altogether the

---

[30] Compare 'That in which we are related – that we have suffered more profoundly, also from each other, than men of this century are capable of suffering – will link our names again and again, eternally. . .' (EH 'Why I Am So Clever' 6); and, 'Well, then! I am, no less than Wagner, a child of his time; that is, a decadent: but I comprehended this, I resisted it. The philosopher in me resisted' (CW Preface).

first tragic philosopher, even when considered among the pre-Socratics (EH 'Why I Write Such Good Books' BT 3), and that he promises us nothing less than the coming of a new tragic age (EH 'Why I Write Such Good Books' BT 4).

Thus when it comes to his declaration of war against Wagner, Nietzsche is actually true to his word here: '*other* musicians don't count compared to Wagner' (CW Second Postscript), for Wagner is the whole corruption in art, not just part of it. This is what makes overcoming him, by definition, a *vital act* of philosophical and artistic necessity. So here again we find the same logic that we found through our analysis of section 11: what is a warning about Wagner from one side is really at the same time gratitude and praise for him on the other, and it is also why Nietzsche's subsequent digression into Brahms is ultimately a red herring.

Indeed, if anything, Nietzsche's remarks about Brahms only reinforce the distinction that other musicians fail to come anywhere near Wagner's 'sudden, downward motion' into the abyss: Brahms 'does *not* create out of an abundance, he *languishes* for abundance' (CW Second Postscript). Brahms's music is the music of yearning and dissatisfaction, and in particular, 'he is the musician for a certain kind of dissatisfied woman' (CW Second Postscript).[31] But even this type of dissatisfied woman – Clara Schumann by all accounts – still lingers far behind the female Wagnerian known as Cosima. Indeed, fifty steps beyond Brahms's 'dissatisfied woman' you get the female Wagnerian, 'just as fifty steps beyond Brahms you encounter Wagner'.[32] So when it comes to the whole 'German misunderstanding' about the

---

[31] There is no doubt that this remark is a reference to Clara Schumann (1819–96), who was at one time the wife of the composer Robert Schumann (1810–56), as well as being a composer in her own right. At nearly twenty-five years his senior, Robert Schumann had been Brahms's early champion, and was directly responsible for promoting his music after he and his wife heard him play some of his piano music in their home in early 1853. It is reported that Brahms loved Clara, and his letters to her strongly suggest that interpretation, but he never tried to consummate his love, even long after Robert died (see Swafford 1997). Interestingly, Schumann had been one of Nietzsche's musical 'consolations' before he encountered Wagner. See SL (1969: 12 [KSB 2: 121]), letter to Carl von Gersdorff, 7 April 1866.

[32] Needless to say, when it came to *his* female Wagnerian, Nietzsche could not help but add that she is 'more interesting, and above all *more charming*'.

rivalry between Brahms and Wagner, Nietzsche essentially settles the problem in relation to declining cultures: Brahms could hardly compete with Wagner because Wagner was ahead of the curve in every respect. Remember, the decay in music was universal. It was everywhere. Wagner simply seized upon and accelerated the decay by transforming the old forms into enlivenment and pathos at any cost, because he was a born actor. Brahms, however, was a musician, so he tried to resolve the decay by purely musical means, something that was in effect no longer possible. Consequently his music ends up languishing after the old forms, the grand style, and all that had once been. Brahms, Nietzsche tells us, 'becomes cold and of no further concern to us as soon as he becomes *the heir* of the classical composers' (CW Second Postscript). But this is no real solution, for there is a necessary cycle to everything in nature, and culture is no exception. That means, as far as Nietzsche's case of Wagner is concerned, that one must accept that corruption is the fate of music. Wagner's 'grand style' introduced theatricality and effects, and ultimately the emergence of acting into music. Wagner toppled over all the other art forms in existence and then consolidated them through his actor's genius, and now, like it or not, he lords it over us. Nothing, therefore,

> can cure music *in* what counts, *from* what counts, from the fatality of being an expression of the physiological contradiction – of being *modern*. The best instruction, the most conscientious training, intimacy on principle, even isolation in the company of old masters – all this remains merely palliative – to speak more precisely, illusory – for one no longer has the presupposition in one's body, whether this be the strong race of a Handel or whether it be the overflowing animal vitality of a Rossini. – Not everybody has a *right* to every teacher: that applies to whole ages. (CW Second Postscript)

Before leaving the discussion here about the fatality of Wagner, Nietzsche once again makes an appeal to resisting Wagner in the hope that there still might be some vestige of vitality left in Europe to finally overcome him, although the mood here is considerably more subdued than it was in the opening of the first postscript.

> To be sure, the possibility cannot be excluded that somewhere in Europe there are still *remnants* of stronger generations, of typically untimely human beings: if so, one could still hope for a *belated* beauty and perfection in music, too, from that quarter. What we can still experience at best are exceptions. From the *rule* that corruption is on top, that corruption is fatalistic, no god can save music. (CW Second Postscript)

With this entry, we arrive at Nietzsche's epilogue, and with it his attempt to finally 'wash his hands' of the case of Wagner. Once again, Nietzsche begins by reaffirming his commitment to the idea of ascending and declining cultures. But since the discussion that ensues takes for granted that Nietzsche has defined himself and his project as the antipode to Wagner's, the epilogue itself effectively becomes Nietzsche's last attempt to fully articulate the relationship between vitalism as an ontology and its implications for culture in the wake of Wagner. Indeed, as he rattles through all those predicate terms that are supposed to neatly fit into the binary categories of either ascending or declining life – 'affirmation of the will' and 'master morality' in the former category, 'negation of the will' and 'slave morality' in the latter – Nietzsche's intent is to map these vitalistic presuppositions on to the cultures that exemplify them, and in the process to 'situate' both Wagner and himself as Wagner's 'antipode' within this cycle of ascending and declining life.

This is the key to Nietzsche's entire argument against Wagner: vitalism as an ontology entails the unconditional affirmation of the will in which one must be 'strong enough' to affirm life. In the process, becoming oneself the *expression* of that affirmation is how one *creates*, how one 'makes music', from the materials of life. Because there is a connection between one's vital force and that which is created from it, all 'genuine art' by definition flows from these vitalistic presuppositions.[33] So while the 'classical', 'Roman' and

---

[33] Every age has the virtues of either ascending or declining life, Nietzsche tells us, and 'aesthetics is tied indissolubly to these biological presuppositions' (CW Epilogue).

'pagan' cultures become, as they are here, synonyms for ascending life because they created art out of an abundance of vitality, the 'Socratic', 'Gospel' and 'Christian' cultures become synonyms for declining life because they did just the opposite. With this connection between vitality, creativity and the flourishing of a culture, it is an easy matter to deduce where Wagner with his *Parsifal* 'fits'.

To be clear then, one cannot help but find this conception to be implicitly, if not explicitly, phallic. The very idea that Nietzsche can resolve the question of where Wagner and his art as culture 'fit' within the macrocosmic cycle of ascending and declining life is to settle the question once and for all about whose art is more vital, and therefore more 'fertile', for the promise of a new tragic age. In this respect, it is easy to see that Nietzsche's solution to the problem of culture at the microcosmic level is in the same stroke his final retaliation against Wagner for the terrible slander that had been perpetrated against him. Remember that to suggest, as Wagner's letter to Dr Eiser surely had, that the cause of Nietzsche's nervous symptomology was excessive masturbation is at the same time to imply that Nietzsche's vital force became 'depleted' and 'exhausted' without ever creating or generating anything.[34] And of course, if Nietzsche is depleting his vital force on the physical plane, it stands to reason that he can hardly be sublimating it for creative acts on the affective and mental planes – a 'slander' that surely runs afoul of Nietzsche's preferred teachings in his most vociferous, final works.[35] The idea therefore that Nietzsche could even *presume* to discuss harnessing his 'creative instincts' for the purposes of life, and especially for art, would sound downright ridiculous if you happened to be Wagner, and were reading Nietzsche's doubtful first efforts to criticise the creative moment

---

[34] See Gilman (2007) for a solid account of Dr Eiser's correspondence with the Wagners and the catalytic role he played in Nietzsche's final break with Wagner.

[35] Nietzsche's late works, especially *Twilight of the Idols*, are riddled with the idea that the creation of art is the sublimation and expression of one's sexual drives. For an excellent discussion of Nietzsche's sense of sublimation and its relation to the integration of self – a notion that includes, of course, the beginnings of the 'microcosm' of culture – see Gemes (2009).

of the artist – indeed to say *anything* meaningful about the artist in his relation to culture.[36] And yet the pressure behind what had begun as an abstruse and diffident first formulation for overcoming Wagner – that one must become an 'irreducible cultural unit' to combat the bombast of Bayreuth – steadily intensified until his obsession and fixation against Wagner was brought to the precision of a fine point in *The Case of Wagner*. Indeed, the ideas of 'depletion', 'exhaustion' and the 'degenerating instincts for life', as we know perfectly well, pervade *The Case of Wagner* as a whole, and are the terms that Nietzsche obsessively discharges as the watchwords for the 'desolate malignancy of Wagner's old age', as well as where his art as culture 'fits' within this cycle of ascending and declining life. And since there is a kinship between the microcosmic and macrocosmic levels of life, by siding with the 'Socratic', the 'Gospel' and the 'Christian' cultures in creating his *Parsifal*, Nietzsche is telling us that Wagner embraced all that is waning and moribund at the macrocosmic level. This of course means that Wagner's vitality, his will-to-affirm and to create, are in reality akin to the degenerating instincts for life at the microcosmic level.

Is it any wonder then that the virtues of 'overcoming' Wagner at the microcosmic level are akin to the virtues of ascending life at the macrocosmic level – the very problem that Nietzsche not only introduces in his preface to the *The Case of Wagner*, but that frames his problem as a whole? For Nietzsche, the will-to-power is the correct ethical deduction of Schopenhauer's metaphysical principle,[37]

---

[36] Wagner had spent a good deal of time perusing the first part of *Human, All Too Human* between 1878 and 1879, as Cosima's diary entries testify, and took note of a number of passages which, fairly or unfairly, criticised his art. In this connection, two passages in the diaries are quite interesting, because they criticise Wagner on some of the very subjects that Nietzsche would eventually and exclusively claim for himself: inspiration in art and philosophical timelessness. As cited previously, the diary entry that discusses Nietzsche's denial of inspiration is dated 27 July 1878 and deals with HAH1 155, while the diary entry of 22 March 1879 is noteworthy in that Wagner had taken note of one of Nietzsche's earliest criticisms of his art, namely, that it was too *untimely* (see CWD 2: 123, 27 July 1878, and CWD 2: 280–1, 22 March 1879).
[37] On this point, see UF 9[42], autumn 1887.

and so it is no surprise that he should harness this principle as the foundation of ascending vitality and the philosopher's own call to action to overcome himself in order to become an 'irreducible cultural unit', when a fateful sickness, such as Wagner's music, threatens him more globally with declining life.

In the context of the epilogue, what is so fascinating about the structure of Nietzsche's entire argument against Wagner is how committed he is to the miserly logic of binary and mutually exclusive categories such as those of ascending and declining life. Nietzsche behaves as if the qualitative nature of life itself could be fixed to discrete and unambiguous value quanta, and then somehow measured and categorised according to the law of non-contradiction. And yet this is precisely what makes his argument against Wagner work in terms of situating both Wagner and himself as Wagner's 'antipode' within the wider, macrocosmic framework of ascending and declining life. The 'microcosmic Wagner' must be seen as the definitive embodiment of degenerating instincts, while the 'microcosmic Nietzsche' must be seen as the definitive embodiment of overflowing instincts and the vitality and creativity to overcome him. And given, finally, that there is a kinship between the microcosmic and the macrocosmic levels of life, and that Wagner's degenerating instincts seemingly outpaced those 'universal signs of decay' at the macrocosmic level, all that is declining in form is in effect made to go through the 'microcosmic Nietzsche' as a kind of clearing house for ascending vitality towards the rebirth of culture, which, in *Zarathustra*, promises us nothing less than the coming of a new tragic age. Hence the categories here must be rigid and inflexible, and as a matter of fact it plays to Nietzsche's advantage that they should appear to be so, especially when it comes to discussing these 'opposite forms in the optics of value' (CW Epilogue). For what matters to Nietzsche is not what is 'true' or 'untrue' about life, but whether the thing itself *categorically belongs* to the *ascending or declining form of life*, and therefore whether the thing itself can be consistently experienced or perceived as the opposite or the antipode of its other.

In this sense, we finally get to the source of Nietzsche's exasperation and *ressentiment* in accusing Wagner of being an actor.

For Wagner, as it turns out, was seemingly able to inhabit *both values at once*, something that Nietzsche vehemently condemns here as false, and about which he desperately tries to set us to rights in showing that opposites really are opposites in what remains of the epilogue. But if we are supposed to believe the story Nietzsche tells us in *Ecce Homo* about how *he* overcame decadence in order to charge Wagner with it, then *only Nietzsche* had been fortunate enough to inhabit both the ascending and declining types of life at once, and consequently *only Nietzsche* had been gifted with the ability to detect 'a subtler smell for the signs of ascent and decline than any other human being before me'. This is precisely what allows him to proclaim his authority as the teacher of decadence *par excellence*.[38]

As we have already seen, the same exact valuations occur when it comes to considering *Parsifal* vis-à-vis the art of *Zarathustra*. As the reader may recall, all opposites in Zarathustra were blended into ever higher unities in which 'the highest and lowest energies of human nature, what is sweetest, most frivolous, and most terrible wells forth from one fount with immortal assurance' (EH 'Why I Write Such Good Books' TSZ 6). In fact, it is this ability to accept oppositions and then to *transcend them as opposites* that makes the psychological type of Zarathustra possible, and the highest type of everything that exists. After all, the vitality that *is* comprehends both its ascending and declining forms but is neither form exclusively, for 'to know both' and 'to be both' is to comprehend opposites *as* opposites but not to be comprehended by either. This is what gives the artist *qua* artist the most comprehensive vision of existence as a whole, and it is also what bestows genuine authority on the nature of one's art as a vital deed. And since this level of profundity is, according to Nietzsche's own account in *Ecce Homo*, made possible through the deed of *Zarathustra*, it follows that Nietzsche cannot possibly admit that Wagner might have already achieved the same exact thing. Therefore, Wagner's

---

[38] 'I know both, I am both', he tells us in EH 'Why I Am So Wise' 1.

instincts are false, and consequently he is the actor. Nietzsche urges us to come to our senses when he tells us that

> What alone should be resisted is that falseness, that deceitfulness of instinct which *refuses* to experience these opposites as opposites – as Wagner, for example, refused, being no mean master of such falsehoods. To make eyes at master morality, at *noble* morality . . . while mouthing the counterdoctrine, that of the 'gospel of the lowly,' the *need* for redemption! (CW Epilogue)

Wagner is the actor because he will do anything to safeguard the validity of his art, even if that means disingenuously playing both sides in the 'optics of value'. And since *Parsifal* is a 'Christian' work and so exclusively belongs to one side of the optics of value – to declining life – there can be no possibility that Wagner's instincts, and therefore his art, belong to the ascending form of life. Hence Nietzsche here chastises those Germans and Christians who are fools enough to be duped by Wagner's 'staged religion', which panders to the current degenerative tendencies of modernity. 'I admire, incidentally, the modesty of the Christians who go to Bayreuth. I myself wouldn't be able to endure certain words out of the mouth of a Wagner. There are concepts which do *not* belong in Bayreuth' (CW Epilogue).

But if we as readers are supposed to conclude that Wagner's art is contradictory and false, then what follows amounts to an extraordinarily embarrassing public revelation about Wagner's person that is surely intended to shore up the reason. At the same time, Nietzsche's strike here is no doubt intended to get to the core of his oft-repeated dictum that there is no distinction between the doer and the deed – that the contradictory nature of Wagner's art can ultimately be traced back to the contradictory nature of Wagner's being.

For those 'in the know', it was no secret that Wagner had a penchant for robing himself in silks and satins and other fabrics of the fairer sex. And while Cosima frowned on this particular proclivity of Wagner's sensuality, it was just this tendency towards the vital other and the opposite of one's own being that the artist, in Wagner's philosophy, yearns to embrace, and to which he 'must wed himself' in order to beget the genuine work of art.[39] After all, to recognise that the essence of the creative moment entails both fertility and receptivity is to grasp that the artist in principle must be capable of uniting both. Thus to provoke the fruitfulness of the creative moment, the process of sublimation, in Wagner's eyes at any rate, could only begin by uniting the physical experience of those opposites, and it was a process that Wagner, with his predilection for perfumes, powders, silk and lace, wholeheartedly adopted.

Unfortunately, not all members of the Wagner household saw eye-to-eye on this point. The master's negligees were often enough a source of consternation for the sexually repressed Cosima, who could hardly understand the necessity of sublimation in the creative process itself, and so Wagner was left to find other forms of femininity to satisfy his delight in the shared pleasures of sensual love. In his later years, however, Wagner did manage to find this kind of sensuous excitement in the young and beautiful Judith Gautier, and in letters to his muse and the passionate object of his attachment, Wagner made it clear that for the sake of 'mornings well spent on *Parsifal*', it was necessary that his boudoir should be adorned with silk-covered chaises longues 'which I shall call "Judith"', rose-scented cushions, and small pieces of furniture with floral patterns on yellow satin.[40] Wagner's preferred colour for this iridescent fabric appears, however, to have been pink – '*my* pink, very pale and delicate' – and he was ready to request large quantities from Judith in Paris, the capital

---

[39] '[I]f I wish to demonstrate that music (as a woman) must necessarily be impregnated by a poet (as a man), then I must ensure . . . that she is made pregnant only by the man who yearns for womankind with true, irresistible love. The necessity of this union between poetry and music in its fullness and entirety (a union desired by the poet himself) was something I could not demonstrate simply by means of abstract and aesthetic definitions. . .' (SLRW: 220–1, letter to Franz Liszt, 25 November 1850; compare Wagner's summary teachings of it in PW 2: 375–6, 'Opera and Drama'). Once again, interested readers will notice the striking ideological parallels in Schopenhauer's own account of the metaphysics of the beautiful, which indicates that the creation of art must be understood as a vital act (PP 2, 'On the Metaphysics of the Beautiful and Aesthetics', 215).

[40] SLRW: 877, letter to Judith Gautier, 22 November 1877.

of decadence itself, to ensure maximal comfort and pleasure as he toiled away on *Parsifal*. These demands, which he underscored with particular stress, were needed for 'the peaceful tranquillity of creative seclusion'.[41]

No doubt Nietzsche knew the score here. After all, he had once played the role of Wagner's valet, and so knew full well his predilection for silk underwear.[42] So in Nietzsche's frame of reference, the false and contradictory nature of Wagner's art was due entirely to the false and contradictory nature of Wagner himself, where once again, the 'optics of value' necessarily reared its ugly head. While composing a music drama that celebrates the renunciation of the world and the austerity of the will, Wagner was surrounding himself, as Köhler once observed, with a 'veritable Gesamtkunstwerk of the senses' (2004: 584). Thus by suggesting, as Nietzsche does here, that *Parsifal* is a 'version of Christianity for female Wagnerians, perhaps *by* female Wagnerians', and then going on to describe Wagner as 'one of the female species' (CW Epilogue), Köhler concludes quite rightly that Nietzsche 'outed' Wagner (2004: 587), and in the process returned just deserts for the embarrassing revelation Wagner had made about Nietzsche's proclivity for self-abuse six years previously.

In Nietzsche's frame of reference at any rate, to entertain the proposition that Wagner's *Parsifal* was close to the meaning or essence of Christianity when its composer was indulging his appetite for rose powders and brocade was about as ridiculous as entertaining the proposition that Cosima's father, Franz Liszt, should become a church elder, effectively in charge of disseminating its dogmas (CW Epilogue). Once again, for anyone 'in the know', here was another eccentric performer and showman who had not only been a notorious womaniser in his youth, but had turned over the responsibility for Cosima's upbringing to his lover's old governess so that he could pursue his career as a concert pianist around Europe. Eventually a series of personal tragedies in his life did turn him towards the church, and ultimately he joined

---

[41] SLRW: 878–9, letter to Judith Gautier, 18 December 1877.
[42] SL (1969: 147 [KSB 5: 190]), letter to Richard Wagner, 27 September 1876.

the Third Order of Saint Francis in 1857 and became 'Abbé Liszt'. Yet perhaps most significantly and to the point, Liszt was responsible for having made Wagner. Not only did he promote Wagner's music in Europe at a time when nobody else would have taken that gamble, it was through his personal and professional support that Wagner's *Lohengrin* was first premiered,[43] and through this, his fledgling career finally gained traction. Thus for Nietzsche's purposes, Liszt and Wagner were two of a kind. What these two actors and performers had to do with Christianity was incompatible with the optics of their values. Resorting once again to *ad hominem* arguments – Nietzsche's preferred method – he wants us to conclude that their entire show of piety was just that: a public relations stunt for declining life. 'The need for *redemption*, the quintessence of all Christian needs, has nothing to do with such buffoons . . . the Christian wants to be *rid* of himself. *Le moi est toujours haïssable.*'[44] The *only* way in which they might excusably be Christians, then, is the extent to which both might hate themselves for being the actors (and therefore the fakers) that they are. And with this remark, Nietzsche resumes his paean to 'noble morality' and the 'affirmation of the will', reinforcing once again that these predicate terms belong by definition to ascending life, and that they are the touchstone of what belongs to his philosophy. With this latter assertion, Nietzsche proceeds to underscore his argument that he is Wagner's 'antipode'.

Noble morality, Nietzsche tells us, is all self-affirmation, all self-glorification, and therefore all great and beautiful art belongs here. When one is wholly of this type, he continues, one cannot help but have an instinctual aversion to all that grows on impoverished soil: 'one cannot dissociate from [noble morality] an instinctive aversion *against* decadents, scorn for their symbolism, even horror: such feelings almost prove it' (CW Epilogue). Nietzsche then reminds us that the 'noble Romans' experienced Christianity

---

[43] Liszt was instrumental in getting Wagner's *Lohengrin* premiered in Weimar in August 1850 at a time when Wagner himself was in exile in Switzerland as a political refugee for having participated in the unsuccessful Dresden uprising of May 1848 (SLRW: 199, letter to Franz Liszt, 21 April 1850).

[44] 'The "I" is always hateful' (CW Epilogue).

in exactly the same way; that is, as 'an abominable superstition' – once again underscoring in the process the intimate connection that exists between the microcosmic and macrocosmic levels of ascending and declining life. Thus as Nietzsche seeks to sum up his case against Wagner, he reiterates his final warning against the hypocrisy that follows from transgressing these 'opposite forms in the optics of value'. Nobility and enslavement, affirmation and negation, master morality and slave morality – each term is an attribute of vitality that categorically belongs to either the ascending or declining form of life, and is therefore binary and exclusive of its other. 'One looks in vain for more valuable, more *necessary* opposites', Nietzsche here pontificates. Opposites really are opposites, and the fact that Wagner can seemingly inhabit contradictory values with such innocence defines what modernity is (CW Epilogue). The fact too that the 'modern Christian *Junker*' – another contradiction in terms – innocently believes that the Wagner of silks and satins is the second coming of Christ shows just how little they understand of these necessary opposites.

> Biologically, modern man represents a contradiction of values; he sits between two chairs, he says Yes and No in the same breath. Is it any wonder that precisely in our times falsehood itself has become flesh and genius? that *Wagner* 'dwelt among us'? It was not without reason that I called Wagner the Cagliostro of modernity. (CW Epilogue)

Wagner is the actor and faker *par excellence* who, with his contradiction of values, with his 'Yes and No in the same breath', has accelerated the downfall of a declining culture. This is what Nietzsche means when claiming that Wagner 'sums up modernity' (CW Preface). Hence it is precisely here that those who are 'authentic' must 'take sides' against themselves and stand unequivocally, categorically for one set of values as the 'antipode' of those who contradict one another and are at bottom rooted in sheer performance. Considering that the philosopher's duty is to overcome their time within themselves, and that Nietzsche's time in particular was the degeneration of all culture into acting for effect – in a word Wagnerism – Nietzsche is saying, in not so many words, that he must overcome his own tendency for performance in order to pave the way for a culture that would be, in a very real sense, post-Wagnerian.

Now whether he managed to overcome his penchant for theatrical melodrama and histrionic effects in his own right is an altogether different proposition, but in the final paragraph of the epilogue, Nietzsche leaves wiggle room for himself – naturally – since it goes almost without saying that he must win against Wagner in 'knowing both' and 'in being both' in order to overcome the 'most instructive case' of what is contradictory and false – Wagner. 'But all of us have, unconsciously, involuntarily in our bodies values, words, formulas, moralities of *opposite* descent', Nietzsche concedes here. 'We are, physiologically considered, *false*.' Truly, for where else would we begin in our attempt to diagnose the modern soul? And yet,

> With a resolute incision into this instinctive contradiction, with the isolation of its opposite values, with the vivisection of *the most instructive* case. – The case of Wagner is for the philosopher a *windfall* – this essay is inspired, as you hear, by gratitude. (CW Epilogue)

Indeed it was, for if Wagner somehow forced Nietzsche to take sides against himself, there should now be no question that Nietzsche believed his *Zarathustra* was the beginning of this post-Wagnerian confrontation, of saying only Yes to the creative deed that is life. This is finally what it means to 'make music from the materials of life' over and against the case of Wagner.

Conclusion

Coming full circle

We have offered a detailed textual analysis of *The Case of Wagner* which has examined what Nietzsche is saying (and doing) in challenging Wagner to a duel; we have also offered an account of what we believe to be the most logically coherent and internally consistent structure at the base of Nietzsche's dynamic and lifelong obsession with Wagner. We have shown that Nietzsche's philosophical alignment with Wagner is intimately bound up with the ontological commitment to vitalism, from which certain definite consequences were deduced about the nature of life and the meaning of art and its relationship to culture. This commitment to vitalism, then, is the crux of the entire matter. For if the category of life truly has ontological priority over the categories of mind or intellect, then it follows that the concept is, in some sense, derived from a creative source, and that all concepts that fail to ground themselves in the creative matrix of life are deemed to be, in a very real way, *severed* from that source. Hence the primary and original significance of the concept is *generative*, not 'critical' or 'dissuasive', so it should come as no surprise that attempting to sever the intellect from its creative roots results in its 'devitalization'. Only art and the creative deed more generally embody the principle of life directly, for as the microcosm (the artist) is to the macrocosm (life itself), both are rooted in creative origins and ends. This is precisely what makes art the immediate vital act of life and the truly metaphysical activity of human beings.

Furthermore, it is this ontological commitment to vitalism that frames the narrative we find about the tragic age of the Greeks, whose art as culture had flourished until the 'common bond of its religion and primeval customs was pierced and severed by the sophist needles of the egoistic spirit of Athenian self-dissection' (PW 1: 136, 'Artwork of the Future'). Through this counter-movement, the figure of Socrates, the very embodiment of 'Athenian self-dissection' and therefore the central figure symbolising the divorce of the intellect from its creative roots, becomes a 'turning point in world history' for the devitalisation of the intellect, the decline of the tragic age, and thus the destruction of art as culture (BT 15).

With this narrative presupposed, it was at this critical juncture that the 'artist of the future' would materialise in order to restore the unity of rationality and vitality for the rebirth of art as culture. At the time of *The Birth of Tragedy* and of Nietzsche's 'pro-Wagnerian' commitments more generally, this idea was symbolised by the figure of the 'music-making Socrates' as a cultural form; yet as we have shown, ultimately Nietzsche disputed both the capacity and authenticity of Wagner as the philosopher and artist most uniquely capable of embodying this figure.

In this respect, we witnessed how Nietzsche appealed to Wagner's own theoretical arguments about the conditions between vitalism and art and its relationship to culture in order to hold Wagner and his 'artwork of the future' to account for its failure to live up to its own principles. For once Nietzsche could convince his readers that Wagner's art had typified the features of a 'declining form', while at the same time showcasing his *Zarathustra* as the embodiment of philosophical music (or musical philosophy), and thus the consummation and fulfilment of the unified teachings of Schopenhauer and Wagner for culture, it followed that Nietzsche could declare himself the true 'music-maker' for the tragic culture in perfect consistency with his pro-Wagnerian period.

Thus we have shown that *The Case of Wagner* is a dispute over the nature of music itself in which the very terms of the dispute derive both their charge and significance from the ontological commitment to vitalism and its connection with art as the truly metaphysical activity of human beings. In other words, to affirm life by 'setting my misery to music'[1] is the wisdom of the philosopher in confronting the problem of suffering (the *what*) and communicating it in an immediate and irrefutable way (the *how*). This is precisely why the cultural form of the 'philosopher who practices music' carries so much theoretical weight for Nietzsche over and against Wagner in his 'post-Wagnerian' works – that same Wagner, be it remembered, who had turned the 'most vital art form' into a 'narcotic of the worst kind' (AT 6) – for not only does the cultural form implicitly rely on Wagner's own theoretical architecture of culture under the presupposition that vitalism and its expression in art govern the decline and rebirth of culture that divides historical epochs, but it is these same presuppositions that now govern, through the mouth of Nietzsche–Zarathustra, the demise of the pessimism of degenerating instincts, from Socrates to Christianity to Schopenhauer and Wagner, and through it to the rebirth of a new tragic age. For the individual who represents both the ascending and declining types of life at once, and is therefore capable of uniting two opposing cultures within himself, as Nietzsche plainly says in *Ecce Homo*, that person 'breaks the history of mankind in two. One lives before him, or one lives after him' (EH 'Why I Am a Destiny' 8).[2] With this declaration Nietzsche becomes, as he had once claimed he would of Wagner, 'in good measure his heir'.[3] In this regard, then, we have a better sense of the significance of Nietzsche's parable of *Zarathustra*, with its promise of a new Dionysian world-view, which was born 'exactly in that sacred hour in which Richard Wagner [the 'old god'] died in Venice' (EH 'Why I Write Such Good Books' TSZ 1).

---

[1] SLRW: 379, letter to Cosima von Bülow, 1 March 1858.
[2] In this connection, there is probably no better self-confession on Nietzsche's part than the one he made to August Strindberg in late 1888 when he said, in the context of praising his own *Ecce Homo*, that 'I am strong enough to break the history of mankind in two.' SL (1969: 330 [KSB 8: 509]), letter to August Strindberg, 8 December 1888.
[3] SL (1969: 208 [KSB 6: 333–4]), letter to Peter Gast, 19 February 1883.

A dangerous game

With these explanations, we have finally resolved the meaning of Nietzsche's enigmatic case of Wagner, not only in terms of the charges it contains, but also in terms of the theoretical edifice from which those charges are sanctioned. As we noted previously, Wagner was the central philosophical and artistic problem of Nietzsche's project as a whole, for in Nietzsche's estimation, Wagner either united or came closest to uniting philosophy and art for the purposes of culture. Thus to triumph over Wagner meant that Nietzsche had to challenge Wagner on his own terms. But if the central issue at stake in challenging Wagner to a duel and in *winning that duel* was that Nietzsche and not Wagner would be seen as the 'philosopher who practices music', then the real significance of Nietzsche's duel with Wagner lay precisely in the fact that it entailed reaching into his own 'bag of tricks' in order to overcome him. Looking at our analysis of the five main charges as they occur in *The Case of Wagner*, this is exactly what we discovered, for when the charges in question were in any way related to Nietzsche's 'psychological unity', and especially when they concerned the deed of *Zarathustra*, there was nothing but legitimacy and authenticity spreading everywhere, whereas in Wagner's hands they are tricks pure and simple.

It is here, incidentally, that we finally have a very suggestive reason as to why *Parsifal* cannot succeed when it comes to Nietzsche's attack on it in *The Case of Wagner*. Nietzsche's attack has comparatively little to do with the oft-cited cover story that Wagner started talking about a Christian conversion experience in connection with it during their final meeting in Sorrento in November 1876, and that this somehow offended the sensibilities of Nietzsche's newly found 'free spirit'.[4] Nietzsche had long been aware of Wagner's intentions towards it as a project, for not only had the original prose sketch of *Parsifal* been drafted four years before Nietzsche even met Wagner,[5] but Nietzsche himself

---

[4] Nietzsche's notes on his final conversation with Wagner are in KSA 14: 161.
[5] See BB, 46–61, 'Parzival' sketch (27–30 August 1865).

had heard the prose sketch read out loud for him at Christmas in 1869, and had experienced, according to Cosima's diary entry, 'renewed feelings of awe'.[6] The reason *Parsifal* cannot succeed is that, if it does, Nietzsche would be forced to admit that Wagner had won the duel between them, and with it the right to inherit the mantle of the 'philosopher who practices music'. Therefore *Parsifal* does *not* win, and so we necessarily get, on the one hand, *Zarathustra* 'outdoing' *Parsifal* in *Ecce Homo*, while on the other we get the very musical, very theatrical tirade against it in *The Case of Wagner*.

On this point, an observation that Ridley makes about the value of what Wagner attempted to do with *Parsifal* dovetails very nicely into our discussion of Nietzsche's competition with Wagner. Following Michael Tanner's reading of *Parsifal* in certain important respects (Tanner 1979: 205–18), Ridley notes that,

> Far from *flattering* 'every nihilistic' instinct, 'every religious expression of decadence', as Nietzsche claims, Wagner sets out in *Parsifal* to understand and inhabit those instincts and expressions, so as to diagnose and *overcome* the impulses lying behind 'the whole counterfeit of transcendence and beyond'. Wagner's art, that is, is engaged in an enterprise that is Nietzschean to its core. *It is, in fact, an exercise in just the kind of musical philosophy for which Nietzsche longed most ardently.* (Ridley 2014: 232, our emphasis)

How true Ridley's conclusion is becomes apparent once we consider, on the one hand, Nietzsche's frank and 'un-theatrical' reaction to the prelude,[7] and then his 'competition' with it in *Ecce Homo*, in which we find *Zarathustra* 'outdoing' *Parsifal* on some of the very qualities that Nietzsche cited to Gast in his letter with genuine wonder and enthusiasm (EH 'Why I Write Such Good Books' TSZ 6).

While the analysis we have presented here is by no means exhaustive, it is sufficient to call into question how far or in what

---

[6] CWD 1: 176, 25 December 1869.
[7] SL (1969: 260 [KSB 8: 12–13]), letter to Peter Gast, 21 January 1887.

way Nietzsche actually possessed an epistemic gap to critique Wagner, since in the final analysis it is precisely this epistemic gap that has been driving and continues to drive the modern permutations of Nietzsche's case of Wagner. Now certainly one might object to the idea that Nietzsche needs to have an 'epistemic gap' in order to criticise Wagner. The very fact that there continues to be a 'case' against Wagner proves in some sense that Nietzsche put his finger on something about him. In that respect (so the argument goes), one need not entertain, much less endorse, Nietzsche's competition with Wagner in order to take his case of Wagner seriously. To respond to these objections, we need only point out that the 'purely negative case' against Wagner, especially in its modern permutations, would never have existed in the first place if Nietzsche had not found it necessary to build a competing case for himself. In other words, Nietzsche could hardly 'compete' with Wagner, much less declare himself the 'winner' of that competition, if he had not constructed a negative case of Wagner on the one hand in order to build a positive case for himself on the other. It is here that we must understand that Nietzsche's 'purely negative case' against Wagner is *necessary* in that it establishes the very parameters for Nietzsche's positive case for himself, and thus his 'success' in overcoming Wagner.

Again it might be true that we need not entertain, much less endorse, Nietzsche's case for himself, but in order for the charges in the 'purely negative case' against Wagner to stick, we must surely ask ourselves whether we are comfortable with the fact that Nietzsche's act of 'overcoming Wagner' reaches into what he claims is Wagner's 'bag of tricks' in order to do so. It is precisely on this point that Nietzsche's 'epistemic gap' becomes important, for it is principally in virtue of this gap that he believes he can frame his negative case against Wagner. If the only issue at stake were Nietzsche's 'purely negative case', there would be no reason to expect that Nietzsche's act of 'overcoming Wagner' should in any way depend on Wagner. Wagner's bag of tricks, which Nietzsche spends so much of his energy castigating in *The Case of Wagner*, would have to be 'tricks' in the unconditional sense, and could not be rehabilitated, or in any way qualified, when it comes to Nietzsche's act of overcoming Wagner. But this is nowhere near the case. Nietzsche's case of Wagner is completely tied up with Nietzsche's case for himself, and in that sense we might even come to expect that Wagner's bag of tricks should become fair play in building a case for himself – and this is precisely what we *do* find. Because what is at stake with Nietzsche's case of Wagner is his competition with Wagner over who more consistently united, or came the closest to uniting, philosophy and art for the purposes of culture, Nietzsche is necessarily committed to helping himself to the very 'tricks' that he accuses Wagner of pandering to in the negative case, and in the process, he introduces what we consider to be a very dangerous game.

Once we understand, therefore, that Nietzsche's case of Wagner is, more than anything else, a case of *psychological hegemony* over the philosopher and philosophy that speaks music, the inevitable conclusion we must draw is that carving out Nietzsche's case of Wagner in the purely negative sense is doomed, for what is driving the case of Wagner at a very deep level is precisely this competition with Wagner. In this respect, there is something quite peculiar about the case of Wagner having become a 'genre', and specifically one whose afterlife has been systematically negative from Nietzsche onwards. While Heidegger, Adorno and, more recently, Lacoue-Labarthe were all involved in mainly negative debates about Wagner, their debates and, as it were, their 'cases' against him are fundamentally different from Nietzsche's, inasmuch as Nietzsche's case of Wagner is completely bound up with the case that Nietzsche makes for himself.

For the case of Wagner to exist as a genre and to be a genuine continuation of the debate that Nietzsche supposedly inaugurated, the so-called 'negative debates' about Wagner would effectively need to raise questions surrounding Nietzsche's case for himself. If the central debate invoked by the case of Wagner as a genre is, as Badiou seems to think for instance, the debate about whether Wagner created a new situation with respect to the relationship between philosophy and music (Badiou 2010: 56), then the debate that is inextricably bound up with Wagner would be one that actually considers whether *Nietzsche* is every bit as responsible, and in fact the principal party to blame, for having appropriated 'music' as a means to convey an ideological agenda. Frankly, after an admission such as the one we encounter in section 106 of *The Gay Science*, Nietzsche could hardly be exonerated from the charge of knowing the power of music as an advocate, especially when it comes to the art of 'seducing' people's ears and hearts to both error and truth alike. When that is combined with the means with which the philosopher must convey his conceptions with certainty, what we find is precisely what we could call transmitting an ideology in an immediate and irrefutable way. This is the essence of the philosopher who speaks music. Yet these points somehow completely elude Badiou, even though his 'lessons on Wagner' are fundamentally organised around this very theme.[8] So while perhaps we need not entertain, much less endorse, Nietzsche's offering of *Zarathustra* as the legitimate counter-offer to rival Wagner, we are still left with the question of whether Nietzsche 'succeeded' precisely because he was able to make the charges in the so-called 'purely negative case' against Wagner stick. Perhaps Nietzsche did exactly what he said he did after all: he simply wrote a 'page of "music" about music'[9] from which the charges against Wagner have been parroted ever since, while Nietzsche's case for himself as the 'philosopher who speaks music' has been implicitly and unconsciously endorsed by the very fact that his charges against Wagner have rarely, if ever, been critically examined. (On this point, perhaps Thomas Mann is a notable exception.)[10]

But as we have tried to demonstrate, Nietzsche's charges against Wagner remain ambiguous precisely because they imply a direct competition with Wagner in which Nietzsche's polemic ceremoniously ejects through the front door the very elements that eventually creep in through the back door in the name of his 'self-overcoming'; and in the specific charges we considered, the art of seduction, gesture, theatricality and histrionics all played

---

[8] 'I should mention at the outset an underlying thesis, which I have no intention of proving myself, that posits music as a fundamental operator in contemporary ideology. I'm taking "music" in its loosest sense here, not as art or intellectuality or thought, but simply what declares itself as such' (Badiou 2010: 1).

[9] SL (1969: 340 [KSB 8: 553–4]), letter to Carl Fuchs, 27 December 1888.

[10] See especially Mann (1933; 1966; 1985).

a part – qualities that are supposedly found only in Wagner's 'bag of tricks'. And this is only the tip of the iceberg as far as the charges in *The Case of Wagner* are concerned. Therefore we would need to ask whether Nietzsche succeeded in becoming the musical philosopher that he promised he would, and whether he won the duel with Wagner by the sheer skill of his linguistic legerdemain in crediting Wagner's 'bag of tricks' to the good purely in relation to his 'psychological unity' of self-overcoming, and yet labelling those same 'tricks' as symptoms of decline with regard to Wagner's art. Given that Nietzsche knows all about Wagner's 'bag of tricks' and uses them to 'overcome Wagner', so that his 'purely negative case' against Wagner is conditioned from the outset, it would be debatable at best to take on board the charges against Wagner without in some sense implicitly endorsing the success of Nietzsche's case for himself. What this means, purely and simply, is that we must be able to resolve how far or in what way Nietzsche's criticisms of Wagner actually implicate Nietzsche and the case he built for himself in the process. This is the only way in which the so-called case of Wagner as a genre would be a genuine continuation of the genre that Nietzsche supposedly inaugurated.

Failing this, to continue to believe that the Wagner criticism of the present day is somehow the genuine continuation of the genre that Nietzsche supposedly inaugurated can only be a gesture towards Nietzsche's case of Wagner in the most superficial sense, for if all we mean by the case of Wagner as a genre is having a suspicious look at Wagner, then we are misapprehending Nietzsche's case of Wagner in the most fundamental sense. In this respect, then, Badiou's desire to take on Wagner simply because 'taking on Wagner constitutes a genre to which I would like to contribute one more variation' (Badiou 2010: 55) completely misses the point; and indeed his 'lessons on Wagner' read as if what is at stake is nothing more than the gesture of making a case for the sake of it.

We must recall that Nietzsche's case of Wagner is *necessarily* bound up with the case he made for himself, and in this sense the questions surrounding *his* case are still very much open for debate. But to take on Wagner because others have also taken him on, to have a suspicious look at Wagner because others have done the same, whether to prosecute or defend him, ends up reducing Wagner and his art to the banalities of the *Jetztzeit*, in which the concern for 'Wagner's relevance for today' becomes a foil for the term 'modernity' itself, as if it were somehow the last and conclusive term beyond the 'ancient' and 'medieval' in the tripartite periodisation theory of history, and as though there would finally be some sort of culmination and fulfilment for modernity in criticising him.

Nietzsche's case of Wagner is a 'musical case' for himself, and it was a case that was necessarily mounted at Wagner's expense. Wagner was not in error when, always acutely perceptive of the world around him, he remarked of Nietzsche that 'that bad person has taken everything from me, even the weapons with which he now attacks me. How sad that he should be so perverse – so clever, yet at the same time so shallow!'[11] And as Lesley Chamberlain has astutely commented, 'Nietzsche set himself up as Wagner's competitor, and in more ways than he could control. Wagner and his music became the principal leitmotifs in the score of Nietzsche's life while the prose came closer and closer to music' (Chamberlain 1996: 66). Truly, as Ridley has noted, the very fact that no other philosopher has been translated *into* music 'by composers of the calibre of Mahler, Delius and Richard Strauss, for instance, nor [. . .] had so clear an influence upon writers and poets of the stature of D.H. Lawrence, Rilke, Yeats and Thomas Mann, to name but a few' (Ridley 2007: 141–2), should give us a very clear indication that when it came to music, it was *Nietzsche* who wished for a case to be made for himself. If Wagner really has turned into a sort of critical hermeneutic focal point in terms of the relationship between philosophy and its artistic condition, as Badiou seems to think (2010: 71–2), then that is only because Nietzsche's *competition* with Wagner has made him so. So if we intend to be clear regarding in what respect 'philosophy and its artistic condition' have been merged, then we really ought to begin precisely where our work has begun; that is, by evaluating how far or in what

---

[11] CWD 2: 128, 2 August 1878.

way rationality and creativity are fused in the philosophical act. In this sense Nietzsche's case for Wagner, which is at the same time Nietzsche's case for himself, becomes the *de facto* proof over which a fundamental truth of the Wagnerian thesis was fought: as life has no higher source than its own creation, art is necessarily the immediate vital act of life.

But if this so, what then is the relationship of the principle of creativity and the purely creative to the more traditional philosophical notions of 'reality' and 'truth'? It is surely not the case that all thinking is wishful thinking, and yet on this question it is noteworthy to re-emphasise how the formal portion of *The Case of Wagner* closes with the 'three demands' that Nietzsche places on art, which deal precisely with this question of 'authenticity' and 'truth':

1 That the theatre should not lord it over the other arts
2 That the actor should not seduce those who are authentic
3 That music should not become an art of lying (CW 12)

In looking over Nietzsche's 'demands' here, it becomes extremely difficult to figure out in what sense he believed he could claim that he was any more 'authentic' than the artist that he very theatrically condemns in *The Case of Wagner*; but they give us a very good indication of the principal issues that are truly at stake in Nietzsche's case of Wagner as a genre, and why they matter for philosophy.

Glossary of Key Terms

Decadence: although this term has a very wide application in broader Nietzsche scholarship, it has a surprisingly technical definition in Nietzsche's Wagner criticism. In the most fundamental sense, the term decadence is a privative concept and is used to describe the absence of formal coherence, whether of large-scale structures as in the case of architecture or music, or of organisational power and thus harmony in the sense of coordination and agreement of its parts as a whole. The term also has a normative connotation which is intimately bound up with Nietzsche's commitment to vitalism as an ontology, for that which observes and accords with the principles of life, taken either in its broader sense or in its more circumscribed biological sense, is deemed to be well ordered or in high form. It is this normative connotation that is often applied to individuals, groups and cultures as such, suggesting that those who are accused of decadence either no longer accord with the principles of life and are thus in 'declining form', or no longer observe them and instead fight against them, and so are in effect 'deteriorating from within'.

As one might expect, both senses of the term are applicable to Nietzsche's Wagner criticism. According to Nietzsche, the overall architecture of Wagner's compositions does not cohere through large-scale rhythmic structures or some other uniform time metric which might organise the composition as a whole. Instead, Wagner's practice in composition was to include detailed performance markings in the score from one bar of music to the next. The effect of this formalised performance system broke down any sense of finding large-scale rhythmic structures in the composition, since the realisation and interpretation of the music increasingly depended on actualising these individual rhythmic units for the sake of its performance, and consequently, its overall effect. This, then, is the descriptive sense in which Wagner's music is decadent.

At the same time, Wagner's aversion to large-scale structure in favour of indulging in the infinitesimal and enlivening the smallest articulations of sound performance was natural to him, because both Wagner and his art were in 'declining form'. This is the normative sense in which Wagner and his art are decadent. When Nietzsche accuses Wagner of ushering in the degeneration of all art into acting for effect, the accusation is made principally in view of Wagner's 'declining form' as well as the advanced or accelerated degree of that deterioration towards formlessness when compared more broadly with his milieu. It is this that puts Wagner and his art in the vanguard of modernity.

The music-making Socrates: this term, originally introduced in the so-called 'Wagner sections' of *The Birth of Tragedy*, specifically refers to the form of a culture central for the rebirth of tragedy, and thus stands as the hypothetical resolution to the ills of the Socratic culture and its attendant effect on the state of the modern music drama – in other words opera – that is the foil of the essay more generally. The term itself also obliquely nominates Wagner and his art as a herald of this coming form and therefore as the pre-eminent modern example of these 'ever-new configurations of genius' that will bring about the rebirth of tragedy. Nietzsche is not very specific about what the term includes, either at the individual level or as the form of a culture more broadly, but there are very clear diagnostic implications entailed by the term, especially when contrasted with the Socratic culture. Thus in contradistinction to the Socratic culture, which is argued to have divorced rationality from vitality, and which led as a consequence to the decline of art at the hands of science, this term signifies a cultural form in which the rational and creative drives must rebalance, realign or reunify for the purposes of art and life. As philosophy and music are the apogee of these drives united, they are the intellectual art forms for culture *par excellence*.

When Nietzsche later revised his narrative of the rebirth of tragedy in the *Attempt*, the term itself had come to signify the form of a culture which confronts the 'burden and weight of existence' in order then to 'make music' from the materials of life. At the individual level, the term thus represents the primary activity of the tragic philosopher in affirming existence as opposed to those 'intoxicating escape routes' which Nietzsche accused Wagner and his art of positing as a solution. Accordingly, the philosopher who makes music from the materials of life became part and parcel with the pessimism of strength and thus the tragic concept, while the 'Wagnerian solution' so to speak belonged to the pessimism of degenerating instincts and thus the Socratic culture in declining form. From *The Birth of Tragedy* to *The Case of Wagner*, 'the philosopher who makes music' is therefore the central symbol for culture around which Nietzsche's confrontation and competition with Wagner revolved. See also **pessimism of strength** and **pessimism of degenerating instincts**.

Pessimism of degenerating instincts: this term, which is paired with the **pessimism of strength** as a contrast, is a species concept of pessimism that attempts to distinguish, in the main, the doctrine of ethics that follows from a depleted, exhausted and devitalised orientation to the problem of existence. Originally introduced in the *Attempt*, this term is the natural consequence of those who fail to affirm the principle of life because of the implicit hopelessness or fruitlessness that seems to be entailed in the nature of sentient existence. Accordingly, life is seen as an insoluble intellectual problem from which, according to Nietzsche, 'escape routes' are devised, most notably those that appeal to the 'moral interpretation and significance of existence'. This term is paired with the Socratic culture of *The Birth of Tragedy*, and is specifically identified in the *Attempt* as the species of pessimism responsible for declining cultures, most notably that of the tragic age of the Greeks. Finally, it is this term that allows Nietzsche to reclassify the original heroes of *The Birth of Tragedy* – Schopenhauer and Wagner – as inconstant and inconsistent adherents of vitalism who, accordingly, shift from being symbols who had prefigured the rebirth of a new tragic age into symptoms of a declining culture. Compare **pessimism of strength**.

Pessimism of strength: this term, which contrasts with the **pessimism of degenerating instincts**, is a species concept of pessimism that attempts to distinguish the doctrine of ethics that follows from affirming the nature of sentient existence in an unqualified or uncompromising way. This term, which is formally introduced in the *Attempt*, stands for an ethical doctrine that far more consistently implies the metaphysics or ontology of vitalism in its purest sense, as the latter entails an unconditional affirmation, not the negation, of the will for life. Notably, this doctrine is paired with the tragic age of the Greeks which, according to Nietzsche, allowed their art as culture to flourish, but it is also implicitly paired with the rebirth of a new tragic age more generally, as those who accord most fully with the principles of life admit vital forms and thus allow the creative principle to flourish as the primary activity, even despite the horrors or terrors of existence. Thus in deriving an ethical principle that was far more consistent with the ontology of vitalism than the ethics found in either Schopenhauer's philosophy or Wagner's art, it is this term that allows Nietzsche to suggest himself as legitimate successor of the pre-Socratics in the *Attempt* and the origin of the emerging tragic concept, in contradistinction to either Schopenhauer or Wagner, the original heroes of *The Birth of Tragedy*. Compare **pessimism of degenerating instincts**.

Vitalism: this term suggests an ontology that is fundamentally identical with life, although life in this sense is not identical with the organism as such, nor is it exclusively defined in relation to the metabolic and reproductive functions of biological phenomena. In this respect, life is not solely an object of scientific inquiry. The term life, especially as it features in Wagner's theoretical works, has a much broader connotation and includes a philosophical orientation that gives the categories of life itself priority over those of mind or intellect, and thus is seen as the ultimate ontological category.

In particular, the activity of the intellect (scientific or otherwise) is deemed to arise within, and to operate from, the matrix of life itself, and so is viewed as a mere by-product or effect of life. Accordingly this orientation radically subordinates intellect to both the will and to psychological factors more generally, as the underlying assumption is that mind or intellect does not have the power to comprehend life, as it is deemed to be secondary and derivative. This is certainly the case, in varying degrees, in the philosophies of Schopenhauer, Wagner, and Nietzsche. Thus while it might be possible for science to determine mathematical entities with conceptual rigour and to explain one phenomenon through another as terms in a relationship, what we mean by 'life' forever escapes this kind of analysis. Therefore what vitalism understands by the term life itself, as distinct from what may be thought through its concept, points to a reality that can never be known in the exclusively conceptual sense.

Wagner as the sign of decline: see **decadence**.

Guide to Further Reading on *The Case of Wagner* and *Nietzsche Contra Wagner*

Aaron Ridley, 'Nietzsche and Music': examines the special place music has in Nietzsche's philosophy and argues vis-à-vis *Parsifal* that philosophy as music is at the very basis of Nietzsche's competition with Wagner.

Aaron Ridley, *Nietzsche on Art*: an overview of Nietzsche's philosophy of art that examines the development of his aesthetics in relation to some of Nietzsche's most celebrated themes and argues its importance to understanding Nietzsche's philosophy as a whole.

Bryan Magee, *Wagner and Philosophy*: a very readable introductory survey of the philosophical influences on Wagner and the themes that preoccupied his thinking in the creation of his art.

Christopher Middleton, *Selected Letters of Friedrich Nietzsche*: an excellent and economical digest of Nietzsche's correspondence that illuminates much of Nietzsche's more private thoughts and helps to situate many of the themes in his philosophy more broadly.

Daniel Conway, 'The Case of Wagner and Nietzsche Contra Wagner': a detailed examination of the themes found in both works, which are linked to those found in Nietzsche's wider philosophy.

George Liébert, *Nietzsche and Music*: an excellent and insightful study of Nietzsche's relationship with music and its effect on his wider philosophy.

Julian Young, *Friedrich Nietzsche: A Philosophical Biography*: a well-researched and highly detailed study of Nietzsche's life and works that is perhaps the definitive modern biography.

Martin Geck, *Richard Wagner: A Life in Music*: a remarkably insightful modern biography that combines meticulous research with skilful analysis in examining Wagner's life and thought as embodied in his music.

Martin Gregor-Dellin, *Richard Wagner: His Life, His Work, His Century*: a thorough, detailed and excellent biography of Wagner that provides a balanced examination of his life and works.

Michael Tanner, *Wagner*: a very concise, very readable study of each of Wagner's music dramas, focusing on their major themes and defending common misconceptions surrounding Wagner and his art.

Roger Scruton, 'Nietzsche on Wagner': a concise overview of Nietzsche's relationship to Wagner and how it is understood in Nietzsche scholarship more broadly, as well as an examination of some of the charges that make up *The Case of Wagner*.

Stewart Spencer and Barry Millington, *Selected Letters of Richard Wagner*: an outstanding compilation of Wagner's correspondence, which contains a wealth of insight into Wagner's life, his works and his philosophy.

Bibliography

Adorno, Theodor W. 1981. *In Search of Wagner*, trans. Rodney Livingston. London: Verso.
Aristotle. 1934. *Nicomachean Ethics*, trans. H. Rackham. 2nd edn. Cambridge, MA: Harvard University Press.
Badiou, Alain. 2010. *Five Lessons on Wagner*. London: Verso.
Borchmeyer, Deiter. 1991. *Richard Wagner: Theory and Theatre*, trans. Stewart Spencer. Oxford: Clarendon Press.
Came, Daniel. 2005. 'The Aesthetic Justification of Existence', in *A Companion to Nietzsche*, ed. K. Ansell-Pearson. Oxford: Blackwell, 41–58.
Chamberlain, Lesley. 1996. *Nietzsche in Turin: The End of the Future*. London: Quartet.
Conway, Daniel. 1997. *Nietzsche's Dangerous Game: Philosophy in the Twilight of the Idols*. Cambridge: Cambridge University Press.
— 2012. 'The Case of Wagner and Nietzsche Contra Wagner', in *A Companion to Friedrich Nietzsche: Life and Works*, ed. Paul Bishop. Rochester, NY: Camden House, 279–308.
Fischer-Dieskau, Dietrich. 1978. *Wagner and Nietzsche*, trans. Joachim Neugroschel. London: Sidgwick and Jackson.
Förster-Nietzsche, Elisabeth. 1912–15. *The Life of Nietzsche*, trans. Anthony M. Ludovici and Paul Cohn. 2 vols. New York: Sturgis, Walton and Co.
Geck, Martin. 2013. *Richard Wagner: A Life in Music*. Chicago: University of Chicago Press.
Gemes, Ken. 2009. 'Freud and Nietzsche on Sublimation', *Journal of Nietzsche Studies*, 38: 38–59.

Gemes, Ken, and Chris Sykes. 2014. 'Nietzsche's Illusion', in *Nietzsche on Art and Life*, ed. D. Came. Oxford: Oxford University Press, 80–106.

Gilman, Sander. 2007. 'Nietzsche, Bizet, and Wagner: Illness, Health, and Race in the Nineteenth Century', *Opera Quarterly*, 23: 247–64.

Gilman, Sander (ed.). 1987. *Conversations with Nietzsche: A Life in the Words of His Contemporaries*, trans. David J. Parent. Oxford: Oxford University Press.

Gregor-Dellin, Martin. 1983. *Richard Wagner: His Life, His Work, His Century*, trans. J. Maxwell Brownjohn. London: Collins.

Köhler, Joachim. 2004. *Richard Wagner: Last of the Titans*, trans. Stewart Spencer. New Haven: Yale University Press.

Liébert, Georges. 2004. *Nietzsche and Music*, trans. David Pellauer and Graham Parkes. Chicago: University of Chicago Press.

Loeb, Paul S. 2010. *The Death of Nietzsche's Zarathustra*. Cambridge: Cambridge University Press.

Magee, Bryan. 2000. *Wagner and Philosophy*. Harmondsworth: Penguin.

Mann, Thomas. 1933. 'Nietzsche and Music', in *Past Masters and Other Papers*, trans. H. T. Lowe-Porter. New York: Alfred A. Knopf, 141–6.

— 1966. 'Nietzsche's Philosophy in the Light of Recent History' (1947), in *Last Essays*, trans. Richard and Clara Winston. New York: Alfred A. Knopf, 141–77.

— 1985. 'The Sorrows and Grandeur of Richard Wagner', in *Pro and Contra Wagner*, trans. Allan Blunden. Chicago: University of Chicago Press, 91–148.

Nehamas, Alexander. 2000. 'A Reason for Socrates' Face: Nietzsche on "the Problem of Socrates"', in *The Art of Living: Socratic Reflections from Plato to Foucault*. Berkeley: University of California Press, 128–56.

Nietzsche, Friedrich. 1933. *Thus Spake Zarathustra*, trans. A. Tille. London: J. M. Dent.

— 1967. *The Birth of Tragedy/The Case of Wagner*, trans. Walter Kaufmann. New York: Vintage.

— 1968. *Twilight of the Idols/Anti-Christ*, trans. R. J. Hollingdale. Harmondsworth: Penguin.

— 1969. *Selected Letters of Friedrich Nietzsche*, ed. and trans. Christopher Middleton. Chicago: University of Chicago Press.
— 1974. *The Gay Science*, trans. Walter Kaufmann. New York: Vintage.
— 1980. *Kritische Studienausgabe, Sämtliche Werke*, ed. G. Colli and M. Montinari. 15 vols. Berlin: de Gruyter.
— 1985. *Selected Letters of Friedrich Nietzsche*, ed. O. Levy, trans. Anthony M. Ludovici. London: Soho Book Company.
— 1986. *Kritische Studienausgabe, Sämtliche Briefe*, ed. G. Colli and M. Montinari. 8 vols. Berlin: de Gruyter.
— 1989. *Ecce Homo/The Genealogy of Morals*, trans. Walter Kaufmann. New York: Vintage.
— 1993. *The Birth of Tragedy*, trans. Shaun Whiteside. Harmondsworth: Penguin.
— 1995a. *Human, All Too Human 1*, trans. Gary Handwerk. *The Complete Works of Friedrich Nietzsche*, vol. 3. Stanford, CA: Stanford University Press.
— 1995b. *Unfashionable Observations*, trans. Richard T. Gray. *The Complete Works of Friedrich Nietzsche*, vol. 2. Stanford, CA: Stanford University Press.
— 1998. *On the Genealogy of Morality*, trans. Maudemarie Clark and Alan J. Swensen. Indianapolis: Hackett.
— 1999. *Unpublished Writings from the Period of Unfashionable Observations*, trans. Richard T. Gray. *The Complete Works of Friedrich Nietzsche*, vol. 11. Stanford, CA: Stanford University Press.
— 2003. *Writings from the Late Notebooks*, ed. R. Bittner, trans. Kate Sturge. Cambridge: Cambridge University Press.
— 2005. *Nietzsche Contra Wagner*, trans. Judith Norman, in *The Anti-Christ, Ecce Homo, Twilight of the Idols and Other Writings*, ed. A. Ridley and J. Norman. Cambridge: Cambridge University Press.
— 2009. *Writings from the Early Notebooks*, ed. R. Guess and A. Nehamas, trans. Ladislaus Löb. Cambridge: Cambridge University Press.
— 2011. *Dawn*, trans. Brittain Smith. *The Complete Works of Friedrich Nietzsche*, vol. 5. Stanford, CA: Stanford University Press.
— 2013. *Human, All Too Human 2 and Unpublished Fragments from the Period of Human, All Too Human 2, Spring 1878–Fall*

1879, trans. Gary Handwerk. *The Complete Works of Friedrich Nietzsche*, vol. 4. Stanford, CA: Stanford University Press.
— 2014. *Beyond Good and Evil/ On the Genealogy of Morality*, trans. Adrian Del Caro. *The Complete Works of Friedrich Nietzsche*, vol. 8. Stanford, CA: Stanford University Press.
— 2017. *Selected Works for Piano*, ed. Nicholas Hopkins. New York: Carl Fischer.
— 2019. *Unpublished Fragments from the Period of Thus Spoke Zarathustra, Summer 1882–Winter 1884*, trans. Paul S. Loeb and David F. Tinsley. *The Complete Works of Friedrich Nietzsche*, vol. 14. Stanford, CA: Stanford University Press.
Plato. 1926. *Laws*, trans. R. G. Bury. Cambridge, MA: Harvard University Press.
Ridley, Aaron. 1998. *Nietzsche's Conscience: Six Character Studies from the Genealogy*. Ithaca, NY: Cornell University Press.
— 2002. 'What is the Meaning of Aesthetic Ideals?', in *Nietzsche, Philosophy, and the Arts*, ed. S. Kemal, I. Gaskell and D. Conway. Cambridge: Cambridge University Press, 128–47.
— 2007. *Nietzsche on Art*. London: Routledge.
— 2014. 'Nietzsche and Music', in *Nietzsche on Art and Life*, ed. D. Came. Oxford: Oxford University Press, 220–35.
Schopenhauer, Arthur. 1966. *The World as Will and Representation*, vol. 2, trans. E. F. J. Payne. New York: Dover.
— 2009. *The Two Fundamental Problems of Ethics*, trans. Christopher Janaway. Cambridge: Cambridge University Press.
— 2014. *The World as Will and Representation*, vol. 1, trans. Judith Norman, Alistair Welchman and Christopher Janaway. Cambridge: Cambridge University Press.
— 2014. *Parerga and Paralipomena*, vol. 1, trans. Sabine Roehr and Christopher Janaway. Cambridge: Cambridge University Press.
— 2015. *Parerga and Paralipomena*, vol. 2, trans. Adrian Del Caro and Christopher Janaway. Cambridge: Cambridge University Press.
Scruton, Roger. 1997. *The Aesthetics of Music*. Oxford: Clarendon Press.
— 2004. *Death-Devoted Heart: Sex and the Sacred in Wagner's Tristan and Isolde*. Oxford: Oxford University Press.

— 2014. 'Nietzsche on Wagner', in *Nietzsche on Art and Life*, ed. D. Came. Oxford: Oxford University Press, 236–51.

Small, Robin. 2005. *Nietzsche and Rée: A Star Friendship*. Oxford: Clarendon Press.

Soll, Ivan. 1990. 'Pessimism and the Tragic View of Life: Reconsiderations of Nietzsche's Birth of Tragedy', in *Reading Nietzsche*, ed. R. Solomon and K. Higgins. Oxford: Oxford University Press, 104–32.

Swafford, Jan. 1997. *Johannes Brahms: A Biography*. New York: Alfred A. Knopf.

Tanner, Michael. 1979. 'The Total Work of Art', in *The Wagner Companion*, ed. P. Burbridge and R. Sutton. London: Faber and Faber, 140–224.

— 1996. *Wagner*. London: Harper Collins.

Wagner, Cosima. 1938–40. *Die Briefe Cosima Wagners an Friedrich Nietzsche*, ed. E. Thierbach. 2 vols. Weimar: Nietzsche-Archiv.

— 1978/1980. *Diaries*, ed. Martin Gregor-Dellin and Dietrich Mack, trans. Geoffrey Skelton. 2 vols. London: Collins.

Wagner. Richard. 1893–97. *Richard Wagner's Prose Works*, trans. William Ashton Ellis. 8 vols. London: Kegan, Paul, Trench & Trübner.

— 'The Artwork of the Future', in *Richard Wagner's Prose Works*, I: 69–213.

— 'Beethoven', in *Richard Wagner's Prose Works*, V: 61–126.

— 'A Communication to My Friends', in *Richard Wagner's Prose Works*, I: 269–392.

— 'The Destiny of Opera', in *Richard Wagner's Prose Works*, V: 131–55.

— 'Opera and Drama', in *Richard Wagner's Prose Works*, II: 1–376.

— 'Public and Popularity', in *Richard Wagner's Prose Works*, VI: 51–82.

— 'The Public in Time and Space', in *Richard Wagner's Prose Works*, VI: 85–94.

— 'Religion and Art', in *Richard Wagner's Prose Works*, VI: 211–52.

— 'What is German?', in *Richard Wagner's Prose Works*, IV: 151–69.

— 1980. *The 'Brown Book': The Diary of Richard Wagner, 1865–1882*, trans. George Bird. London: Victor Gollancz.
— 1987. *Selected Letters of Richard Wagner*, ed. and trans. Stewart Spencer and Barry Millington. New York: W. W. Norton.

Westernhagen, Curt. 1981. *Wagner: A Biography*, trans. Mary Whitall. Cambridge: Cambridge University Press.

Young, Julian. 2010. *Friedrich Nietzsche: A Philosophical Biography*. Cambridge: Cambridge University Press.

Index

actors, 183, 239
  in declining cultures, 179
  Wagner as actor, 149–53,
    155–6, 158–64, 179–80, 191,
    195, 198, 221–8
Adorno, T., 2n, 235
Advaita Vedanta, 5
Aeschylus, 166, 167
  cultural significance of, 33,
    39, 62
ancient music drama, 21, 22,
  166, 167
art
  authenticity in, 191
  decline of, 25, 153, 178
    (*see also* culture: decline of)
  and life, 6, 11, 24–6, 32–3, 35,
    229, 239
  Nietzsche's demands on, 183,
    239
  and suffering, 72–3
  see also modern art
art forms, 19–21, 22, 206
artist-as-velleist, 119–20

artistic genius, 69, 73–4
artists of the future, 22–3, 24–5,
  160, 189, 230
'Artwork of the Future,
  The' (PW, Wagner), 6, 9,
  14–26
  ancient tragedies, 167
  art forms and, 19–21, 22, 167
  artists of the future, 22–3,
    24–5
  'Athenian self-dissection', 20,
    21, 25, 34, 213, 230
  Greek tragedy, 19, 20–1
  language as 'music,' 78, 81,
    84, 85
  luxury, 101, 150
  rebirth of culture, 159–60
  theatricality and effects, 133
  vitalism, 15–18, 24–6
Assorted Opinions and Maxims
  (HAH2, Nietzsche),
  143–4
'Athenian self-dissection', 20, 21,
  25, 34, 213, 230

Attempt at a Self-Criticism
 (AT, Nietzsche), 8–9, 11,
 41–63
 critique of Schopenhauer,
  50–1, 52, 53
 critique of Wagner, 51–3
 'making music' from the
  materials of life, 48–9
 microcosmic approach to the
  problem of culture, 44–8
 Socratic culture, 41
 thematic consistencies between
  The Birth of Tragedy and, 42–3
authenticity, 158, 178–9, 182,
 191, 230, 239
Avenarius, F., 124n

Badiou, A., 235, 236, 237, 238
beauty, 132–3
'Beethoven' (PW, Wagner), 5, 6
Beyond Good and Evil (BGE,
 Nietzsche), 81–6, 178, 182
Birth of Tragedy, The (BT,
 Nietzsche), 8, 10–11, 26–40,
 134, 230
 decline and rebirth of culture,
  32–40
 historical Socrates, 26–8, 30–1,
  35, 36
 Kaufmann translation, 4–5
 metaphysical theses, 6
 'music-making Socrates', 10,
  26, 28–30, 32–3, 34, 35,
  36–7, 38, 40
 thematic consistencies between
  Attempt at a Self-Criticism
  and, 42–3
Bizet, G., 108–11, 202

Borchmeyer, D., 4
Brahmanic culture, 42n, 43
Brahms, Johannes, 215, 216–17
Bülow, H. von, 135, 136–8,
 136n, 142

Carmen (Bizet), 108–11
case of Wagner as genre, 2, 3, 13,
 235, 237, 239
Case of Wagner, The (CW,
 Nietzsche), 1–3, 7, 12–13,
 98–183, 184–228
 Bizet v. Wagner, 108–11
 charges against Wagner, 107–8,
  232, 236–7
 decline of culture, 212–15
 female Wagnerian, 206–11,
  216, 225
 German resistance to W.,
  184–6
 Kaufmann translation, 114n
 music, 190, 193–4, 213–17,
  230–1
 Nietzsche's demands on art,
  183, 239
 'overcoming' Wagner, 212, 216,
  217–18, 220–1
Parsifal (Wagner), 202–3, 232–3
'philosopher who practices
 music', 63
Wagner as actor, 149–53,
 155–6, 158–64, 179–80, 191,
 195, 198, 221–8
Wagner's art as theatricality
 and effects, 125–33, 152,
 165–7, 202
Wagner's German identity,
 186–9

INDEX

Wagner's music as decadent, 101–2, 108, 111–15, 121–3, 150, 167–8: artist-as-velleist, 119–20; *The Ring*, 115–17
Wagner's music as 'idealistic', 145–9
Wagner's music as rhythmically, harmonically and formally flawed, 125, 133–4, 140–5
Wagner's prose works, 169–74
Chamberlain, L., 86, 238
Christianity, 51, 146–8, 192, 193, 225, 226–7
cognition, 18
'Communication to my Friends, A' (PW, Wagner), 170
composition, 153–5
Conway, D., 60n, 96n, 121, 125n
creativity, 32, 96, 219
culture
archetypes of, 42–3, 45
Brahmanic, 42n, 43
decline of, 101, 178–9, 212–15: and rebirth, 12, 13, 32–40, 61, 100, 159–60
European, 10, 186, 189
forms of, 218–19
and geography, 109, 110, 174
German, 186
German reformation of, 39–40, 69
Hellenic, 42n, 45
and life, 100, 185
macrocosmic approach to the problems of, 67, 70

microcosmic approach to the problem of (individual level), 44–8, 64–5, 68, 70–1, 88–9, 219
modern, 100
organic logic of, 13, 33, 35, 41, 61
Socratic, 10–11, 33, 34, 35–6, 41, 42n, 45, 52, 180, 213
tragic, 41, 52
and vitalism, 25–6
see also Socratic culture; tragic cultures

Dante, 195, 204-205
'David Strauss, Confessor and Writer' (DS, Nietzsche), 70
Dawn (D, Nietzsche), 71–5, 149
decadence, 144, 153, **240–1**
Ecce Homo (EH, Nietzsche), 104–6, 222
literary, 155–6
in Wagner's music, 101–2, 108, 111–15, 121–3, 150, 167–8: artist-as-velleist, 119–20; *The Ring*, 115–17
Socrates as the physician of, 55, 57-58
Socratic culture, 69, 150
degenerating instincts, 48, 53
pessimism of, 47, 52, 60, 65, 102, 123, **242**
Socrates and, 57, 58
Socratic culture and, 45, 46–7, 180, 186, 207
'Destiny of the Opera, The' (PW, Wagner), 5, 161
dialectics, 56, 57

Dionysian future of music, 93
Dionysus, 50–2, 199, 207, 209
drama, 22, 23, 156, 160, 166–7;
    see also music dramas
dramatic action, 23, 50, 151,
    166-167
dramatic poems, 151
dream world, 5–6

Ecce Homo (EH, Nietzsche),
    87–97
    decadence, 104–6, 222
    Dionysus, 199
    Zarathustra, 98–9, 128, 156–8:
    as counter-offer to Wagner,
    195–7, 198, 201; music,
    177–8; and Parsifal, 205,
    222, 233
effect, 161
effects and theatricality, 125–33,
    130n, 152, 165–7, 202
European culture, 10, 186, 189
existence, 42–3, 44, 66, 68,
    74, 102–3

female Wagnerian, 206–11,
    216, 225
Flying Dutchman, The (Wagner),
    112–13
Fuchs, C., 153, 156, 202

Gast, P., 175–6, 204
Gautier, J., 224
Gay Science, The (GS, Nietzsche),
    75–81, 83, 173, 177, 236
Geck, M., 4
genius, 69, 73–4
geography, 109, 110, 174

German culture, 186
German identity, 186–9
German music, 51, 213
German philosophy, 37
German reformation of culture,
    39–40, 69
German resistance to Wagner,
    184–6
'German style', 83–4
Germans, 81–4, 132–3, 167, 172,
    173–4, 178, 194
Geyer, L., 188
Goethe, J.W. von, 114–15
Greek tragedy, 6, 19, 20–1, 33, 34,
    36, 229–30

harmony, 50, 141–2
hearing, 20
    inability of Germans to, 82–85,
    86
Hegel, G.W.F., 170–4
Heidegger, M., 2, 235
Hellenic culture, 42n, 45
historical Socrates, 26–8,
    30–1, 35, 36, 49, 53–4,
    56–8, 100
Human, All Too Human (HAH1,
    Nietzsche), 67, 69–71, 113,
    114, 157–8n, 190, 220n
humanity, 14–18, 20

idealism, 145–9
ideas, 80
individuals, 74, 88–9
'inner' man, 19–20, 23, 23n,
    133
intellect, 15, 17, 24, 25, 99–100,
    185, 229

INDEX

Kant, I., 37, 114
Kaufmann, W., 4–5, 91n
Köhler, J., 5n, 208, 210n, 225
Köselitz, H., 175–6, 204
Lacoue-Labarthe, P., 235
language, 78, 79, 81–5, 150–1, 177, 178
Leibniz, G., 79n
Liébert, G., 134, 142
life, 156, 160, 185, 218
   and art, 6, 11, 24–6, 32–3, 35, 229, 239
   Nietzsche's 'post-Wagnerian' conception of culture, 99, 100
   and science, 15–18, 24, 46–7
   value of, 55–6
   see also existence
'light-world', 5, 6
Liszt, F., 225–6
Loeb, P., 86
logic, 29–30, 134
Lohengrin (Wagner), 226
luxury, 101, 150; see also decadence

'making music' from the materials of life, 48–9, 66, 96, 218–19, 228
Manfred Meditation (Nietzsche), 135, 137–8, 140, 141, 142
Meistersinger (Wagner), 167
melody, 50, 151
metaphysics, 191–3, 193
mind *see* intellect
modern art, 21, 22, 71–2, 100
modern culture, 100

modernity, 121–2, 123, 125, 134, 153, 163, 167–8, 227, 238
morality, 46, 102, 123, 163, 226–7
music, 183, 212, 238
   Beyond Good and Evil (BGE, Nietzsche), 83–4
   The Case of Wagner (CW, Nietzsche), 103–4, 190, 193–4, 213–17, 230–1, 239: Bizet v. Wagner, 108–11; as language, 150–1, 161
   Dionysian future of, 91, 93, 199
   The Gay Science (GS, Nietzsche), 75–6, 77–81
   German, 51, 213
   as language, 150–1, 161
   and language, 177
   Leibniz, 79n
   and rebirth of culture, 100Schopenhauer and, 5, 44n, 49–50, 92, 118, 121
   see also 'making music' from the materials of life; 'philosopher who practices music'; 'philosopher who speaks music'; Wagner's music
music dramas, 23, 35
   ancient, 21, 22, 166
   decadence, 108, 111–15
musical composition, 153–5
'music-making Socrates', 10, 26, 96, 230, **241–2**
   decline and rebirth of culture, 32–3, 34, 35, 36–7, 38, 40, 59
   Nietzsche as, 54
   Platonic dialogues, 28–30

nature, 14–18, 20, 24
Nehama, A., 62
Nietzsche, E., 211n
Nietzsche, F. W.
    biographers of, 3n
    compositional instinct, 134–5, 136–40
    as heir of pre-Socratics, 60, 64–7
    musical competence, 134n
    obsession with Wagner, 1–2
    as 'philosopher who practices music', 12, 149–50, 215, 232
    as 'philosopher who speaks music', 59, 86, 87, 93, 94, 95, 177
    'post-'/'contra-Wagnerian' conception of culture, 61
    'post-'/'contra-Wagnerian' position, 8–9, 11, 12, 43–4, 54–5, 60, 66, 67–8
    'pro-Wagnerian' conception of culture, 62–3
    'pro-Wagnerian' position, 8, 9, 54–5
    as 'psychological unity' of Schopenhauer and Wagner, 95–96, 98, 199, 206, 232, 237
    Wagner's intellectual influence on, 7, 8
    as W.'s 'true heir', 189, 215, 231
Nietzsche Contra Wagner (NCW, Nietzsche), 1, 7–8, 76n, 122
noble morality, 223, 226

'On Religion' (PP 2, Schopenhauer), 162

On the Genealogy of Morality (GM, Nietzsche), 119, 120, 172
optimism, 46 'outer' man, 19–20, 133
'overcoming' Wagner, 212, 216, 217–18, 220–1, 234

Paerga and Paralipomena, vol. 2 (PP 2, Schopenhauer), 162
Parsifal (Wagner), 205, 232–3
    ascetic ideal, 120
    Christianity, 223, 225
    German culture, 188–9
    modernity, 121
    religion, 115, 148, 163, 208
    theatrocracy, 194, 202–3
passion, 140–1
performance markings, 153–5
pessimism, 42, 45
pessimism of degenerating instincts, 47, 52, 60, 65, 102, 123, **242**
pessimism of strength, 44, 46, 48, 52, 58, **243**
Phaedo (Plato), 28–30
'philosopher who practices music' / 'philosopher who speaks music', 11, 13, 39, 40, 54, 63, 79n, 81, 96, 231, 236
    as catalytic agent of culture, 60–2
    commitment to make music, 66
    musical language, 79
    Nietzsche as, 12, 59, 86, 87, 93, 94, 95, 149–50, 177, 215, 232
    physicians of culture as, 100

rationality and vitality, 73
and Socrates, 35, 38, 57, 58
Wagner as, 175, 178
Zarathustra as, 90–1, 93–4
see also 'music-making Socrates' philosophers, 50, 72–3, 88–9, 162
artists of the future as, 24–5
and music, 79–80
as physicians of culture, 58, 72, 100, 101–2
Wagner as, 106–7
philosophical vitalism, 11, 74
philosophy, 29, 79n, 96, 110, 178, 181, 191–3
phrase markings, 153–5
Plato, 10–11, 55
Platonic dialogues, 11, 28–32
poetry, 21, 22, 79, 85, 160
poets, 23, 23n
pre-Socratics, 38, 46, 60, 62–3, 64–7
principle of sufficient reason, 169
'Prize Essay on the Freedom of the Will' (FW, Schopenhauer), 171
'Problem of Socrates, The' (TI, Nietzsche), 55–8
prose works, 86, 169–71
psychological hegemony, 96n, 118, 235

rational philosophers, 80
rationality, 30–1, 32, 33, 57, 73, 96
reality, 5–6
reason, 17–18, 21, 24, 51, 56, 57, 91n, 169, 185

redemption, 112, 112–13, 115, 149, 195, 207, 226
religion, 21, 148, 162; see also Christianity
'Religion and Art' (PW, Wagner), 146–7, 193
rhythm, 78, 79, 126, 142–3, 153, 155, 201
rhythmic perturbations, 153, 155, 203
'Richard Wagner in Bayreuth' (WB, Nietzsche), 86, 92, 94, 96, 106–7, 126–8, 198
Ridley, A., 119, 233, 238
Ring (Wagner), 115–17
'Feuerbach ending', 117–18n

Salomé, L., 79n
Schopenhauer, A., 37, 39–40
art and life, 180–1
effect on Germany, 115
music, 5, 44n, 49–50, 79n, 92, 118, 121
Nietzsche's critique of, 50–1, 52, 53, 59–60, 65
Nietzsche's 'pro-Wagnerian' conception of culture, 62–3
philosophy, 79n, 191–3 principle of sufficient reason, 169
suffering, 72, 89n
truth, 162–3
vitalism, 11, 59-60, 63 will, 44n, 49–51, 150
'Schopenhauer as Educator' (SE, Nietzsche), 68, 96, 103, 176
Schumann, C., 216, 216n
Schumann, R., 216n

science
    as cultural form, 53
    and life, 15–18, 24, 46–7
    limitations of, 30, 34–5
    scientific method, 69
    scientific world-view, 45, 47–8
Scruton, R., 134n, 141
self-creation, 105–6
Socrates
    as catalytic agent of culture, 60–2, 63
    decadence, 123
    decline of culture, 178
    historical, 26–8, 30–1, 35, 36, 49, 53–4, 56–8, 100
    'music-making', 10, 26, 96, 230, **241–2**: decline and rebirth of culture, 32–3, 34, 35, 36–7, 38, 40, 59; Nietzsche as, 54; Platonic dialogues, 28–30
    Nietzsche's critique of, 55–8
Socratic culture, 10–11, 33, 34, 35–6, 41, 42n, 45, 52, 180, 213
'sound-world', 6
suffering, 66, 72, 89, 89n, 90, 96, 231

Tanner, M., 4–5, 233
theatre, 183, 239
theatricality and effects, 125–33, 130n, 152, 165–7, 202
theatrocracy, 191, 194
theoretical man, 27, 28, 30, 53, 100
Thus Spake Zarathustra (TSZ, Nietzsche), 149, 175–6, 178, 205, 208; see also Zarathustra

tone poetry, 23, 23n
tragedy, 46; see also *Birth of Tragedy, The* (BT, Nietzsche); Greek tragedy
tragic cultures, 41, 52
Tristan and Isolde (Wagner), 116, 135, 138, 139, 141–2, 167
'Tristan chord', 141
truth, 162–3, 239
Twilight of the Idols (TI, Nietzsche), 55–8, 123

Unconscious, 91n
unconscious life-pulse, 18, 21, 25
Unfashionable Observations (UO, Nietzsche), 95
Unfinished Fragments and Notebooks (UF, Nietzsche), 1
    German reformation of culture, 39–40
    music, 109
    'music-making' and historical Socrates, 35
    Nietzsche as artist and philosopher, 176
    philosophers, 50
    pre-Socratics, 38, 63
    scientific world-view, 48
    Socrates, 58, 62
    Wagner as actor, 129
    Wagner's music: effects, 131, 132; as a means, 152; popularisation of, 178; rhythmic, harmonic and formal flaws, 143
    Zarathustra, 94n
    uniting philosophical and artistic drives, 11, 25, 33

as the 'meaning' of the duel
with Wagner, 103, 110,
175-178, 190, 206, 232, 235
see also 'philosopher who
practices music'

vanity, 113
velleity *see* artist-as-velleist
vision, 20
vital time, 19, 19n
vitalism, 11–12, 15, 63, **243–4**
'The Artwork of the Future'
(PW, Wagner), 15–18, 24–6
Attempt at a Self-Criticism (AT,
Nietzsche), 51, 59
The Case of Wagner (CW,
Nietzsche), 99, 218, 229–30
philosopher as physician of
culture, 58
Zarathustra, 206
vitality, 47–8, 57, 73, 219; *see also*
vitalism
von Hartmann, E., 91n

Wagner, C.
father, 225
female Wagnerian, 207–11, 216
Hans von Bülow, 135, 136n
Parsifal (Wagner), 233
and R. Wagner's decadence,
112–13, 114, 115
sexuality, 224
Wagner, R.
as actor, 149–53, 155–6, 158–64,
179–80, 191, 195, 198, 221–8
biographers of, 4
case of W. as genre, 2, 3, 13,
235, 237, 239

as composer, 92
as contemporary of Aeschylus,
39
critique of Nietzsche, 69
decline of culture, 212–15
German identity, 186–9
German resistance to, 184–6
intellectual influence on
Nietzsche, 7, 8
Nietzsche's charges against,
107–8, 232, 236–7
Nietzsche's critique of, 51–3,
59–60, 65
Nietzsche's obsession with,
1–2, 220
as philosopher, 106–7
as 'philosopher who speaks
music', 175, 178
political exile, 14
prose works, 86, 169–74
reality and dream world,
5–6
see also 'Artwork of the Future,
The' (PW, Wagner)
Wagner's art as theatricality
and effects, 125–33, 152,
165–7, 202
Wagner's music, 60, 75–6, 78
attack on, 51–3
as decadent, 102–3, 108,
111–15, 121–3, 150, 167–8:
artist-as-velleist, 119–20; *The
Ring*, 115–17
as 'idealistic', 145–9
as rhythmically, harmonically
and formally flawed, 125,
133–4, 140–5
suffering and, 76n, 231

Westernhagen, C., 4
will, 44n, 49–51, 91n, 150, 185, 218
World as Will and Representation, The (WWR, Schopenhauer), 49–50, 92, 169, 192, 205–6

Young, J., 3n, 60n, 117n, 134, 134n

Zarathustra, 12, 98–9, 128
  as counter-offer to Wagner, 86–7, 88, 194–8, 198–202
  and German language, 82
  music, 177–8
  and *Parsifal*, 205, 206, 222, 233
  as 'philosopher who speaks music', 90–1, 93–4

EU representative:
Easy Access System Europe
Mustamäe tee 50, 10621 Tallinn, Estonia
Gpsr.requests@easproject.com

www.ingramcontent.com/pod-product-compliance
Lightning Source LLC
Chambersburg PA
CBHW050212240426
43671CB00013B/2305